RAILS
NEWQUAY

Railways - Tramways -
Town - Transport

by
John Vaughan

THE OAKWOOD PRESS

British Library Cataloguing in Publication Data
A Record for this book is available from the British Library
ISBN 978 0 85361 677 1

Typeset by Oakwood Graphics.
Repro by PKmediaworks, Cranborne, Dorset.
Printed by Cambrian Printers, Aberystwyth, Ceredigion.

Standard gauge rails first reached what was then the hamlet of Newquay in 1849 with the arrival of Treffry's Newquay Tramway. However, there was no passenger service until the CMR opened its Newquay terminus in June 1876. Standing at the terminus with an auto-coach in the 1920s is one of the classic GWR prairie tanks, No. 4554.   *M. Dart Collection*

Title Page: One of the last acts by the erstwhile British Rail (BR) in the 1990s was to place 'Newquay Branch Line' branding notices at strategic locations, in the perhaps optimistic hope of encouraging rail travel. However, would-be passengers would travel in a diesel unit and not in the 0-6-2T steam locomotive depicted! This example was at Par.   *Author*

Front cover: Newquay harbour in about 1900 finds commercial sailing vessels at the 1872-built central jetty being loaded with china clay. A couple of empty wagons can be seen on the old tramway lines within the compact harbour complex, which was accessed via a steep tunnel through the cliffs.   *Author's Collection*

Rear cover: A typical Newquay branch train of the 21st century, in the shape of class '150/2' No. 150219, is seen at the single track terminus. The first passenger train arrived in 1876, some 132 years earlier than when this scene was recorded.   *Author*

Published by The Oakwood Press (Usk), P.O. Box 13, Usk, Mon., NP15 1YS.
E-mail: sales@oakwoodpress.co.uk
Website: www.oakwoodpress.co.uk

Contents

Just before the turn of the 20th century the growing town of Newquay had become sufficiently important for the GWR to name one of its 'Duke' class 4-4-0 locomotives after the town. Here No. 3274 *Newquay* stands at Truro station in Edwardian times.

P.Q. Treloar Collection

Introduction

The town of Newquay is situated on the northern coast of Cornwall in a location of immense contrasts. These contrasts reflect the influence 19th and 20th century man has had in the development of a small coastal hamlet of the Georgian era into a substantial holiday resort of the 21st century. These contrasts relate to the magnificent natural beaches and cliffs in the area, the headland with its fine Victorian edifices, and the bars, night clubs, restaurants, tacky gift shops and diverse architecture in the town. There is further contrast between summer and winter, not only in terms of climate but because during the summer months the population of Newquay quadruples in size.

In terms of local industries and employment there have been radical changes during the past 150 years. In centuries past the primary occupations were from the sea, especially in terms of pilchard and later herring fishing, and from the land, including agriculture and farming, and various mining activities. From 1849, when a tramway to Newquay was built, the commercial activity at the harbour hugely increased. A number of cottage industries grew rapidly from the turn of the 20th century, particularly clothing and knitwear but by far and away the greatest influence was the development of tourism.

This development was greatly facilitated by the availability of public transport, especially the coming of the railway to Cornwall in 1859 and to Newquay in June 1876, which brought visitors to the Atlantic Coast from every rail-connected part of the UK. From a population of 489 in 1840 Newquay had grown to 2,935 in 1901 and well over 20,000 in 2001. It is estimated that during the peak summer months the population can exceed 100,000!

From the late Victorian era entrepreneurs realised the potential of the leisure industry and huge hotels started to appear around Newquay. This was the age when only the wealthy could afford to travel. The medical profession of the era recommended fresh air, a relatively good climate and the seaside environment to cure all manner of ailments. Large mansions began to appear along the cliff tops and rows of terraces for the growing number of middle class families were built, along with all the key facilities of a growing community such as stores, schools, hospitals, banks and public buildings.

An early guide book paints a rosy image of the blossoming Newquay in the 1920s:

> The breezy little town of Newquay, situated so pleasantly among the glorious cliffs and sunlit headlands of the coast of North Cornwall, is becoming more and more popular by the year. Time was when accommodation for visitors was scanty and unsatisfactory, and the journey from London or any of the big centres of busy life was regarded as something of a feat in the way of travelling. Now, however, the accommodation is unexcelled and, thanks to the enterprise of the Great Western Railway, the run may be made comfortably from London in seven hours. Through trains run to and from Chester and the Midlands via Bristol.

The feature also mentions travelling to Wadebridge by rail, 'where the Newquay coach may be picked up', referring to the London & South Western Railway (LSWR) route into Cornwall.

In the Edwardian era direct trains from London to Newquay operated and on summer Saturdays in particular thousands of holidaymakers would arrive in

This ancient photograph of Newquay Harbour dates back to 1881, eleven years before the Atlantic Hotel was built on the Headland, top left. The central stone jetty was built by the CMR in 1872/3 and was connected to land by a wooden trestle, above which can be seen the Active fish cellars, demolished in 1905. Only wooden sailing ships populate the harbour and two railway wagons full of china clay are being unloaded.   *Newquay Old Cornwall Society*

Even in Edwardian times the inhabitants of Newquay enjoyed their pint of bitter. There were six malt houses in Newquay and the building on the right, in Beach Road, was the Steps Malt House. Young ladies pose for the camera with the sea visible in the background. The historic building was yet another victim of a Newquay road widening scheme.   *Author's Collection*

Newquay by train. The service between Newquay and Par gradually increased in frequency and in 1905 another railway line from Truro via Chacewater, St Agnes and Perranporth to Newquay opened. Between the two World Wars growth was significant and the holiday trade boomed. By this time road coaches and buses were providing an alternative means of transport but it was the family car in the post-depression years of the 1930s that started to have the greatest impact. Also, by the late 1930s, domestic air travel was becoming established.

In the post-World War II era the holiday trade quickly became re-established and Newquay was proving to be as popular as ever. Further significant growth occurred as many of the old residences referred to earlier were converted into small and not so small hotels and guest houses to cater for the new 'bed and breakfast' brigade. Although a variety of water sports had always been enjoyed, surfing became increasingly popular and the beaches, breakers and tidal patterns at Newquay resulted in the town becoming the 'Surf Capital of England'.

The 1960s and 1970s were decades of transition for Newquay. While the resort remained popular, the foreign package tours, in particular to Mediterranean resorts, began to increase their share of the vacation market. In many cases a new generation of jet plane resulted in travellers from the Midlands and the North in particular arriving at foreign destinations in far less time than they could travel to Cornwall. Also, by comparison, the Cornish weather was unpredictable. A growth in caravan parks, self catering holidays and an improvement in facilities, such as the provision of en-suite bedrooms, helped the fight back but the Cornish holiday industry realised there was no room for complacency. By 2007 the holiday seasons were lengthening and there are now over 5 million visitors to Cornwall every year.

Gradually travel patterns have changed and now the car is king, which in the height of the season gives rise to the most hideous traffic jams on some of the roads around Newquay and certainly on the A30 artery. The use of aircraft has hugely increased and some 400,000 passengers used Newquay Airport in 2007. The numbers arriving by train has significantly decreased but the Newquay branch line retains the distinction of being the only Cornish branch to enjoy through trains from distant locations on time-dated Summer weekends.

I have made a special study of the fascinating Newquay branch and its branches for 40 years and I am delighted to have had the opportunity of preparing this book for the Oakwood Press, which is not only the most comprehensive account of 'Rails to Newquay' ever written but also provides a summary of the town's history, industries and transport. Every photograph shows a moment in history and I hope that all readers enjoy this unique compilation spanning some 150 years. Some rare historic photographs have been previously published but the overwhelming majority have never been seen before. The help provided by many contributors is recognised on the Acknowledgements page.

John Vaughan
Goring by Sea
West Sussex

The extent of the town of Newquay by the 1930s. Top left is Fistral beach and bottom right Tolcarn Junction with the railway to Chacewater heading due south and the Par line heading to the east. *Reproduced from the 6", 1933 Ordnance Survey Map*

Chapter One

The History of Newquay

Although the growth of Newquay during the past century and a half has been phenomenal there is evidence of human occupation going back over 3,000 years to the Bronze Age. Other remains suggest Iron Age activity. The primary evidence of these early citizens is substantial earthworks or 'barrows' that are still visible in a number of areas in and around Newquay. These prehistoric burial places are mostly round in shape and it is thought that only those at the top of the social hierarchy were entombed therein.

These early inhabitants were actively engaged in a variety of trades and it now seems hard to accept that they travelled to many parts of Europe and North Africa, various buried artefacts demonstrating without doubt that these folk were far from primitive. Evidence shows that items originating in the Baltic countries, Egypt and even far away Greece were transported to Cornwall. The resident tribes were involved in metalwork, possibly from minerals found in local iron lodes and tin laden streams, and the female population were expert spinners and weavers, with ancient spindle whorls of the era having been found locally. Barrows have been located at East Pentire, Trevelgue Head, Cliff Castle (Porth island), Glendorgal and Barrowfields, the latter largely ruined by an insensitive if not greedy 19th century farmer who destroyed many of the barrows to get his hands on the stones for hedging purposes (a Cornish 'hedge' is a stone wall).

Unfortunately, although there are artefacts that have been recovered that prove without doubt that ancient civilisations lived in the Newquay area, few remains of boats, houses and infrastructure have survived the ravages of time, except for a hut circle from the early Iron Age period and earthen ramparts built for defence purposes. It is regrettable that it was not until the 15th century before significant documentary evidence begins to appear to provide a fuller picture of the history of Newquay.

It is common in history books to read that the original name of Newquay was Towan Blistra (hill in the sand) however, such a name was applied only to the Headland and Beacon, beyond what is now the famous Red Lion public house. There was for centuries an old quay located approximately where today's harbour can be found. In the reign of Henry VI parochial history notes show that, '… an indulgence was granted by one Edmund Lacy, Bishop of Exeter on 10 January 1439 for the construction repair and maintenance of a "new keye for the rode of shipping", situated on the sea shore near "Tewen Blustey". In the reign of Queen Elizabeth I the Cornish historian Carew wrote in the year 1602 'neither may I omit "Newkaye", a place in the north coast of this Hundred, so called because in *former* times the inhabitants attempted to remedy a natural defect by art, which conceit [exaggerated notion] they still possess, though lack of means among themselves or in the place has left the result in nubibus [in the clouds], and only left them with the benefit of lester-cocks [a type of web-footed bird] and fisher-boats'.

There are many glimpses of other activities in the Newquay area, such as mine stoping for silver and lead carried out by Burchard von Kranich in the time of Queen Mary Tudor in 1554/1555 and subsequently, during the Elizabethan period in 1579, by Captain Edward Fenton and John Cosworth. Another reference occurs in the reign of James I, when in 1615 the Lord of the Manor, one Thomas Stuer, applied for leave to erect a pier. Thus the question of a quay and harbour, which would inevitably form a focal point of any substantial development, was an issue for many years and it is clear that whatever the state of (dis)repair at any given time the site lent itself to providing shelter for shipping.

In the early 1800s Newquay was little more than a hamlet with a cluster of thatched cottages huddled together to the west of Watergate Bay, under the lee of Towan head. The population in 1800 was about 100 souls. The earliest map on which Newquay is shown appears to be in Borlase's *Natural History of Cornwall* dated 1758. The next name to prominently feature in the history of Newquay is Richard Lomax. He was the Squire of the manor of Towan Blistra, situated in the parish of nearby St Columb Minor and he owned the harbour area and surrounding land. Certainly in 1833 there was a little harbour in the cove below Towan Head with one quay effectively capable of handling small wooden ships of about 80 tons in weight. Lomax was prevailed upon by the local fishermen to build a much larger harbour that would afford not only more space but provide better shelter from the often heavy seas.

The Squire borrowed over £10,000 and built a new harbour with two quays enclosing some three acres of land. Unfortunately, Lomax died on 1st November, 1836 and it was mid-1838 before the harbour was finished. William Carrivick and an auctioneer from Truro called Tippet were his executors and in July 1838 they secured an Act of Parliament to control the harbour, to set shipping dues and to formalise the jurisdiction of the Harbour Master by one mile towards Fistral Bay and half a mile in the other direction towards St Columb Porth. Later that year the executors decided to sell the entire estate manor, which comprised the harbour, 100 acres of arable land, local mines and mineral rights and some 70 acres of land on Towan Head, above Fistral Bay. This estate was purchased outright by Joseph Thomas Treffry from Fowey, a powerful landowner, businessman, visionary and entrepreneur. The development of the harbour and early tramways are described in the relevant chapters of this book.

The first tramway from East Wheal Rose lead mine was opened in February 1849 and this facilitated the transportation of outgoing ores, agricultural produce and, from 1857, when the line to St Dennis and Hendra was opened throughout, china clay and china stone. The horse-operated tramways worked back loads of, primarily, imported coal, fertiliser and timber. As explained in the relevant chapter, the Cornwall Minerals Railway (CMR) took over and upgraded the old Treffry Tramways in 1873/4, to permit locomotive working, constructed a through route to Par and Fowey and finally, in 1876, operated the first passenger train service to Newquay.

By 1877 the CMR ran into financial difficulties and the Great Western Railway (GWR) took over operations, finally acquiring the entire CMR network in 1896. From 1892 the standard gauge CMR was compatible with the GWR main line, permitting through running between Newquay and any part of the national rail network. This event had an enormous impact on the development of Newquay and was to be the catalyst for the rapid expansion of the holiday trade in the area. An early guide book from the late Edwardian era provides an interesting insight:

> This seaside village now fairly takes rank among the most thriving of our holiday resorts. The streets are clean, well-lighted [sic] and well-watered; the shops are good and moderate in their charges; the provision for accommodating visitors in hotels, boarding houses and apartments, is of the best; there are splendid sands for bathing; and the facilities for recreation and sport are ample. Among events of recent years which have helped to augment the fame of Newquay have been the royal visits. In the spring of 1909 H.M. King George V and Queen Mary - then Prince and Princess of Wales - paid the town a visit, and on more than one occasion since the young princes have spent holidays here.

The *Homeland Handbook* of 1922 described for the benefit of would-be holidaymakers what they could expect of the area. The description may be slightly rosy in that it fails to mention gale force winds and very wet days but otherwise it is worth quoting from the 86-year-old booklet:

> The town of Newquay for the most part faces north and west and looks out respectively upon two bays of Newquay and Fistral. In respect of climate it has few equals. The prevailing winds are west and south-west, full from the ocean. The temperature is singularly equable; frost, close to the sea, is almost a phenomenon, and winter frequently passes without snow being seen at all. Running along this part of Cornwall is a narrow dry belt, and consequently Newquay's rainfall is smaller than places on the southern coast of the county, whilst in winter the temperature is generally within one degree of that in the favoured Isles of Scilly. [The description continued]… On the southern side of its hilly backbone there is a beautiful valley and broad tidal estuary. Here, even when boisterous north winds blow, the air is warm and balmy, and in addition to change in climate, there is an entirely different variety of scenery. Instead of high precipitous cliffs we have a wooded creek and verdant slopes patterned with feathery tamarisk, richly coloured rushes and grasses, intermixed with wild convolvulus and other plants peculiar to the spot. [The book describes other forna and flora before stating] The water supply, brought from a granite neighbourhood seven miles away, is absolutely pure. The sanitary condition of the town is most satisfactory; each end is drained by separate systems which empty far out into the sea. The eastern system, which cost £13,000, was completed as recently as 1914.

With endorsements such as this it is hardly surprising that Newquay boomed in the last decade of the Victorian era and the first decade of Edwardian rule. With the growing town came huge hotels, which initially seemed to be out of scale with the surroundings and which dwarfed earlier hostelries such as the Red Lion, later Prout's Hotel, the New Inn, later the Commercial and the Central. The main establishments at the turn of the century were the Atlantic Hotel high above Towan Head, the nearby Headland Hotel, the Great Western Hotel, almost opposite the station, and the Victoria Hotel on a cliff top near the centre of town. The last named caused some excitement by its novel passenger lift that conveyed patrons from the hotel directly to a subway with a direct

In this magnificent view the Victorian stage coach era is well illustrated with no fewer than 20 passengers on board. The coach was operated by the North Cornwall Coach Company Ltd of Wadebridge that operated in the area from 1879 to 1912. These travellers are about to leave the Red Lion Inn to attend a football match in Wadebridge in 1900. As mentioned on page 49, the coach worked a Newquay, St Columb, Padstow and Wadebridge service but the company also operated summer coach excursions in the Newquay and Boscastle areas. *Cornish Studies Library*

The famous Red Lion Inn, once known as Prout's Hotel, was a popular gathering point where several of the Newquay Tramway and Cornwall Minerals Railway celebratory dinners were held. Taken a century after the above photograph the building can still be recognised, notice the twirled iron verandah support in both pictures. It is still possible to enjoy a pint in this historic building above the harbour. *Author*

Newquay is a town of mixed architectural styles. With so many mediocre and aesthetically offensive structures from the 1960s and 1970s extant it is heartening to find a splendid old inn in the centre of town. The Central was so named in 1915, having been the Dolphin when built in 1775, the Old Inn by 1837 and the Commercial on rebuilding in 1859.   *Author*

connection to the sands and a beach in a cove beneath the hotel. In addition to such centres of luxury many lesser hotels also sprang-up.

In 1880 the population of Newquay was 1,800 and they were served by five inns, including Prout's Hotel (the Red Lion, built in 1836). A concert hall was built and in 1891 the first golf links were opened, followed by the Cozy Nook theatre. In 1895 the LSWR extended its North Cornwall line to Padstow and some Newquay visitors chose that route, even though it would end in a 16 mile journey by horse-drawn coach. The population was growing rapidly, from 2,935 in 1901 to 4,415 in 1911 and 6,637 in 1921.

In 1911 a substantial church, St Michael the Archangel, was built on Marcus Hill and was capable of accommodating 1,000 worshippers. Many churches of other denominations were also provided. In 1912 a fine Post Office was built followed by Council Chambers, a Concert Hall and a County Secondary School. In 1912 the Pavilion Theatre was built and gradually a complete small town grew into a major centre of population with retail outlets and financial institutions of every shape and size. World War I came and went and before World War II a 'Holidays with Pay Act' was passed by Parliament, which afforded a growing number of workers the opportunity to spend a week or so away from home. It is estimated that by 1938 one third of the UK population were taking holidays and most of those headed for the seaside. By 1931 the population was 7,651 and new housing estates were springing-up all over the town. During the 1930s many of the early houses were converted to business premises and large hotels continued to be built including the Pentire, the Bewdley, the Fistral Bay and the re-built Great Western.

Frequent visits by members of the Royal Family to Newquay really put the town on the tourist
map. Often Royalty would stay at the Victorian Headland Hotel. One of the well recorded visits
was by the Prince of Wales in 1909 but in this wonderful 1913 view TRH The Prince of Wales
and Prince Albert are seen in their chauffeur driven limousine outside the hotel.

Author's Collection

The current Prince of Wales regularly visits Cornwall to visit the large Duchy of Cornwall
estates and often the Royal Train is used. The Author was on hand at Newquay station in March
1991 to record Prince Charles leaving his private saloon and walking down Newquay's
remaining platform to a waiting car. He had spent the night on the train.   *Author*

All of this development came to a standstill during World War II when the military almost took over the town. Many of the hotels were requisitioned for other uses, such as hospitals and hospices. Large numbers of evacuees from our large cities arrived. There were training centres and many camps in the area, one accommodating 2,000 air cadets. RAF St Mawgan (formerly RAF Trebelzue) developed rapidly and played an active part in proceedings, as did military airfields at Perranporth and St Eval. Many of Newquay's beaches were mined and covered with barbed wire. The timbers of the old CMR trestle in the harbour were part removed and the visitors stayed away.

After the war there was a period of consolidation before the annual holiday machine selected top gear but the recovery was remarkable. By 1951 the town received 20,000 visitors per day and by 1961 this had increased to 50,000, which was four times the total population. In 1971 the population was 14,963 and in season a staggering 70,000 visitors per day were watered, fed and accommodated. Caravan and camping sites grew rapidly and the season gradually expanded from four months, June to September, to seven months, April to October. In 1971 a whopping 68 per cent of visitors arrived by car, 15 per cent by coach and only 13 per cent by rail. A few per cent arrived by air. Since 1971 rail travellers have greatly diminished, discouraged by high fares and a poor service.

Now labelled as the 'Surf Capital of England' Newquay is flourishing. The population is nearing 22,000 and during the peak season 100,000 visitors invade the area on a daily basis. With this influx comes a number of social problems linked with modern urban life such as binge drinking and drug taking but there are still thousands of families who enjoy themselves on the wonderful beaches in the area.

In order to fully appreciate the town of Newquay it is best visited off season when the wonderful coastal setting can be explored at leisure and in some areas of the town it is still possible to park a car! One of the highlights, especially for the visitor who has 'done his homework', is the harbour where there is evidence of the old Newquay Tramway tunnel and the central stone jetty, which was built by the CMR in 1872/3 to increase vessel handling capacity. At high tide it is not uncommon to see seals basking in the harbour. Nowadays fishing largely comprises the capture of lobsters and other shellfish. In the summer the main catch is tourists, tempted on board small pleasure craft and speed boats.

A visit to the historic Red Lion Inn that overlooks the quay is a must and a splendid view of the entire coastline can be had from the nearby Fort Inn. Beyond the harbour on the Headland is the old lifeboat station, last used in anger in 1934 and a remarkable but abandoned 1 in 2¼ launching ramp. The Atlantic and Headland hotels are imposing and although sumptuous, rather gaunt against the Cornish sky. The view from the Headland over Fistral Beach is impressive and on a stormy day the huge Atlantic breakers make one thankful for being on dry land. Also visible on the south side of the headland are the remains of the local squire Treffry's unfinished 'Harbour of Refuge'. On the north side of the Atlantic Hotel is the little Huer's Hut, used by lookouts in the olden days to spot shoals of pilchards. The presence of flocks of seagulls over the shoals were sufficient for each Huer to blow his megaphone-like

This very early mid-19th century engraving shows Treffry's 'Harbour of Refuge' on the western side of Towan Head at Newquay. The harbour was never finished due to Treffry's death in 1850 and over the decades the massive granite wall was gradually destroyed by the power of the sea. To the left is Fistral beach (*see page 90*). *Author's Collection*

A survivor from at least the 14th century is the 'Huer's Hut'. This old building was occupied by the Huers who would keep a lookout for pilchard shoals and sound a horn and shout whenever a potential catch came into view, whereupon much of Newquay's population would take to the boats to take advantage of this seasonal activity. The building was restored in 1838. *Author*

trumpet and shout 'Heva', 'Heva' - 'The Cry is up' – whereupon the townsfolk would stop whatever they were doing and make for the boats. Other natural attractions include the sandy estuary of the River Gannel and various under-cliff caves all along the coastline. Early man-made sites include Tumuli or Barrows at Barrowfields, Porth Island and Whipsiderry. Newquay Zoo is an attraction that boasts a miniature railway and the nearby long-established Trenance Gardens and boating lake are well worth a visit in season.

Although there are several fine old buildings in the area, the local council have been instrumental in approving the demolition of many period structures of note, ranging from the early fish cellars, to Edwardian schools, the original Post Office, the historic whim buildings above the old tramway tunnel, to a shocking act of official vandalism: the destruction of the lovely original granite Newquay railway station building. Fortunately some fine terraces and a handful of old municipal buildings remain. However, planning permission has been granted by the local authority for some truly hideous modern structures and one has to seriously question where the council's interests lie. As a result of insensitive development over the years the centre of the town is an uncomfortable mish-mash of architectural styles, many of which are instantly forgettable and aesthetically offensive. There is no doubt that nature has done a better job of creating beauty at Newquay than the local authority.

The National University Surfing Competition was held at Towan beach at Newquay during March 2008. Competitors and crowds arrived from around the country, with one team noted from Aberdeen! On a very fine 1st March the crowds watch the surfers with the harbour entrance top left at the 'Surf Capital of England'.   *Author*

Newquay Harbour *circa* 1895. The Atlantic Hotel, *top left*, was completed in 1892 but the Fly and Active fish cellars can be seen on the distant North Quay. The latter was demolished in 1905. There are six commercial sailing ships in the harbour, including one at South Quay (*right*) and one at Central Jetty. Both have been loaded with china clay, note the five empty tramway wagons, but there is apparently no revenue earning back load. *Author's Collection*

A turn of the 20th century scene showing Newquay Harbour with half a dozen sailing ships within its confines. Worthy of special note is the Atlantic Hotel, *top left*, and below, to its left, the Red Lion (earlier 'Prouts') Hotel, mentioned in the text. This is one of only four known views of the harbour where a single horse (*just beyond the junction for the central jetty*) can be seen coupled to a couple of china clay wagons. *Newquay Old Cornwall Society*

Chapter Two

Local Industries

In the early days the main industries in the immediate Newquay area were shipbuilding, farming, fishing, mining and explosives, and textiles. However over the years all of these have paled into insignificance when compared with the tourist industry. In addition to the industries detailed in this chapter, within a dozen or so miles of Newquay there were and in some cases still are many other industries. Included in the still active category are china clay extraction and processing, although the nearest rail shipment point to Newquay is the vast Imerys (formerly English China Clays) Rocks works at Goonbarrow Junction, a mile east of Bugle and about 15 miles from Newquay. Also within this radius were considerable quarrying activities and even a number of brickworks, such as Carbis at the end of the Carbis Wharf branch, Trerice once served by a siding on the Retew branch and St Columb.

Shipbuilding

Newquay had both shipbuilding yards and shipowners aplenty. There were also healthy ship repair and sail making businesses in the area. Between the years 1818 and 1916 no fewer than 190 small commercial sailing ships were in the hands of various Newquay-based owners. Records show that one individual owned as many as 18 vessels and that in 1891 there were seven owners with an interest in four or more ships. Shipping patterns at Newquay are of immense interest because they demonstrate the rise and fall of the harbour and give some indication of traffic volumes on the Newquay Tramway. As reiterated in Chapter Five, a random week in May 1849 saw four vessels arriving in the harbour and seven leaving, a projected annual total of between 250 and 300 ships (six per week). By comparison records show that in 1879 a total of 164 vessels used the harbour (three per week). By 1889 this had dwindled to 107 (two per week) and by the early 1920s only one ship in the entire year used the harbour commercially.

There were four shipyards of note. The earliest was Clemens Yard at Quay, within the inner harbour at Newquay. Run by the Clemens from 1849, the first ship that they built was the schooner *Treffry* named after the squire who owned the harbour. The sons of the family moved to Island Cove Yard, off the small island of Killacourt just below the cliffs at Newquay. This yard closed in 1871/2. Quay Yard continued to operate with other owners until 1867. The very last ship produced was a 68 ft schooner named *Forest Deer* that was still afloat until 1932. The most prominent was Clemens Yard beside the River Gannel at Tregunnel and this prolific shipbuilding site was in business from 1839 to 1881. It was owned by the same family throughout. For fitting out, the vessels were often towed to Newquay Harbour. The last ship produced was the schooner *Triumph*. Small ships continued to be built in the area until about 1907. The fourth yard was the John Stephens Yard at Porth, about a mile north of

Most of Cornwall's farms are small in size. In recent decades they have been hugely affected by changes in legislation, from the UK government, the European Commission and by the economics of the supermarkets. Consequently there has been a significant move away from dairy farming and an increase in rearing beef cattle. The five local beasts seen here in echelon are in the latter category.   *Author*

Much of the land along the cliff tops of the Cornish coast is fit only for sheep to graze. For centuries rearing sheep in the Newquay area was a major source of food and revenue, providing not only meat but also wool as a secondary source of income. Furthermore, the climate around Newquay is conducive to early lambing, which guarantees premium prices. This Edwardian scene shows sheep just south of Watergate Bay and Hotel, visible in the distance.
Author's Collection

Newquay. Later owned by Joseph Osborne the yard finally closed in 1880. At many of the yards ship repair activity continued for some years after the cessation of shipbuilding activities.

The decline of shipbuilding at Newquay was no different to many other shipbuilding ports both in Cornwall and in the UK generally. Steamships were gradually replacing sailing vessels and with the steamships being considerably heavier than their predecessors they were unable to use many small Cornish harbours. This concentrated seaborne traffic to the larger and deep water ports. Often sailing ships had to wait for many days before setting sail due to climatic conditions, whereas the steamships could sail in anything but the most severe weather. Due to a heavier payload and more reliable running steam ships cost less to run, in payload ton/mile terms, making the operation potentially more profitable. Between 1880 and 1900 Newquay shipowners lost over 50 sailing ships, and many more during World War I, and with the changing times these ships were not replaced. Improvements in rail services impacted on shipping, with railways arriving in Cornwall from the rest of the UK in 1859, the Newquay branch opening in 1874 (goods), 1876 (passenger) and the broad gauge being abandoned in 1892. Furthermore commodity markets suffered regular depressions, particularly iron ore, but even in the good times more and more minerals were being dispatched to ports on Cornwall's south coast.

Farming

Although much of the land on the cliff tops above the sea at Newquay and along some of the sandy estuaries was comprised of poor grassland, fit only for grazing sheep, much of the surrounding countryside was very fertile capable of producing high yield crops. It was necessary for farmers to fertilise the land with sea sand, seaweed, imported guano (manure) and, where appropriate, lime. The farmers were well placed to increase crop production to feed the growing population.

In the 18th century barley was the primary crop as it was suited to the coastal climate, whereas the area was somewhat damp and at times a little cool for wheat. Corn was grown in abundance and a local mill was built where farmers would bring their corn for grinding. The resulting flour was then transported to local villages by pack horse. This supply chain included villages south of the River Gannel, such as Crantock and Cubert.

The barley was used to make a rather poor bread and it was also malted for beer, which was consumed in some volume. Eventually Newquay boasted six malthouses. The Trenance Valley behind Newquay was very fertile except for the marshland at the very bottom of the valley. There were cider orchards on the lower slopes and the drink became very popular in the mid-18th century. In 1840 about one quarter of the Newquay area population of 489 persons were involved in farming of one sort or the other.

The Corn Law restricted the amounts of corn imported into the country but Newquay was able to produce a surplus that was stored in a granary on North Quay Hill before being shipped to other parts of the UK. There was a lime kiln

There were nine fish cellars in Newquay, some of which dated back to the 18th century. Pilchards were laid out in rows with a liberal sprinkling of salt between the layers, which could be up to six feet in height. Fish oil was drained out and collected separately. The fish were eventually washed and loaded into barrels or 'hogsheads', each containing 3,000 pilchards. This view shows the Active cellar above the harbour's north quay. The Active was demolished in 1905. *Newquay Old Cornwall Society*

The last substantial catch of pilchards at Newquay was in 1893 and from that time local fishermen concentrated on herring fishing. However, even this seasonal activity declined after World War I. In this wonderful old postcard, postally used from Newquay in July 1907, the local fishing fleet is shown in the harbour. The tramway seems to be little used. *Author's Collection*

HARBOUR & FISHING FLEET, NEWQUAY.

at the bottom of South Quay Hill. In the mid to late 1890s, long after the Corn Law had been abolished (in 1849), the price of wheat crashed as ships from all over the world arrived on Cornish shores. There had also been some poor harvests in preceding years. Farmers diversified and more grasslands were put down to accommodate dairy cows, beef cattle, sheep, pigs and poultry. Most of the farms were very small by today's standard, averaging about 50 acres each.

Mechanisation on the local farms increased with tractors replacing horses, combine harvesters replacing binding and threshing machines, rotary mowers, turners and haymakers. Granulated fertiliser and mechanical spreaders replaced a plethora of old manual activities. In dairy farming milking machines and milking parlours have replaced old manual and low volume procedures. Although some hedgerows have been removed in the area many have been retained to act as wind breaks.

Dairying was once the most profitable type of farming in the area but interference by the British Government and the European Parliament, cut-throat competition from abroad and the driving down of prices by major supermarkets have destroyed the viability of many dairy farms. In the 1970s pigs were kept on over 40 per cent of farms in the Newquay area but again low prices in the past couple of decades have seen a reduction in pig farming. Rearing beef cattle has been far more profitable than servicing dairy herds because the needs of the animals and therefore costs are considerably less. However, in 'gross take' across all farms in the area sheep provide the main source of income. The climate is conducive to early lambing and the best prices are paid for early lambs. The wool is also sold, each fleece weighing-in at about 15 pounds. Cabbages, potatoes, cauliflower and broccoli are also grown in the district but not in huge volumes.

Even in the 21st century farming is still an important industry but in the immediate area of the town of Newquay all farmland has been purchased by property developers who have no doubt made considerably more money than the hard working local farmer.

Fishing

Being surrounded by water the County of Cornwall has a great fishing tradition going back to the Iron Age. Numerous fishing villages developed and this included Newquay. Back in the 16th century fishing was described as one of the three biggest industries in the county, the others being mining and farming. Newquay was to develop into one of these villages, growing rapidly from 30 cottages in 1818 to a town of some 7,000 inhabitants a century later. The main source of revenue in the Newquay area was from fishing for pilchards, which, although very lucrative was nevertheless seasonal. The pilchard is smaller than a mackerel but larger than a sardine and they always appeared in large shoals. In season special lookouts were posted to spot the shoals, clues being provided by flocks of sea birds shadowing the fish as well as disturbance to the water and a reddish tinge on the sea, more easily spotted in calm seas. The pilchards headed north from the Atlantic towards the Bristol Channel in deep water but on their return they hugged the coast in shallow water, which is

Around the turn of the 20th century herring fishing was big business in Newquay, resulting in a considerable amount of activity in the harbour area. The better the catch the greater the inclination to celebrate the resulting prosperity. In this scene a local photographer catches the action as hogsheads are filled with fish in what is described as 'a record catch'. Note the old tramway trestle in the background.   *Newquay Old Cornwall Society*

In this wonderfully animated scene in Newquay Harbour fish are being unloaded from fishing vessels as the tide recedes. Most of the fish have already been loaded into the hogsheads and some are being removed by horse and cart. It looks as though some of the crowd could be buyers. Within a decade the fishing industry in Newquay would be all but finished, bringing to an end centuries of tradition.   *Cornish Studies Library*

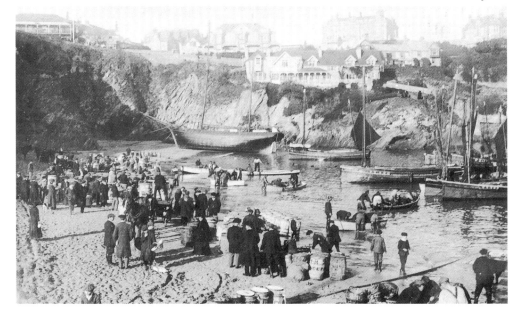

when they were at their most vulnerable from the attentions of the fishermen. After the pilchards had departed the herrings arrived but the former was much more important.

The arrival of the shoals of pilchards could be predicted on a broad brush seasonal basis but they actually needed to be located. The fishing companies appointed special spotters, called 'Huers'. There was a huer's house at the beginning of the headland, located below what is now the Atlantic Hotel. The ancient building was rebuilt in 1835 and it has survived the passage of time. As already mentioned, when a shoal was spotted by the huer he would use a megaphone-like trumpet and shout 'heva', 'heva'. The word would rapidly spread in the town and everybody involved would rush to the boats. In the season many locals left their main employment on a temporary basis to join the seining fleet.

The main fishing process for catching the pilchards was called 'seining'. The seining boats were rowing boats with a crew of seven men. They carried a fine mesh seining net, some 1,000 ft long and 70 ft deep. The net was 'shot' at the appropriate time. Two other vessels were involved, the 'volyer' or follower, which carried a tuck net and a 'lurker' was in attendance. The volyer boat also carried seven men. The end of the seine net was held secure by the volyer while the seine boat rowed quickly round in a circle to trap the fish. The lurker carried the master seiner or overseer. When the fish were encircled each end of the net was tied by ropes. A good catch could amount to over one million fish. The entrapped fish were left in the water for one tide to subdue them. They were then removed by 'tucking' whereby the fish were transferred via a smaller net from which fish were gradually lifted by the basket load, put into the boat and rowed ashore. The fish were then removed to a cellar.

Each collection of seining boats was owned by a company and each of these companies had a fish cellar. Despite the name these cellars were above ground and each had a fish loft. They had to be large enough to accommodate 500 hogsheads (straight-sided barrels) of fish, each containing up to 3,000 pilchards. Huge quantities of salt were used in the process. The fish were laid out in rows with a layer of salt between each row. These stacks would reach about five foot in height when another row was started. The fish were left for five to six weeks during which time the oil drained out under the pressure of the weight of fish in each row, with sometimes a stone weight being added. The oil was sold separately from the fish. The fish were washed a couple of times and placed into casks, although the total function involved a number of specific processes, most of them carried out by women and children. The main markets for pilchards were Catholic countries bordering the Mediterranean.

There were nine major cellars in Newquay. Some dated back to the late 1700s. The oldest was the 'Spy' on Towan Head, the 'Fly', 'The Good Intent' both on the cliffs under the Beacon, just north of the harbour, and 'The Active', at the head of the north pier. The 'Toby' was situated at the lower end of Tower Lane and 'Rose Cellars' was at the top of the road that descended to the harbour. The 'Unity' cellars were at the bottom of Gover Lane and the 'Speculation' was under the cliff by the 'Cozy Nook' theatre. Finally and the last built was the 'Hope', also in Tower Lane. There were also four ancient cellars including 'Point Cellar', the 'Union', the 'Treffry' and the 'Concord', the latter located in nearby

Although significant commercial activities at Newquay Harbour ended in the 1920s there is still a modicum of activity, mainly in fishing for crustacea, especially lobsters. With lobster pots piled high on the old CMR detached central jetty the good ship *Trevose*, No. PW64, is unloaded in September 2007. *Author*

Porth. Sadly, although 'The Toby' was incorporated into a store building, no complete cellar has been preserved, which in view of their importance to the growing town of Newquay seems a great shame.

Unfortunately the pilchard industry gradually dwindled. Not only was there increasing competition and large numbers of pilchards being caught in deeper waters by the drifting process but the actual pilchard shoals changed the habit of a lifetime and ceased to frequent the bays of the north Cornish coastline. The last substantial catch at Newquay was in 1893. From that date full time professional fishermen concentrated on herring fishing, although that too had a seasonal element and could be fished for only a few months of the year. For some years there was a small herring 'fleet' based at Newquay. Herring fishing at Newquay reached its peak just after World War I but then gradually declined.

In recent years there has been a modicum of general fishing by small craft but the emphasis has been on shell fish, including crabs, lobsters and crayfish. In the season pleasure boats use the harbour and wealthy tourists pay handsomely to go shark fishing. In the winter months boats throughout the harbour are under repair and refurbishment and the lobster pots are piled high, especially on the old CMR central jetty. Normally at high tide there are a handful of seals sunbathing within the harbour to the delight of tourists. At low tide the harbour is just about devoid of water. The old tramway tunnel aperture is still visible and the lifeboat house is a focal point. Outside the harbour walls hundreds of surfers wait to catch that super wave to speed them and their surfboard back to the beach. The days of the great Newquay and Cornish fishing industry have now gone but its heritage lives on.

Mining and Explosives

Tin, copper, lead, iron, wolfram, zinc and arsenic have all been mined in Cornwall for many centuries, with a peak of activity during the mid-19th century. The scale of operations was quite breathtaking as rapid growth was commensurate with the demands of the industrial revolution and an increasing population. From the early days of primitive manual mining activities, dating back thousands of years, mechanisation gradually took hold in the 18th century. Water power gave way to steam power and by the mid-19th century engine houses in a variety of shapes and sizes liberally covered the substantial mining areas.

Tens of thousands of tons of ore were raised every year but as the mines were worked more vigorously many became deeper and therefore more expensive to operate. With growing production the transportation of materials became crucial. Although the perils of the sea were always present a vast fleet of small sailing ships operating from a large number of ports on both the north and south coasts of Cornwall coped with payload volumes. Outgoing loads comprised various ores and minerals and incoming commodities included coal and timber for use in the mines and pits and fertiliser. However, the journey between the mines and the ports was grossly inefficient and for decades was entrusted to horses and mules carrying panniers containing the payload. Increasingly, team of horses were employed hauling wooden metal-tyred wagons with a capacity of about three tons. Not only were such journeys slow but loading and unloading was a manual operation and, particularly in the winter months, the primitive non-metalled roads became deeply rutted and wagons frequently became 'bogged-down' in the mud.

Opened in 1891, the very extensive Perranporth Explosive Works on Cligga Head, just south of that town, was owned by the British & Colonial Explosives Company. It was taken over by Noble's Explosives but as the mining industry declined so did the need for explosives and the works closed in 1905. The works was resuscitated during World War I but it closed forever in 1919. The surviving remains are well worth a visit, as seen in this 2007 view looking towards Perranporth. *Author*

The underground conditions in Cornwall's mines during the 19th century were appalling. To reach richer lodes mines became deeper and deeper and the miners were obliged to work in dark and damp conditions hundreds of fathoms beneath the ground, with often only candles providing light. With candles in their hats, miners chip away at the ore, which is being removed by tramway at East Pool, about 16 miles from Newquay, in 1892.   *Cornish Studies Library*

To many the ultimate Cornish icons are the remains of disused engine houses and stacks that litter the countryside in many parts of the county. All along the north Cornwall coast these silent sentinels excite the imagination as to what life must have been like a century and a half earlier. These buildings housed massive coal-fired steam engines that were used as pumping engines for removing water or whim engines for lifting ore, equipment and miners.   *Author*

Slowly the roads improved as finances from the turnpike system became available but it was the introduction of tramways and railways that made the greatest impression in modernising the transportation system. Ports and quays such as Calstock, Looe, Fowey, Par, Pentewan, Devoran, Falmouth, Penzance, St Ives, Hayle, Portreath, Newquay, Padstow, Wadebridge and Bude, plus a handful of minor sites, became rail connected. There were also a huge number of minor tramways incorporated within mining areas and many of the actual mine complexes. Initially these tramways and railways were horse-powered but gradually the steam locomotive arrived, enabling heavier loads to be transported to the ports.

The extraction of china clay and china stone became increasingly important particularly in the Hensbarrow Downs area north of St Austell. There were other areas where china clay was extracted, including pits between Penzance and St Just, on Bodmin Moor and near Helston. Although discovered in Cornwall in 1746, the extraction of china clay was a later development than the mining of ores. By the 1840s only about half a million tons of china clay and stone was produced. This increased to three million tons by the 1880s and over 6,500,000 tons by the turn of the 20th century. To some extent the growth of the china clay industry helped alleviate the unemployment problems caused by the fluctuations and eventual decline of the traditional metalliferous mining industry. However, it must be said that tens of thousands of Cornish miners emigrated to distant lands during the mid-19th century to avoid the mining depression.

Newquay itself was not renowned for its mining activities and china clay and stone were important only because plenty of Cornwall's white gold passed through the town on its way from the china clay producing area around St Dennis, some 12 miles distant, to the harbour for shipment in small wooden coasters. Having said that, there were three local areas in and around Newquay where, for a few decades, mining was important. In fact one of the mines was the largest lead mine in Cornwall.

In Newquay evidence of ancient and middle age mining has been found, particularly at Porth, where activities date back to the iron age. In 1553 at Mount Wise, the hill south of the town, a silver mine was opened and the output was used to manufacture coins of the realm. When Treffry became Lord of the Manor in 1838 he opened the Newquay Silver and Lead Mine at Lehenver, Mount Wise and this was in operation from about 1840 until 1864. In addition to the main buildings there was a counting house, carpenters and blacksmiths shops and Captain's house. After closure the disused mine was the source of water for the town. One adit to the mine was the discharge point for the water and it was located at the foot of the cliffs at Killacourt, where the Cozy Nook Theatre is located.

However, the largest mining area was behind Narrowcliff, where the Tolcarne and Rosecliffe Mine was located. There were five shafts at this point, penetrating a silver/lead ore lode. This mine finally closed in 1868, the area in-filled and covered by houses between about 1900 and 1920. The Fistral Mine on the low cliff was called North Wheal Providence and produced lead. Treffry also opened three small lead mines, Newquay Consuls (on the site of the

present municipal golf course), Tower Consuls and another on the north bank
of the River Gannel estuary by Trethellan Farm, called Chiverton Wheal Rose.
These mines were all defunct by the end of the 1860s. There was a small smelter
on the Crantock side of the Gannel but this closed when mining ceased. Finally
there was a mine on the headland at Porth but some of the extractions were
apparently of very low grade.

As mentioned above there were two other mining areas near to Newquay that
were so large that they relegated Newquay's mines to an almost irrelevant status
by comparison. A vast lead/silver mine was located at East Wheal Rose, near St
Newlyn East. The original mine in the area was called Old Wheal Rose, which
opened in 1811 and closed in 1832. Lead ore recovery became more difficult and
the prices of lead on the markets fell making continued operation uneconomic.
Nevertheless, within a couple of years East Wheal Rose had opened and it became
the largest lead mine not only in Cornwall but in the whole of England. At its
peak 1,250 people were employed at the mine and reference is made to this in
Chapter Five. As stated there, production peaked just after the 1846 disaster when
38 miners were drowned during a flash flood that overwhelmed the pumps.
Treffry opened his tramway in 1849 but unfortunately it was downhill all the way
for the next eight years and the mine closed in 1857. Many years later in 1881
world commodity prices improved and the mine reopened. The engine house
that survives on the land owned by the present-day Lappa Valley Railway dates
from this later period. However, the resuscitation was short lived and the mine
closed forever in 1885. In its time the mine produced a quarter of a million ounces
of silver and over 50,000 tons of lead ore. There was another rich mine nearby
called Cargoll Mine that operated from 1845 to 1882.

The final area of importance was the Great Perran Iron Lode about four miles
south-west of Newquay. This lode was located at or near the surface and so
contrary to, say, East Wheal Rose much of the ore was quarried rather than
mined. The lode ran along part of Perran Beach and inland to Deer Park mine,
near what was to become Shepherds station on the Chacewater to Newquay via
Perranporth railway line. This lode had great potential and after years of taking
iron ore by horse and cart to Newquay and the Gannel estuary for shipment,
from 1874 the area was served by a railway line built by the CMR. The
developer W.R. Roebuck was unlucky because, having spent considerable
capital in the venture, there was a crash in world prices at the very time the
railway opened. The recession was so bad that 18 out of the 25 iron mines closed
during 1874. Contracts could not be met and the railway sued the Cornish
Consolidated Iron Mines Corporation, but the actions were futile because the
iron company went bankrupt and was eventually wound up in the High Court.

The mining and quarrying industries were heavy users of explosives,
including gunpowder and dynamite. As the Cornish mining industry boomed
in the early and mid-19th century explosives were used in increasing volumes.
These substances were unstable and therefore explosives factories were mainly
located in somewhat isolated locations, such as secluded valleys, amongst sand
dunes and on cliff headlands. In the latter category was the substantial
explosive works located on Cligga Head, about eight miles south of Newquay,
just beyond Perranporth. Owned by the British & Colonial Explosives Company

and later taken over by Nobel's Explosives the works produced large volumes of dynamite before production petered-out in 1905. The works was revived at the start of World War I but it finally closed in 1919. The buildings have all since been demolished but there are extensive ruins to explore on Cligga Head. These foundations must not be confused with some old mining remains in the same area. Another gunpowder factory was owned by C.M. Powder Co. Ltd at Treamble, at the end of the branch line from Shepherds, but that too closed several decades ago.

Although not of significant importance, mining around Newquay in the mid-19th century provided full time employment for 10 per cent of the town's workforce and a far greater percentage in the areas surrounding the mines.

Textiles

Newquay may seem an unlikely spot for the development of the textile industry but much of the area, especially the grassy headlands and cliff tops that were not suitable for crops, was ideal for grazing sheep. This process of breeding sheep for meat, wool and skins had of course been in existence for centuries but is was in 1905 that a lady known as Madame Hawke sprung to prominence. In that year Mrs Hawke's husband died leaving her to support six children. She started a modest clothes shop in Newquay and made many of the garments herself with the aid of a hand knitting machine. She sent samples of her work to Debenhams and they were so impressed that they agreed to take her total output. She expanded the business and acquired larger premises. Other factories opened and at its peak no fewer than 450 residents of Newquay were employed in the textile industry. Other factories opened and after World War I there was the Trinity Works, F.C. Hawke & Sons, Hope Knitting Company, Blystra Knitting Company, The North Cornwall Knitting Company, Oakleigh Hosiery Company and the West End Knitting Company all based in Newquay.

During World War I the Drake family took over the Hawke businesses and formed the Newquay Knitting Company. The industry was so large that a separate cardboard box factory was built to serve Newquay's textile companies. The Madame Hawke name is still used but since World War II there was a steady decline in the industry due to cheap foreign imports. After being taken over by Messrs Abbot and Scaddon in 1961 the main factory in Crantock Street closed during the late 1960s thus ending the town's long association with the industry. The site has now been redeveloped to provide private residences and retirement homes.

Tourism

Although the history of tourism is detailed in the previous chapter, when all of the various services are taken into consideration including hotels, catering, entertainment, transport and retail then there is no doubt that more people are employed in the tourist industry than any other and by a considerable margin.

Far left: In 1905 the husband of one Madame Hawke died leaving her to support six children. She opened a clothes shop and made many of the garments herself. The business was a great success. After selling-out after World War I the Newquay Knitting Co. was formed. The business was successful and eventually there were at least eight knitting and clothing companies in Newquay employing some 450 staff. This view shows the shop with the business 'under the patronage of the Royal Family'.

Left: As the town of Newquay grew so did its retail community. In this wonderful item from 1922 one could buy a splendid box camera at Alfred Bond, the dispensing chemist in Bank Street, have your shirt cleaned at the local sanitary laundry (your order being 'greatly esteemed'), catch one of the GWR agent's buses from the station and buy a book at the 'new' Homeland Bookshop.

(Both) Author's Collection

As tourism increased and the town of Newquay grew to accommodate the annual influx, so the number and style of local hotels and guest houses also grew. In this fascinating scene from the late 1930s guests are indulging themselves in a round of putting, while outside the Bay Hotel is a tremendous variety of British-built cars, including Wolseley, Rover, Austin and Standard models, all guaranteed to be painted black!   *Author's Collection*

There is little doubt that the most prestigious Newquay hotels were the Victorian-built Headland and Atlantic establishments with other fine hotels in town, such as the Victoria and Great Western. The Headland seen here (and little changed in well over a century) was often used by Royalty, its coastal views being unparalleled. Towan Head is to the right of this 2007 view.   *Author*

Collecting old postcards and photographs of Newquay Harbour is a fascinating pastime. From the pictures it is possible to estimate the volumes of shipping and tramway traffic in any given year, albeit on a non-scientific basis. In this busy scene there are eight china clay wagons on the quay lines, with one wagon on the south quay (*right*) having its loading chute connected to discharge its cargo into the hull of a small wooden sailing ship. The view is from about 1900 with the Active and the Fly fish cellars centre right.   *Newquay Old Cornwall Society*

In this later view the days of Newquay Harbour as a commercial undertaking are numbered. Four empty GWR china clay wagons wait to ascend the incline to the street tramway but there are no backloads of coal and only two commercial vessels are tied-up. The fish cellars have been demolished, with an estimated date of about 1912. The 1892 Atlantic Hotel is top left, dominating the scene.   *Author's Collection*

Chapter Three

Transport

Shipping

A significant number of the residents of Cornwall who were not employed in the mines or on the land had little choice but to earn a living from the sea. Apart from fishing and shipbuilding the only alternative way of making a living was as a seaman. In 1850 over 100 residents were employed in the industry and as late as the year 1889 no fewer than 70 Newquay families, mainly fathers and sons, were engaged in the shipping trade.

Although the Cornish had been seafarers for centuries the development of lead, tin, copper and iron mining, particularly in the 18th and 19th centuries, produced a massive increase in the number of commercial vessels using Cornish ports. Employment on one of the old wooden sailing ships in the 19th century was no easy option. Depending on the type and size of ship crew numbers ranged from three to twelve. The Captain was truly the master of the ship and he made all important decisions pertaining to its running. As traffic increased the number of shipping companies also increased, with wealthy businessmen funding the construction of ships at the numerous Cornish shipbuilding yards and thereby controlling small fleets of ships. Many ships had a number of owners because shares in them could be purchased in the open market. In this respect the captains were employees of the shipowners and shareholders.

Life as a seaman was tough and the word 'sailor' was very relevant. The work was heavy, the hours long and above all else life at sea was dangerous. On ships with a small crew it was almost impossible to rest during a voyage. There was often no cover over the ship's wheel, leaving mariners to the ravages of the elements. In fog there had to be lookouts, not only for rocks but for passing steam ships that would be unaware of small wooden vessels. Quite often it was necessary to go aloft to tend the sails and rigging, a very difficult task in windy or icy weather. In stormy weather it was often 'all hands on deck' and some of these difficult tasks needed to be carried out in total darkness. In still weather there was endless tacking in order to try and make progress from what would otherwise be a becalmed position. All this had to be accomplished in boots and oilskins, quite a handicap in adverse conditions.

The small sailing ships of the day would weigh-in at anything between 30 and 250 tons. Their size and sail rigging configuration would put them in the categories of smack, sloop, ketch, lugger, schooner (various configurations), brig, brigantine, barque, barquentine, etc. There was always a trade-off between speed and manoeuvrability. In broad terms small sloops with a cargo capacity of 40 to 50 tons were the preferred option for local shipping but as loads and distances increased two-masted schooners and ketches became the most popular types, replacing most of the sloops. In the mid-19th century most coastal traffic was in the hands of three-masted schooners with cargo capacities in the region of 175 tons. These vessels remained the most numerous type until the advent of iron ships with steam propulsion that would signal the end of the era of sail, and of many of the small Cornish harbours, including Newquay.

Most of the really large wooden sailing ships were square-rigged and they were employed mainly on deep sea journeys to distant locations, some travelling as far as Newfoundland. Their deep draft and limited flexibility was a major drawback for coastal use, especially at the multitude of minor Cornish ports but they were in their element on longer journeys. Although there were many minor harbours around the Cornish coast, at some locations small wooden ships were simply 'beached', unloaded and loaded at low tide and re-floated at high tide. Although this system worked to a degree, hauling carts down to sandy beaches and vertically lifting quite heavy loads on board ship did not compare with the efficiency of loading/unloading at a proper wharf, quay or dock.

Climatic conditions had a major influence on shipping. Especially in the winter months Atlantic storms would rage and with no internal combustion engine to power ships out of trouble or to make quickly for the nearest refuge these small ships were very vulnerable. Most harbours had protective sea walls where ships could anchor or berth in relative safety but those that were beached were particularly vulnerable. The number of shipwrecks around the Cornish coast is quite unbelievable and ships foundered in their thousands. The loss of life was huge and slowly but surely a network of coastguards, lighthouses and lifeboats were put into position. Even then they provided no guarantee of safety, as even 21st century events have proved.

A tiny example of disasters affecting North Cornwall ships follows. The *Triumph* built at Newquay in 1881 went missing after leaving Briton Ferry in South Wales on 3rd November, 1915 with a load of coal. It was never heard of again. The smack *Porth* was wrecked at Annet off the Scilly Isles in a blizzard during 1890 with 60 tons of culm on board. Two crew were rescued but one died of exposure. The *Nancy* was driven ashore in a force 10 gale at Welcombe Mouth north of Bude on 21st November, 1874 and all three crew were lost. The *Model* was the very first ship to handle lead ore that arrived at Newquay Harbour via the tramway from East Wheal Rose Mine in 1849. It was stranded in Barnstaple Bay on 13th March, 1911 and was a total loss. On 22nd January, 1868 the *Maria Louisa* was lost with all hands on Treguin Rocks, Mullion Island, bound from Plymouth to Penzance with slates. While riding out a strong north west gale off of Towan Head, Newquay on 29th January, 1877 the *Lizzie May* had to fly distress signals. The crew of six were rescued by lifeboat but the ship foundered and was lost. While heading for Newquay with a load of coal from Cardiff on 28th August, 1874 the *Josephine* foundered 1½ miles north-east of Trevose Head and all four crew (all members of the Hockin family) were lost. The roll call of death and destruction is truly infinite with thousands of morbid entries emphasising the dangers of seafaring in the days of sail.

A tiny handful of Newquay schooners survived World War I and the very last to use the harbour for loading was the Stephens-owned *Hetty* that departed with a load of china clay in 1921, while the last commercial vessel to use the harbour was the *Hobah* that discharged bagged manure on 22nd November, 1922. She sailed for Appledore in ballast. By this time the days of the small coastal sailing vessel were almost at an end, although the schooner *Kathleen & May* continued to serve Cornish ports until 1966, albeit with an engine fitted to supplement sail!

In addition to coasters and general merchantmen there was always considerable fishing activity at Newquay but the shipping arrangements appear in Chapter Two. One other category of shipping was the occasional visit by excursion vessels, normally paddle steamers in the Edwardian era. These ships often worked out of Bristol and they visited various points along the Bristol Channel including Ilfracombe and the Mumbles, west of Swansea. Occasionally they reached Padstow and even less frequently Newquay.

Stories about Cornish smugglers and skirmishes with revenue men are numerous and have been sufficient in number to fill many books. It is easy to take the view that such stories have been hugely exaggerated over the years. However, records from 300 years ago indicate that smuggling was carried out on a substantial scale all around Cornwall's coasts and in fact the activity dates back to at least Tudor times. Perhaps an obvious point should be made here and that is the huge difference between the activities of smugglers and those of pirates, the latter operating mainly on the high seas. Thousands of citizens were involved in the former activity, such was the resentment of high taxes on popular commodities, especially liquor and tea. Their intention was of course to evade import duties and taxes. At Newquay the patrolling 'patch' for revenue cutters, which were mostly armed schooners each with a complement of about a dozen men, was from Land's End to Bideford. Smuggling was on a grand scale, although there was even more activity around Cornwall's southern ports, which were nearer to mainland Europe. One account mentions a rendezvous at night featuring some 60 horses each carrying 1½ hundredweight of tea. Ships

In this animated study from before the turn of the 20th century there are five commercial wooden sailing ships in Newquay Harbour and three railway wagons, one containing china stone and the other two filled with coal. In the background, on top of the distant cliffs, the town of Newquay is growing, with only a few 'gaps' left to be built upon.

Author's Collection

In the days of sail the Cornish coast could be treacherous in bad weather and thousands of ships met their end on the rocks, with a heavy loss of life. With no sophisticated communications systems and primitive weather forecasts it was all too easy for even experienced skippers to be caught unaware. Even with steam power or diesel propulsion the perils of the sea were never very far away and in 1989 the MV *Secil Japan* met its end at Deadman's Cove, near Portreath, just a few miles south-west of Newquay.

Cornish Studies Library

that were intercepted or caught in the act of duty avoidance were found to be carrying significant loads. One ship had 400 gallons of Spanish wine on board, another had 3 hogsheads of tobacco (over 1,740 lb.), 183 gallons of French claret and 163 gallons of brandy. Another ship was carrying 281 gallons of claret, one hogshead of tobacco, 68 gallons of wine and 167 gallons of brandy, plus 32 cwt of candles (another high-cost item)!

A wide range of commodities were handled at Newquay Harbour, although over time there was a change in emphasis. In addition to Newquay Harbour there was a registered port on the Gannel river to the south of Newquay in the 13th century. There was trade with Wales and Ireland and some goods were transferred from beached craft onto barges and conveyed further inland to Trevemper, including Welsh coal for Truro Smelting Works. As already mentioned, early practice involved simply beaching small craft, with horses and wagons travelling down the sands to unload and load, with the craft refloating at the next high tide. The same process took place at Porth, north of Newquay and in the River Gannel. Iron ore was loaded into beached craft off Crantock.

There is evidence that the north quay of the present Newquay Harbour had been *in situ* for centuries, reference thereto being made as long ago as 1439 but the long south quay was added in the Lomax/Treffry era and this not only afforded shipping much greater protection from inclement weather and storms but better loading and unloading facilities. From 1849 the south quay was tramway-connected and from this date all lead and iron ore and coal traffic was handled there. The north quay was used largely by fishing vessels. From 1872 a central jetty was built by the CMR and this doubled the ship handling capacity.

Long before the tramway arrived ores were brought by horse and cart to a point above the harbour and crude chutes were used to channel the minerals down onto the quay. One report mentions that grain was transferred down to the harbour by the same means. The remains of the chute apertures can still be detected in the retaining walls of the harbour.

The central jetty was 200 ft long and 40 ft wide and it was connected to the shore by a long curved wooden trestle. The jetty was tramway-served with a single track feed dividing into two sidings. The Harbour Master instructed the Captains of vessels where they should tie-up. Often vessels were towed out of the harbour by 'hobblers' (horse and rope). In the early days the primary outgoing commodity in tonnage terms was lead and iron ore. Much of this was destined for smelters in South Wales. Incoming tonnage was headed by coal, mostly from South Wales, leading to a very convenient 'out and back' run. As these industries declined the china clay and china stone industry grew and this was to become the main export, mostly to Runcorn for onward transmission to the Potteries by canal. There was also a demand for timber, especially in the mines. Agriculture demanded the importation of manures, fertilisers and limestone, while a number of crops particularly corn and barley were exported through Newquay. There was a wide range of small volume miscellaneous commodities handled and early postcards show both tramway and road going wagons on the quay, all horse-powered.

To the delight of summer tourists seals can often be found basking in Newquay harbour at high tide. The seals are well fed as they follow the tourist boats and receive nibbles in return for providing seasonal entertainment. On the left is the CMR 1872 central jetty while on the right is the south quay, as seen in September 2006.   *Author*

Right: The first formal RNLI lifeboat to arrive in Cornwall was at Padstow in 1856. By 1860 it was Newquay's turn when the *Joshua* was delivered. This was none too soon as during the year 1866 a staggering 1,860 ships were lost around the shores of the UK. In 1895 a new lifeboat station was established on the headland with the lifeboat being launched down a 1 in 2¼ slipway, the steepest in the country. Closed in 1934 the disused structure is still visible and a visit is highly recommended.

Author

Below: The lifeboat was always an important part of the local community and featured in the entertainment provided on Bank Holidays, galas and regattas and of course 'Lifeboat Day'. Crowds would gather to watch the launch, the highlight being when the lifeboat actually hit the water at the bottom of the steep slip. Such an event was recorded in the 1920s. The Newquay lifeboat station closed between 1934 and 1965, although a boat was on station in the harbour during World War II.

Author's Collection

NEWQUAY, LIFEBOAT DAY, LEAVING THE SLIP.

The Lifeboat

As long as there have been ships there have been maritime accidents and disasters. Particularly in the days of sail, ships were extremely vulnerable to the vagaries of the weather. Without modern communications equipment such as radio, radar, reliable weather forecasts and an internal combustion engine ships could flounder in bad weather, even with the most experienced skipper in charge. It is easy to underestimate the power of the sea but a visit to the Newquay headland during a winter gale and visually to experience the enormous seas, leaves the observer under no illusions that the sea was (and still is), according to Rudyard Kipling, a 'widow maker'. Also the Cornish coastline is rugged with small islands and rocky outcrops, an ever-present danger to shipping. Just to give scale to the problem faced, in 1842 no fewer than 600 ships were lost around the shores of the UK and approximately 1,500 lives were lost. By 1866 a staggering 1,860 ships and over 900 lives were lost but by then a random assortment of rescue vessels and organizations had been set up as the Royal National Lifeboat Institution (RNLI) was formed. Their figures show that in 1866 the RNLI saved 1,600 lives, a figure that relates to both British and foreign sailors.

At nearby Padstow there had been a 'Padstow Harbour Association for the Preservation of Life and Property from Shipwreck', which was formed in 1829. In the early days lifeboats had, of necessity, been whatever vessels were available and in the case of Newquay it was normally long narrow gigs that were launched. Newquay had possessed life saving equipment, which included rocket apparatus that had been used since 1844, and it is said that the men had done great service with it in rescuing many crews from stranded vessels. The first RNLI lifeboat at nearby Padstow arrived in 1856. It was not long before additional lifeboats appeared in Cornwall at other strategic locations and in 1860 it was Newquay's turn, when a lifeboat station was established. A full list of Newquay lifeboats appears on page 44.

In 1860 six large horses owned by Georgie Burt left Newquay one morning to collect the new lifeboat called *Joshua*. As the lifeboat arrived in the hours of darkness locals emerged from their dwellings in some numbers forming a procession. A lifeboat house had been built in the town, beyond the coastguard houses in Fore Street, in downtown Newquay. The vessel was later christened and launched at the harbour with the words 'I name you *Joshua*, and when you go forth on the mighty waters may you like Joshua of old and as your name implies, be the saviour of men'. The lifeboatmen put on their cork jackets and before they left the harbour a self-righting demonstration was given with the crew being ejected into the water in the process, much to the excitement of the watching crowds.

The lifeboat was always hauled by a team of horses to whatever beach was deemed to be most suitable to effect a rescue. When the seas were particularly rough the lifeboat could be hauled several miles by road and path for launching because this was a much safer option than launching at Newquay and having to face violent seas before ever reaching a stricken ship and its crew. In 1895 the lifeboat station was moved to Towan Head and the steepest slipway in the country, at a gradient of 1 in 2¼, was constructed to launch the lifeboat into deep

In this very rare and quite remarkable photograph many of the residents of Newquay have taken advantage of a fine day in 1940 to leave the worries of World War II behind by visiting the commercially abandoned harbour to welcome the arrival of RNLI motor lifeboat *Richard Silver Oliver*. The town had been without a lifeboat since 1934 but for the next five years the service would return. Note the long raincoats, short trousers, school caps and the then surviving but disused CMR wooden trestle.

Cornish Studies Library

This most unusual shot of dubious quality depicts a lifeboat exchange at Newquay goods yard, believed to have been recorded in 1920 when the *John William Dudley* was replaced by the *Admiral Sir George Beck*. Although the lifeboats were launched down the steep slipway they had to be hauled by horses back to the lifeboat station, from wherever they landed.   *Cornish Studies Library*

water. The slip was too steep for the boat to be hauled back up the incline to the boathouse and the vessel had to be returned from one of the Newquay beaches to the headland by a team of eight horses. In 1899 a lifeboat house was also built and it survives to this day, albeit not for RNLI use. The building received a Royal visit in 1909 when HRH The Prince of Wales visited the boat house and inspected the *James Stevens No. 5* lifeboat. Between 1864 and 1908 the Newquay lifeboat saved 98 lives, an impressive record and one that demonstrates the perilous nature of a seafaring occupation.

The steep slipway on Towan Head was deemed to be unsuitable in the year 1934 and the station was closed. The reasons given were the lack of availability of horses to return the boat to the station and the arrival at Padstow of a new motor lifeboat that could cover the geographical area formerly covered by the Newquay crews. In 1940 a Newquay lifeboat station was reinstated and located in the harbour as a wartime measure. This was withdrawn after World War II in 1945 and for 20 years Newquay survived without a lifeboat. An inshore lifeboat station was opened within the harbour area from 1965 and the type of vessel was upgraded from a 'D' class to a 'C' class in 1983. In 1984 RNLI Newquay was awarded a 100 years cumulative service award. In 1993 the station was enlarged and a new boathouse capable of accommodating an 'Atlantic' 21RIB lifeboat, a launching tractor and the existing 'D' class vessel was built. The old Seaman's Mission was demolished and a joint RNLI boathouse and Seaman's Mission constructed. This was the first RNLI station to incorporate a church.

In 1995 the 'C' class lifeboat was withdrawn and a relief 'Atlantic' 21 lifeboat placed on duty until later in the year when an 'Atlantic' 75-B715 arrived. A new class 'D' lifeboat D497 was added to the complement in 1996 and the vessel was named in 2005. The Newquay lifeboats continue in service and between 1965 and 1990 there were 590 launches and it is claimed that 207 lives were saved. In recent decades the nature of the work of the lifeboats has changed and rather than mariners coping with the age of sail it is stranded holidaymakers, cut off by the tide, fallen cliff walkers, surfers with cramp, inexperienced yachtsmen and missing children that comprise the majority of call-outs. This does not diminish the lifeboat service, which works in liaison with the coastguard, air/sea rescue services and the seasonal beach lifeguard service.

The lifeboats are still operated by volunteers and indeed when the Class 'D' was called-out recently 17 volunteers answered the call and the first three to arrive actually took out the vessel. For a century and a half volunteers have often put their own lives on the line and the RNLI must be commended for their efforts. It is possible to question their methods of funding and to ask whether they should become the AA or RAC of the seas with boating types paying annual subscriptions rather than asking for donations from the non-boat owning general public. Some would argue that rescue costs should be recovered through billing, especially in respect of those who have been irresponsible, but such notions offend the ethos of the service and so public collections to fund the service are likely to continue in the future.

Throughout the years the Newquay lifeboat has been the focal point of the seafaring community and the local community. Whatever vessel has been in service it has always been incorporated in local parades through the town. On August bank holidays the lifeboat was launched on Towan Head and huge crowds, especially in the Edwardian era, would gather around the slipway to watch the spectacle of the lifeboat hitting the water after the steep and increasingly rapid descent. Also the lifeboat has normally participated in special days in the harbour area including various regattas, gig championships, fish festivals and lifeboat day itself. Both the old concrete slipway and the boathouse on Towan Head and the new lifeboat station within the harbour are well worth a visit.

Newquay Lifeboats' History

1860   Newquay lifeboat station established.
1860   First lifeboat *Joshua* on station.
1865   Lifeboat replaced by a second *Joshua*.
1871   *Joshua* renamed *James & Elizabeth*.
1873   *James & Elizabeth 2* on station.
1873   *James & Elizabeth 2* renamed *Pendock Neale*.
1892   *Willie Rogers* on station.
1895   Slipway at Towan Head completed – steepest ever built.
1899   Lifeboat House built on Towan Head. *James Stevens No. 5* on station.
1917   Lifeboat lost during rescue, crew of five seriously injured.
1919   *John William Dudley* on station.
1920   *Admiral Sir George Beck* on station (last pulling lifeboat).
1934   Station closed.

1940   Station temporarily reopened in Newquay Harbour area as a war time measure.
1940   Motor lifeboat *Richard Silver Oliver* on station.
1945   Station closed after lifeboat withdrawn.
1965   Inshore lifeboat station opened with class 'D' lifeboat. Increasing water sports activity.
1983   Class 'D' lifeboat withdrawn and replaced by 'C' class.
1984   Lifeboat station given award for 100 years cumulative service.
1994   Old Seaman's Mission demolished and a new RNLI joint boathouse and Seaman's Mission constructed. Boathouse incorporated a church and room to accommodate Atlantic 21RIB lifeboat, launching tractor and trailer and class 'D' lifeboat.
1995   Class 'C' lifeboat withdrawn and Atlantic 21 lifeboat replaced by Atlantic 75-B715 vessel.
1996   New class 'D' lifeboat D497 in service.
2005   Newquay's new Class 'D' lifeboat named *Valerie Wilson* and later Atlantic 75 vessel named *Phyllis*.

The various crews of the Newquay lifeboats over the years have received numerous awards for bravery and valour. During World War II a total of 11 lives were saved by the Newquay crews and many others were saved from non life-threatening but still potentially dangerous situations.

The 1899 lifeboat station built on the headland at Newquay has survived the passage of time, despite not being used for its original purpose for well over 70 years. A commemorative plaque appears above the doors. In 1909 the building was visited by HRH The Prince of Wales but problems returning the lifeboat to the headland contributed to its demise in 1934.   *Author*

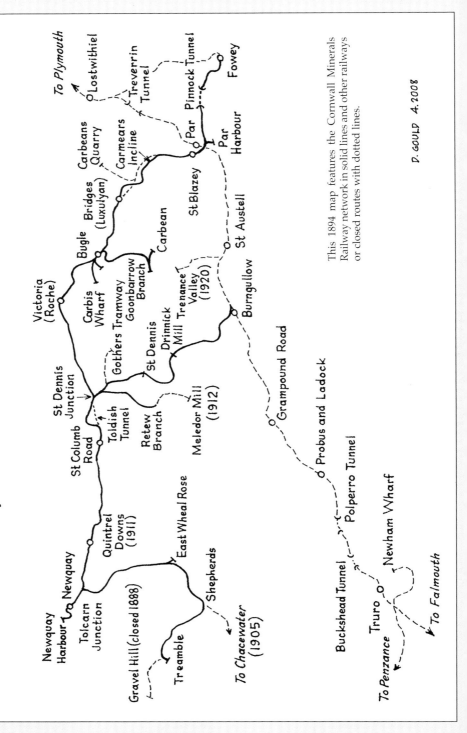

Cornwall Minerals Railway 1894

Newquay Harbour
Newquay
Tolcarn Junction
Quintrel Downs (1911)
East Wheal Rose
Gravel Hill (closed 1888)
Shepherds
Treamble
To Chacewater (1905)
St Columb Road
St Dennis Junction
Toldish Tunnel
Retew Branch
Meledor Mill (1912)
Victoria (Roche)
Carbis Wharf
Gothers Tramway
Goonbarrow Branch
St Dennis
Drinnick Mill
Trenance Valley (1920)
Carbean
Bugle
Bridges (Luxulyan)
Carbeans Quarry
Carmears Incline
St Blazey
St Austell
Burngullow
Par
Par Harbour
Pinnock Tunnel
Fowey
Treverrin Tunnel
Lostwithiel
To Plymouth
Grampound Road
Probus and Ladock
Polperro Tunnel
Newham Wharf
Buckshead Tunnel
Truro
To Penzance
To Falmouth

This 1894 map features the Cornwall Minerals Railway network in solid lines and other railways or closed routes with dotted lines.

D. GOULD 4.2008

Tramways and Railways

The history of tramways and railways at Newquay are fully described in Chapters Five, Six and Seven and only a broad brush oversight appears here.

The first tramway to operate at Newquay was the western sections of the Treffry Tramway, known as the Newquay Tramway, which opened to East Wheal Rose mine in 1849 and to St Dennis and Hendra in 1857. The horse-operated tramway was taken over by the CMR in 1874, with that company upgrading the line to enable steam locomotives to operate. The CMR also extended the original tramway beyond East Wheal Rose to Treamble and Gravel Hill and joined up the missing section of tramway between Bugle and St Dennis Junction and St Blazey to Fowey, thereby linking Newquay with Fowey by rail for the first time. The CMR incorporated many track re-alignments and opened new freight-only branch lines. Operationally the line was taken over by the GWR in 1877 and acquired by it in 1896. CMR trains connected with main line trains at Par from 1879 and after the abolition of the broad gauge on the main line in 1892 through running from distant locations to Newquay was possible.

In 1905 the GWR opened its branch line from Chacewater, via St Agnes and Perranporth, to Newquay giving through connections with the City of Truro. The only remaining horse-drawn section of the old Treffry Tramway, from Newquay station goods yard to the top of the harbour incline and on the quays within the harbour, ceased in 1921/1922. Newquay goods yard was booming and through holiday trains helped establish the town as a prime holiday resort. Over the years there were many changes at the Newquay station site, with new sidings, extended platforms, a new signal box etc. The railway scene became firmly established and there followed a period of consolidation. Even by 1963 there were still through trains on summer Saturdays to Manchester, Newcastle, Wolverhampton and York, as well as two trains to Paddington and one to Nottingham on Friday evening. However in the same year BR closed the Chacewater line and withdrew all goods facilities from the town a year later. Newquay station was heavily rationalised in the 1970s and 1980s with platforms being closed, the old goods yard reduced to carriage sidings and all manual semaphore signalling removed. By the 1990s the branch line had become a single line stub and every siding was removed. The abandoned signal box was burnt to the ground and the original station became derelict before it too was, inexcusably, demolished to make way for additional parking.

The Newquay branch still receives through trains from distant parts on summer weekends and on summer Saturdays in 2007 trains departed for Newcastle and Manchester with three for London. On Sundays there were departures for both Glasgow and London. Otherwise just four round trip workings per day are operated by one- or two-car diesel units that travel the 20¾ miles from Par station in about 50 minutes! Other than during the peak weeks of summer there are no Sunday trains. A short section of awning and a brick shelter are the only creature comforts provided for potential passengers at Newquay. The train service is appalling with, in 2008, no train from Par to Newquay between 14.00 and 19.28 hours! The first connection from London arrives at Newquay just before 15.00. The first train from Newquay is at 10.18 forcing early travellers onto buses, which the train operating company (First Group) also owns!

This early 20th century scene could have been taken decades earlier and it shows a typical stagecoach of the era in Newquay. The heavily laden North Cornwall Coach shows a routeing of Newquay, St Columb, Padstow and Wadebridge on its side, although it is in fact on excursion duty. Top right is an 'AA' sign, that organization being formed in 1905 and which started recommending hotels in 1912. Motor buses had taken over many routes by this time and the days of the coach were numbered.   *Cornish Studies Library*

From a few hundred cars registered in Cornwall in 1907 there were a staggering 320,000 cars and vans recorded in 2007. The social impact of the motor car has been remarkable, bringing with it both huge benefits and growing problems, witness the traffic jams and parking problems in Newquay during the peak summer months. Displaying the famous 'AF' Cornish registration letters, these sporting types are enjoying themselves near Newquay in 1911, with no jams to worry about!   *Cornish Studies Library*

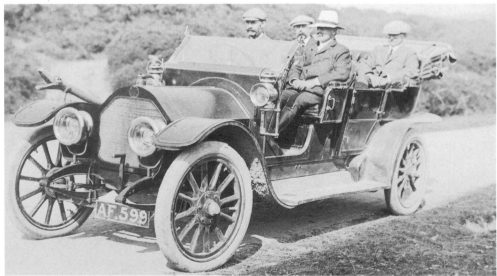

Road Transport

Horse-drawn stage coach and mail services in Cornwall date back to the late 18th century and services greatly increased in number once the Turnpike Trusts started to improve roads, costs being met through the imposition of tolls. The greatest period of road development occurred between 1820 and 1849. Major towns such as Falmouth, Truro, St Austell and Bodmin were well served but in this era Newquay was but a tiny hamlet and the first coach services to reach the area ran from Bodmin to Wadebridge, Wadebridge having been connected to Bodmin (but not the 'outside world') by rail since 1834.

One of the first stage coach services to serve Newquay was operated by the North Cornwall Coach Company. It placed its 'Pioneer' coach on the road between Wadebridge, Camelford and Launceston in 1879. The services connected with the LSWR's coach at Camelford. In the later years of the 19th century and in early Edwardian times the company ran a Wadebridge, Padstow, St Columb to Newquay service, as illustrated. The primary coaching 'inns' in the town of Newquay were the Atlantic Hotel and the Red Lion Inn. Before the company ceased trading in 1912 the North Cornwall operated summer coach excursions to Boscastle and Newquay.

As soon as the internal combustion engine was applied to road vehicles at the turn of the 20th century it was not long before motor buses were taking over from horse-drawn coaches on a number of routes. However, in certain areas horse-drawn coach services survived well into Edwardian times. Strangely it was the GWR that was to pioneer scheduled road motor services in Cornwall and in 1903 it was operating a service from its branch line terminus at Helston to the Lizard. This was followed by services from Newlyn to Marazion and Penzance to Land's End. In East Cornwall the GWR operated a motor service from Saltash to Callington in 1904. Development was rapid and by the end of 1904 it was running a fleet of 36 motor buses. The great advantage of the motor bus in Cornwall was the transportation of the population to remote areas, often on a door to door basis, thereby obviating the need to consider further railway lines and the related capital cost. The real explosion in motor bus services occurred after World War I when the GWR operated a complete network of routes. The LSWR also operated buses in Cornwall but on a smaller scale than the GWR. The LSWR were later to be linked with the Southern National Company.

In the meantime private car ownership and the use of motorised commercial vehicles increased as gradually the internal combustion engine made an impact on the local and county road transport scene. However, as far as the general public were concerned the motor bus was the primary opportunity to experience horsepower from a non-equestrian source.

There were of course a number of other bus operators emerging to cover particular local routes and to cream-off some of the lucrative traffic. At that time there were no restrictions or licensing arrangements and anyone could acquire and run a bus and charge whatever fares they thought the market would bear. The GWR continued to expand, however, and it became one of the largest fleet operators in the UK. Other operators also found scope to grow, for example the

The motor bus arrived in Newquay in Edwardian times with the primary operator being the Great Western Railway! In 1929 the GWR transferred its bus operations to the Western National Omnibus Company. In this vintage view 1934 Dennis Ace OD 7793, a 20-seater with Eastern Counties coachwork, operated as No. 704 by Western National, is seen before working a Newquay to Crantock and Cubert service. Note the 'chock' under the rear wheels, suggesting a weak handbrake. *Author's Collection*

Over the years the motor bus developed into a more reliable, better performing and more comfortable mode of transport and by the 1930s substantial half-cab coaches provided many creature comforts. In its Cornish timetable for 1934 Western National produced this artistic impression showing its vehicles serving 'seaside & country - through the West of England'.
Author's Collection

pioneer of charabanc tours in Newquay was Woodward's Garage, which ran 16 tours in the summer of 1920.

In places the GWR had buses competing with its trains, a situation reflected in comparatively recent times with the privatisation of British Rail and the appointment of Train Operating Companies. Complaints were lodged by a number of independent operators and they alleged that the GWR did not have Parliamentary authority to operate road services. Accordingly the GWR applied for such powers that were granted in the Great Western Railway (Road Transport) Act, passed in 1928. The terms of the Act also allowed the GWR to expand its road services and the railway company acquired a substantial stake in the National Omnibus & Transport Company. This company purchased both the Devon and Cornwall Motor Transport companies. It should be stated that by this time motor buses and coaches had greatly improved with pneumatic tyres, better suspension, more comfortable seats and more power. Consequently the long distance motor coach business began to grow.

In 1929 the GWR transferred out all of its motor bus operations (except a single service in Weymouth) to the newly formed Western National Omnibus Company, a division of the GWR/National Omnibus companies. This company was to become dominant in the West Country for several decades, although operations stretched as far as Gloucestershire and Wiltshire. In 1931 the National Omnibus & Transport Co. Ltd was purchased by Thomas Tilling Ltd. A new Road Traffic Act had been passed on 1st August, 1930 that not only provided for the legal licensing of vehicles, drivers and services but brought the industry under the control of area Traffic Commissioners. There was considerable consolidation of bus services in the 1930s as smaller operators sold out, being either unable or not inclined to comply with the new regulations.

After World War II the industry, in common with the railways, was in a run-down condition with ageing vehicles that had been poorly maintained. Long distance express coach services had been suspended from October 1942 and were only reinstated in the spring of 1946. In the 1947 Transport Act certain large bus companies, including Thomas Tilling Ltd., came under the control of the British Transport Commission, which in fact ended up owning more than half of the UK road transport passenger industry. In practice the company continued to operate as before but with the share capital government owned. Petrol rationing ended in 1950 and there followed a brief golden age for motor buses before the motor car ownership became relatively common place. Prior to World War II car ownership had been the privilege of the upper and middle classes but this was about to change as Britain was told that it had 'never had it so good'. Between 1953 and 1979 the number of bus and coach passenger journeys decreased by three to four per cent every year. This started a spiral of price increases. Government meddling continued with a 1962 Transport Act that placed the shareholdings of government-owned bus undertakings under a newly formed Transport Holding Company. After yet another Transport Act the National Bus Company was formed in January 1969. This was a holding company with some 40 subsidiary companies that had a great deal of local autonomy. As far as the West Country was concerned the old Southern National Omnibus Company Limited became dormant and all operations were merged into the time-honoured Western National Omnibus Company Limited.

CRIDDLE & SMITH, Ltd.,

COMPLETE HOUSE FURNISHERS,

UPHOLSTERERS,
SANITARY BEDDING MANUFACTURERS.

HOUSE AGENTS.

- AUCTIONEERS, VALUERS, Etc. -

HOUSES FURNISHED AND UNFURNISHED.

FREE REGISTER ON APPLICATION.

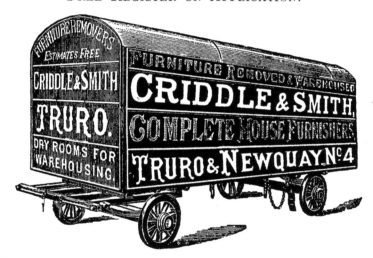

REMOVAL CONTRACTORS.

FURNITURE WAREHOUSED IN
— LARGE DRY STORES. —

Fore Street, NEWQUAY.

Telegrams —" Criddle Smith, Ltd., Newquay."   'Phone **45** Newquay

Single- and double-deck Western National buses served Newquay over the years and veteran Leyland Titan 'TD1' YD 2529, fleet number 3123, was one of them. Dating back to the late 1920s the vehicle was re-bodied with a Beadle highbridge example in 1943. The company served Cornwall for several decades, even though effectively owned by Thomas Tilling and after World War II coming under the control of the British Transport Commission. *Courtesy J. Hicks*

Despite the presence of the Western and Southern National bus companies there was still room in Newquay for independent operators. These companies operated some rural bus routes, school contracts and day excursions for tourists. One of the best known firms was Hawkey's of Newquay and here one of their Leyland Royal Tigers, PAF 36, is seen in the town during the 1950s. *Author's Collection*

TOURS *by*
Red and White Coaches

NEWQUAY MOTOR CO., LTD.
6 EAST ST. · NEWQUAY
TELEPHONE 3321

Another Newquay operator that operated a wide range of tours and excursions was the Newquay Motor Company of East Street. Their 'Red and White Coaches' were used on 'splendid and skilfully planned Coach Tours, with the scenery best seen from the vantage point of a comfy seat in a luxury Motor Coach', according to their own brochure, seen here with a Bedford Duple coach on the cover.

Author's Collection

I.9

THE
WESTERN NATIONAL
OMNIBUS COMPANY LIMITED

FOR BUS SERVICES, EXCURSIONS AND TOURS.
" ROYAL BLUE " EXPRESS SERVICES AND HIRE
OF PRIVATE COACHES IN THE

Newquay Area

Address your enquiries to the Company's Local Office—
I EAST STREET, NEWQUAY   Tel. 2322/3

A/W. 485

The following 38 years have seen a multitude of changes with mainly local authority controls over bus services in their areas increasing but under a central government umbrella. Certain freedoms have been extended to allow competition but this has enabled some of the larger companies to 'cherry-pick' the most lucrative routes. In some extreme cases major operators have squeezed-out local operators, sometimes by employing questionable tactics. There have also been radical changes in financial accountability and national and local funding has permitted a number of hitherto unthinkable events to occur, such as free bus travel for all persons of pensionable age.

In Newquay the history of motor buses go back to early Edwardian times. Since then the growing town has been well served by all major bus operators operating in Cornwall, due to a rapidly growing town and a burgeoning holiday industry. One of the fascinating aspects of Newquay's bus and coach operators has been the existence of local operators not only for local routes but for local tours for tourists. However, they had to compete with the large and well established Western National who also operated out of Newquay. They were competitive and could offer a wide range of tours. An excerpt from their 1934 guide makes fascinating reading:

The Western National Tours are operated with the finest and largest fleet of Touring Coaches in Cornwall. The long experience gained by the Company is used to advantage in the design of coaches, selection and training of expert drivers accustomed to the hilly district, and in a daily inspection of all motor vehicles. The luxurious Coaches and Saloon Omnibuses are the acme of comfort, and for safety and reliability the Company's coaches stand alone, embodying as they do all the essential features of high-class touring-cars. It is marvellous to reflect how these motor coach tours and omnibus services have opened-up the countryside to the holidaymaker, who, but a few years ago, would have been unable to reach many of the places now visited by coach tours or omnibus services. It is no longer necessary to be rich in order to tour through the loveliest scenery in our land.

There is not the space to provide a history of the dozens of coach companies that have operated in the area over the years but the Southern National Omnibus Company Limited also reached Newquay. Locally Woodward's

Although for decades the Western National Company dominated Newquay bus services and the Southern National Company also visited the town, primarily from former Southern Railway haunts in north Cornwall, local bus and coach operators also found a number of niche markets, particularly summer season coach tours. Shown here are two of the post-war companies advertising in a local guide book, Hawkey's of Newquay (*above*) and the Newquay Motor Co. Ltd (*below*), both of East Street. *(Both) Author's Collection*

The main Newquay bus garage was just north of the station, on a site adjacent to the old gas works. In this 1972 scene two former Southdown Motor Services Leyland Leopard single-deck buses are visible (note the CUF Brighton, Sussex registrations), while on the right is an ex-Maidstone & District Leyland Atlantean double-decker, 50 DKT.   *Bill Walker*

The 2008 Newquay bus scene features primarily the Western Greyhound Company that has been rapidly growing, with their vehicles almost taking over the streets of the town. Founded in 1997 the company took over a number of local firms. It now has over 20 routes and operates about 90 buses, many of which are these small Mercedes Vario midibuses. This trio are seen at Newquay bus station in 2007, adjacent to the route of the old Newquay Tramway alignment, which dates back to 1849.   *Author*

BRYMON
AIRWAYS
FIRST FLIGHT COVER

FIRST SCHEDULED FLIGHT
JERSEY — NEWQUAY
Aircraft: Britten-Norman 2A 'ISLANDER'
Reg'n: G-AXXJ   Flight No: BL410/216
Pilot: Capt. A.F. Roberts   Flying Time: 1 hr 15 min

BRYMON
22 APR 1973
NEWQUAY

Although the first aircraft to land in the Newquay area was back in 1912, nearly a century later the primary commercial activity in the area is at Newquay Airport. For decades the site was controlled and maintained by the adjacent RAF St Mawgan. Back in the 1970s Brymon Airways built up a domestic network of routes, including a Newquay to Jersey service, commemorated by this 1973 first day cover, showing a Britten-Normander 'Islander' aircraft. The company was taken over by British Airways in 1993.   *Author's Collection*

Newquay Airport has now been in operation since the 1930s and slowly facilities and services have improved. Many operators have come and gone but at the time of writing Air SouthWest, British Airways, Flybe, BMIbaby, Ryanair and Skybus all serve Newquay airport. Passenger numbers have increased ten-fold from the 1990s with 400,000 using the airport in 2007. Here an Air SouthWest flight comes to a standstill in 2007.   *Author*

Garage, Hawkey's Coaches and the Newquay Motor Company Limited were important firms as was the Harris Company in nearby Summercourt, Hockings of Newquay and Hubber of Newquay (Streamline Coaches). The latest company to make a really significant impression on the local area has been Western Greyhound, which started in 1997 and which uses the old Harris yard mentioned above for storage and maintenance. They also have a modern purpose-built depot. Western Greyhound was launched by former First Group employee Mark Howarth, being the former Managing Director of First Western National, his wife and Robin Orwell, another First Group man.

The company established itself quickly after taking over the business, order book and two contracts of Cornishman Coaches. Just weeks later R&M coaches of Newquay called it a day and Western Greyhound took over and moved into their East Street offices. These offices had once been owned by Hawkey's Motors whose name was inscribed in the external masonry. Pleasure Travel mini coaches ceased trading and Western Greyhound took over all contracts, private hires and tours run by that company. In December 1998 Rural Challenge money became available and slowly but surely the firm grew, new routes were opened up and the age and size of their bus fleet was significantly improved. The company now runs over 80 buses on 20 routes covering a significant part of the county. The company became the only independent coach company based in Newquay. After a full decade the company is still growing and the town and the bus station buzzes with swarms of their short wheelbase Mercedes midibus vehicles.

The motor car and commercial vehicles have continued to grow in significant numbers during the past century and now over 80 per cent of Cornish households have access to a motor vehicle or vehicles. There are a staggering 320,000 cars and vans registered in Cornwall and with a population in excess of 500,000 and growing, the number of motor cars and lorries on Cornwall's roads can do nothing but increase, notwithstanding the high cost of petrol and diesel fuel.

Air Travel

To the layman or the casual visitor to Cornwall the county is not readily associated with air travel. Once away from Heathrow and Gatwick they might think that air travel ends at Bristol, Exeter or Plymouth. However they would be surprised to know that over the years well over 60 sites in Cornwall have been the focus of some form of aeronautical activity. In terms of air services for visitors and holidaymakers wishing to fly to Cornwall then Newquay airport would be paramount but Penzance Heliport and Land's End Airport are both busy in moving large numbers of passengers from the Cornish mainland to St Mary's on the Scilly Isles, with over 300,000 per annum being carried in recent years.

The first flight in Cornwall took place in July 1910 when the pioneer airman Claude Grahame-White flew from Penzance, firstly a short distance inland and then over the town and across Mounts Bay, where the British Home, Atlantic and Mediterranean fleets were anchored. He and his aircraft had arrived by train and the wagon containing the Farman aeroplane was shunted into sidings

During World War II there were RAF airfields all over the county. In the environs of Newquay the main bases were at RAF St Eval, RAF Trebelzue (renamed RAF St Mawgan) and RAF Perranporth. The specific functions of these airfields and the many squadrons using them varied immensely. Fighters, bombers and reconnaissance aircraft were the main users and at St Mawgan there was an important American presence. This perfect Spitfire replica is located beside Newquay Airport on the A3059 road, bringing back memories of the past. *Author*

South of Newquay is Perranporth Airport, which opened on 28th April, 1941, comprising 338 acres and being located on the cliff tops at an altitude of 320 ft. The RAF base had a fine wartime record with its squadrons of 'Spitfires' defending coastal towns and protecting the south-west sea lanes. Now a civil airport, it features a splendid fire fighting vehicle in the shape of this vintage Land-Rover. *Author*

at Ponsandane near Penzance and the parts assembled in a nearby field. The next airman to fly in the county and the first to arrive in Cornwall by air was the French pioneer pilot Henri Salmet who crossed the River Tamar in June 1912. He landed at Newquay on 11th June, 1912 and his Bleriot monoplane was the first aircraft to visit the town. In the ensuing years there were increasingly regular appearances of aircraft in Cornwall, including air circuses and pleasure flights. Eventually proper civil airfields were built in a number of locations. There was plenty of airship activity during World War I and a few active military airfields but it was World War II that saw almost an explosion of airfields throughout the county. The history of aviation in Cornwall is not for this book, suffice to say that in the Newquay area RAF Perranporth, RAF St Eval and RAF Trebelzue, renamed RAF St Mawgan on 24th February, 1942, were all active during the war with a wide variety of squadrons and aircraft occupying these bases, with a multitude of functions, including bombers, fighters and reconnaissance aircraft.

The first scheduled air passenger service in Cornwall was in 1934 when Provincial Airways offered two flights per day between Plymouth and Hayle, later extended to Newquay and Penzance, before going into liquidation in 1935. Air services throughout Cornwall came and went but one pre-war working worth noting was in May 1939 when Western Airways operating DeHavilland Dragon aircraft started a Swansea to Penzance (St Just) service, which also called at Newquay. With the outbreak of war all civilian flying was banned. Trebelzue airport was requisitioned as a satellite to nearby RAF St Eval. However, the old airfield was not really up to the job and it was relegated to a dispersal area once new runways had been built nearby, with the new site being called RAF St Mawgan. In 1944 the main runway was extended, a new control tower was built and hardstandings completed. At 400 ft in altitude and with a cliff-top runway, St Mawgan sometimes had operational difficulties and over the years there were a number of accidents, involving fatalities. The base performed many functions but trans-Atlantic flights were a speciality and the base was well used by our American allies, who risked their lives in the skies over Europe on our behalf. From 1947 the base was placed on a care and maintenance basis, until 1951.

From 1946 civil flying became de-restricted and small independent airlines began to appear. In the summer of 1950 Fingland Aviation started a Manchester to Newquay service and although short-lived it was the start of post-war civil aviation activity at St Mawgan. Air displays were held regularly from 1952. There was plenty of military and civil activity in the following years and in 1959 Starways of Liverpool introduced a Douglas 'DC3' and 'DC4' service to Newquay on summer Saturdays. The multifarious roles of St Mawgan included BOAC using the site as a base for its newly delivered Boeing '707' aircraft from the USA. By the end of the 1990s, following strategic reviews, RAF St Mawgan started to be run down after half a century of military use. By 2006 it was clear that the installation would eventually become a non-operational site and simply mothballed as being surplus to requirements. This posed a problem for the local authorities because the military had maintained and controlled the civil Newquay Airport.

A small passenger terminal on the other side of the St Mawgan site, which had become Newquay Airport, was enlarged and rebuilt to cater for a growing trade amounting to 400,000 passengers in 2007. There was rebellion by some airlines when Cornwall County Council declared that it was going to charge a levy of £5 per departing passenger to pay for improvements at Newquay.

Cornwall has been served by many airlines over the years but some have fallen victim in a competitive environment and have ended up in receivership. The routes serving Newquay have also been many and varied. The non-exhaustive list of airlines that have operated commercially into or out of Cornwall are Aquila Airways, Alidair, Fingland Aviation, Murray Chown Aviation, Melba Airways, Olley Air Services, Starways, Mayflower Air Services, Scillonian Air Services, British Westpoint, Westpoint Aviation, British Eagle International Airlines, Solair Flying Services, Intra of Jersey, BEA, British International Airways, British Midland, Newquay Air, Scillonia Airways, Dan-Air, Westward Airways, Brymon Airways, Severn Airways, Air Anglia, Skybus and Isles of Scilly Skybus, British Airways, Air SouthWest, Ryanair and Flybe.

Newquay Airport presently has routes to London, Exeter, Bristol, Cardiff, Dublin, Leeds and Manchester and all the indications are that traffic will increase. The main operators are Air SouthWest and British Airways. The growth in flying is recognised by Western Greyhound buses which has a frequent and dedicated bus service between airport and town.

There are many artefacts at Perranporth airfield, including an RAF memorial, fighter pens and this control tower, suitably modified since World War II. There is plenty of activity in terms of both fixed wing and helicopter traffic, as well as an air school and glider club. Below the control tower is a fine café that makes a change from the usual tourist traps, seen here in September 2007.   *Author*

Chapter Four

The Treffry Tramway

The Treffry family was one of the great Cornish names of the industrial revolution. The Treffry estate comprised not only a grand mansion called 'Place' at Fowey but large tracts of land, farms, pits, mines, mineral rights, ports and a wide range of other commercial undertakings. The family had been landowners in the area since the Norman conquest! Other great family names included in the aristocratic roll-call in Cornwall were Rashleigh, Hawkins, Fortesque, Robartes, Basset, Fox, Taylor and many others. They all had enormous influence in the county in providing all types of employment by creating and maintaining a Cornish economy that for some decades was of national significance. Perhaps the most enterprising of the Treffry family was Joseph Treffry Austen who was born in 1782, the son of Joseph Austen of Plymouth and Susanna Ann Treffry. When the only male heir in the direct line of accession, William Esco Treffry, died the young Joseph Treffry Austen inherited the entire Treffry estate.

This was a formidable undertaking with huge responsibilities. Nevertheless Austen was a remarkable entrepreneur and a man of great vision and energy. In 1811, at the age of 29, he was involved in building new facilities at Fowey Harbour when the construction of a new quay was instigated. His idea was to extend Fowey so that it became a significant rival to the relatively nearby port of Charlestown, just south of St Austell, which at that time was the primary port for the shipment of the products of the pits and mines. The quay at Fowey was completed and commissioned in August 1813. Austen said of Fowey: 'I consider it to be better calculated than any other harbour in the West of England for Wet and Dry docks, on a scale suitable for merchantmen'. Austen involved himself in the running of Wheal Regent mine in Crinnis Woods to gain practical experience of managing such an installation.

Austen's problem was that the output from the family owned pits and mines was growing rapidly and this output had to be conveyed to local ports for shipment. Although there were minor tramways in numerous mine complexes the first tramway in Cornwall built specifically for the purpose that he had in mind was the Poldice Tramway that ran from the mines around St Day and Scorrier to Portreath, owned by the Basset family, on the north Cornish coast. This tramway of approximately 4 ft gauge carried ore in horse-drawn wagons down from the mines for transshipment at a small artificial harbour. The tramway was successful and Austen had a vision of building a similar tramway to suit his own purposes, particularly to transport ore from his own vast Fowey and Par Consuls, his other mines, clay pits and granite quarries on high land near Luxulyan and also at Mollinis, between Bodmin and St Austell. Although all of his major undertakings were within a 15 mile radius of Fowey the terrain was difficult in transportation terms. Austen eventually changed his surname to Treffry by deed poll, thereafter being known as Joseph Thomas Austen Treffry.

In the early days of the mines the transportation of minerals was by teams of mules and horses, with bags or sacks draped each side of every beast in a sort of

Treffry's Tramways were in operation between 1841 and 1872. Few photographs exist that pre-date the CMR, which took over most of the original lines in 1874. The standard gauge lines were worked by horses, except on three inclines. Although only a few hundred yards away from the tramway, this very old scene at Rocks china clay works shows overburden being removed by horse to expose the clay beds, a scene that must have been very similar to Treffry's operations, except for the gauge of the track. *ECC/Courtesy M. Dart*

The land and mine owning entrepreneur, who first had the vision of linking the north and south coasts of Cornwall by tramway, was Joseph Thomas Treffry. The family 'seat' was at 'Place' in Fowey, seen here on the left. The estate owned much of Fowey Docks and all of Par Harbour. With Fowey church competing for attention a Western National bus is about to depart for St Blazey and Par in the early 1930s. *Author's Collection*

equine balancing act. By the start of the 19th century the output from many mines was so large that wagons were employed, each vehicle containing about 3 tons of ore and drawn in most cases by a team of horses. In fine weather this new traffic worked moderately well but during the winter months and after heavy rain the primitive roads became badly rutted by the metal tyres on the wagons making the roads impassable. The huge volatility in the prices of metals on the international commodity markets put marginal costs into focus and the transportation of materials was an important factor in determining profitability. Furthermore in the early part of the 19th century the steam engine was making an ever increasing impact in the mining industry, not at that time for hauling freight but as stationary pumping engines to remove vast quantities of water from the mines and whim engines for extracting material from the ever increasing depths of the major mines.

The employment of steam engines with their voracious appetite for coal resulted in a huge demand for the mineral, which was not naturally available in Cornwall. Fortunately much of the ore exported from Cornwall was shipped to smelters in South Wales, where there was an abundant supply of coal and so most of the vessels conveying outbound minerals had a guaranteed return payload of coal. Care had to be taken in the shipment of china clay and china stone to prevent the load being contaminated by other substances. This requirement for the 'black stuff' made transportation even more critical and made the accurate cost/benefit analysis of any proposed railway, tramway or canal crucial to viability.

Treffry's mind had been working overtime on the transportation problem. As early as 1815 he had seriously considered building a canal from Padstow on the north Cornish coast to Fowey on the south coast but a survey indicated that the obstacles would be insurmountable. An early attempt to build a railway from Fowey Consuls, located on the hills above St Blazey and Tywardreath (which in fact was an amalgamation of five established mines), to Fowey had been thwarted by the rival Rashleigh family who owned some of the land through which the railway would need to pass. As already mentioned the Rashleighs owned Charlestown and the last thing they wanted was a rival creaming-off much of their trade. However Treffry had a trick up his sleeve because he owned coastal land at Par and he developed a grand vision whereby he would create an artificial tidal harbour to suit his purposes. The transport problem was acute and in 1825 Treffry stated that 'one hundred mules and thirty wagon horses are insufficient to bring the increased quantity of ores to Fowey'.

By 1828 Treffry had his plans for a brand new Par Harbour prepared. This massive project included a vast 1,200 ft stone breakwater that would protect the harbour area from the storms and gales that regularly battered the Cornish coasts. He dismissed the idea for an inner lock system, such as that employed at nearby Pentewan, to avoid a narrow channel being regularly blocked by shifting sand and silt. Instead he decided to make the harbour tidal and so virtually enclosed an extensive 35 acre site. This area would need to be dredged, no mean feat bearing in mind that in those now far-off days mechanical assistance from heavy machinery was simply not available. The grand plan would take 10 years to complete, although as early as 1833 the first vessels were using a temporary pier within the harbour area.

To complement the building of the harbour Treffry planned and built a canal from Ponts Mill, some two miles inland, where the ores from his Fowey Consuls

In order to gain elevation between the transhipment point at Ponts Mill, about two miles north of Par, and the quarries, mines and pits between Luxulyan and Mollinis near Bugle, a substantial incline was built. Opened in 1841 the 2,840 ft Carmears Incline, seen here in Edwardian times, was powered by waterwheel with a cable hauling wagons up the 1 in 9 gradient. Its use after the 1874 opening of the locomotive-worked and realigned Newquay branch line was very limited before the rails were lifted. *M. Dart Collection*

mine would be deposited, having travelled down an incline plane. This incline plane was a major engineering work, being half a mile in length and incorporating an 840 ft granite-lined tunnel, being 9 ft wide and 9 ft high. The double track narrow gauge incline, costing £2,819 to build, had been completed by 1835. Two other but lesser incline planes were later built nearby, one to the actual loading point on the new canal. A complete tramroad system linked the various mines and buildings that comprised Fowey Consuls.

The first activity in canal construction was to drain the salt marshes between Ponts Mill and the sea and to dredge, deepen and straighten the Par river, which was undertaken in the latter part of 1833. The canal was 8 ft deep at Ponts Mill, 6 ft deep at Par and 12 ft wide throughout. The canal ran down to the new harbour at Par resulting in a relatively straightforward interchange from barge to ship. During the construction, provision was made for an associated tow path. Research shows that the canal and the incline plane were ready for service in 1835 but no information was gleaned about the original canal vessels. However it is recorded that on 11th June, 1838 two canal boats were ordered at a cost of £21 each and in 1843 two more were acquired at £17 each.

Although Treffry owned many mines at this time Fowey Consuls was the largest. It is now hard to imagine the scale of operations at Fowey Consuls and the adjacent Lanescot Mine and how important in employment terms the mines were to become. In 1836 the workforce amounted to 1,680 persons, comprising 920 men, 240 women and 520 boys. By this time Fowey had produced 99,400 tons of copper ore and Lanescot 63,123 tons. The mines grew in depth and a huge Cornish beam engine with an 80 inch cylinder was installed to cope with water removal. This was designed by William West of St Blazey and built at the famous Harveys Foundry at Hayle. When installed it was the most powerful steam engine of its kind in Cornwall. Five other steam whims were ordered to join the numerous water pressure (as distinct from steam) engines. The mine areas were like a small working village with barracks for the workers and a wide range of facilities for the era. In 1837 Fowey Consuls produced its greatest tonnage ever, 15,254 tons, sold at £5 12s. 0d. per ton realising £85,434 19s. 0d.

In 1835 Treffry publicly announced to much excitement his intention of linking the north and the south Cornish coast, not by the abandoned canal idea, but by a tramway. This was effectively the birth of the Treffry Tramway system that would have a profound impact on the Cornish minerals scene and in the very long term the town of Newquay. His first objective was to link Par Harbour with Mollinis, near Bugle, where he had extensive mining and clay pit interests. He also intended to serve granite quarries in the Luxulyan area. He enlisted the support of other important mine owners but fell foul of the influential Bodmin to St Austell Turnpike Scheme committee, who accused Treffry of 'attempting to promote Par Harbour and his proposed tramway thereto at the expense of Charlestown and their proposed turnpike road' (which was to run from Bodmin to Roche and through the central china clay district to St Austell and the Pentewan Tramway terminus, with a further extension from St Austell to Charlestown). Various rival schemes were proposed but all failed, no doubt to the delight of the Treffry camp supporters.

The next event, which was a master stroke by Treffry, was to purchase outright Newquay Harbour and surrounding land, much of it comprising the

A standard gauge railway track ran between these walls until approximately 1930. The line ran from the eastern end of the Treffry viaduct to Colcerrow, Carbeans and Cairns quarries. The latter became disused from about 1880. Wagons were horse drawn and the main payload was granite, used in a wide range of applications in the construction industry and in later years taken to a siding at Luxulyan for loading onto railway wagons. *Author*

Wheelpit China Stone Mill was opened on the site of the old waterwheel about 1890, after the closure of the Carmears Incline. China stone for grinding was brought down to the area in horse-drawn wagons via the old Treffry Tramway. Once ground, the material was conveyed in slurry form down to Ponts Mill via a 6 in. diameter pipeline. The works ceased operations in 1908 but some of the old machinery can still be seen. This view at Wheelpit dates back to 1990. *Author*

Manor of Towan Blistra, from the executors of the estate of Richard Lomax who died in 1836. Lomax had started to modernise the harbour at Newquay but it was Treffry who would finish the job by building new quays and planning for the harbour to be served by a tramway that would bring ores and china clay from the mines and pits and take backloads of coal and timber to these centres of industry. The agricultural community was not forgotten and it was envisaged that fertiliser, manure and limestone would be imported and various crops and farm produce exported. The price tag for this wonderful acquisition was a snip at £7,000. The *West Briton* newspaper commented 'we may look for the diffusion on the north coast of that wealth and prosperity which through Mr Treffry's spirited and unwearied exertions we have witnessed in the south'.

Treffry also took a financial interest in certain lead and silver mines in the Newquay area, including the Newquay Lead and Silver Mine, which was just south of Lehenver Lane, now called Mount Wise. He also had a lead smelter at Par but the output of lead ore from his various mines was insufficient to keep the installation in full work. In 1847 he started up three further lead and silver mines in the Newquay area; Newquay Consuls on Fistral Beach, Tower Consuls a short distance inland at a site now known as Tower Road and Chiverton Wheal Rose. None of these mines was long-lived and they were in operation for only a few years, with the Lehenver Lane mine lasting a little longer, but all closing in the 1860s.

Treffry's Tramway from Ponts Mill to Mollinis got off to something of a false start and over a period of 18 months the original contractor seemed to be making little progress against the rugged topography of the steep Luxulyan Valley. Treffry enlisted the support of his steward William Pease to become what, in today's world, would be called Project Manager. In 1837 both the surveying and the quantity surveying had been completed for the Ponts Mill to Colcerrow Quarry section, which was to include a 2,840 ft incline that would raise the tramway by some 300 ft at a gradient of 1 in 9. Located on the eastern side of the valley, wagons would be hauled up and down the mostly single line by cable with power being provided by a substantial water wheel at the top of the incline. To power the waterwheel and to supply the lower mines a complex series of leats were constructed 3 ft wide and 15-18 inches deep.

Treffry's transport system was all coming together as Par Harbour became fully operational in 1840 and the first stage of the tramway from the head of the canal at Ponts Mill to Colcerrow Quarry was opened in 1841. The opening of the Colcerrow line was an important stage but to reach Mollinis the tramway had to cross the deep Luxulyan Valley by an impressive 98 ft-high 648 ft-long granite viaduct, comprising 10 arches. The viaduct doubled as a tramway and a waterway, the water being carried beneath huge granite slabs that formed the foundations of the tramway. The five to six ton granite blocks used in the construction of the viaduct were conveyed from the quarry to the viaduct site via the new tramway. The viaduct cost £6,708 to build and construction took three years to complete. It was appropriately called the Treffry viaduct and today it is, arguably, his finest memorial. An entry in the *West Briton* newspaper in August 1843 mentioned that the Ponts Mill to Mollinis tramway was 'nearing completion'. The standard gauge line opened in 1844 with Treffry, Pease, Rendell (line Engineer) and local dignitaries riding the entire length of the line powered by water and cable and by

This March 1989 view shows the remarkable 1842/3 Treffry viaduct in the heart of the Luxulyan Valley. Set in a wonderfully tranquil location the surviving edifice is 650 ft-long and an impressive 98 ft-high. It contains 200,000 tons of granite and took three years to build. Originally the tramway track ran across the viaduct on granite slabs and beneath them was, and still is, a leat which carries water to the waterwheel area. *Author*

The existing Newquay branch line runs beneath the Treffry viaduct, seen here, on its way from Par to Luxulyan and beyond. Above the central support can be seen the family's coat of arms, which appears only on the north side. Although its main purpose had been served by 1872/3 it was still used by horse-drawn wagons until about 1929/30. The structure is a wonderful memorial to Treffry who was so influential in this part of Cornwall in Victorian times. *Author*

horse. It should be mentioned that Mollinis was not only accessible to a large number of china clay pits but also to a number of tin mines.

The opening of this line was a major objective realised but he was not a man to rest on his laurels and he continued on the acquisition trail. This included extending his estate of china clay pits and further developing Par Consuls. To the irritation of others, especially Treffry's competitors, in November 1843 he also announced his intention to continue with his earlier plan to link the north and south coast of Cornwall by rail and this would involve not only continuing the line from Mollinis to Newquay but that there would be a branch from St Dennis penetrating clay country as far as Hendra and eventually St Austell via Trevisco and St Stephen. Treffry had had the foresight to contact the Hon. G.M. Fortescue, a major landowner in the china clay area whose land the proposed railway would pass, and Sir Christopher Hawkins promising another branch line to Hawkins' vast East Wheal Rose lead mine on Newlyn Downs.

A major work on the Newquay Tramway section of Treffry's Tramways, between St Columb Road and St Dennis Junction was Toldish tunnel. The narrow 530 yds-long bore could accommodate only horse-drawn standard gauge wagons and it was in operation from 1857 until 1872/3, a mere 15 years! A new deviation line was built by the CMR in 1874 for use by locomotives and a further minor deviation occurred in 1904. The portals, seen here in 1966, survive but are now inaccessible.   *Maurice Dart*

Photographs of the Newquay Tramway system pre-1873/4, when the CMR took over, are extremely rare. However, this scene from the turn of the 20th century showing standard gauge horse-drawn three-plank wagons removing overburden from Wheal Remfry China Clay Pit at Retew would have been very similar to the scene on the original tramway. Men and boys were employed in the mines and pits.   *Author's Collection/Courtesy ECC*

Treffry became an even more powerful individual and he held a number of senior posts. He was Sheriff of Cornwall and a Director and Board member of the Cornwall Railway (CR), being appointed Chairman in 1844. This gave him enormous influence and prestige and his contacts included Isambard Kingdom Brunel, with, arguably, Treffry showing greater foresight in adopting standard (then 'narrow') gauge for his tramways! However, this high pressure existence took something of a toll on Treffry and in 1846 he was taken ill, leaving much of the day to day management of the estate to his able steward William Pease. Nevertheless in September 1846 he entertained HM Queen Victoria and Prince Albert at his fine home in Fowey after they had visited his Fowey Consuls mines. Certain earthworks were undertaken between Mollinis, effectively Bugle, and St Dennis (Junction) and work had started in earnest at the Newquay end of the proposed tramway but at least for the time being the plan to continue the tramway beyond Par to Fowey was abandoned and all efforts were focussed on the Newquay 'end' of the route.

However, it is worth noting that this section of tramway was extended from Ponts Mill to Par Harbour in 1855 thus avoiding the time consuming and expensive requirement of transhipping the contents of loaded wagons onto and off of canal barges, thereby saving cost and time in the overall transport process. Subsequently the canal closed. The tramway operated, without interruption, until 1872/3.

Chapter Five

The Newquay Tramway and Harbour

At the Newquay end of the envisaged route the tramway is often referred to as the 'Newquay Tramway' as distinct from the 'Treffry Tramways' and to differentiate between two lines that were destined not to be joined until 1874. On the Newquay Tramway the primary loads in tonnage terms were to be lead ore from the large East Wheal Rose Mine, iron ore from the yet to be developed Perran Lode and china clay from the St Dennis and Hendra areas on the fringe of the Hensbarrow Downs, which would later feature significantly when most of the ore traffic ceased. The plan was for the standard gauge tramway to rise from Newquay Harbour by a 1 in 4½ (average) incline through an 80 yds-long tunnel. From the top of the tunnel the tramway would run on fairly level ground through the streets of Newquay to a site that would later become Newquay goods yard, adjacent to the future Newquay station. Initially the tramway would then run to East Wheal Rose mine and a second line to the St Dennis and Hendra area would follow. Work on the tramways started in earnest in 1844, with some resources being diverted from the completed Mollinis section of the Treffry Tramway.

The Treffry Records, Acc. No. DDX55 County Records Office, Truro show that as early as 27th July, 1838 an Act of Parliament had been passed for 'Maintaining the Pier and Harbour (etc.) at Newquay' and this demonstrates the foresight of Treffry in knowing precisely what his intentions were, from the time of acquisition of the Newquay Harbour area from the Lomax estate. Treffry now owned ports on both the north and the south coast and as forecast years before it would now be his objective to link them by rail. His plans were to be the origins of the Newquay branch line nearly 40 years later. On 23rd May, 1844 An Act of Parliament was passed (cap. xxiii) to 'Amend an Act for Maintaining the Pier and Harbour of Newquay in the County of Cornwall, and to make certain Tram Roads in connection therewith'. This document is a wonderful insight into Treffry's plans and contains a wealth of detail, some of which is summarised here.

The Act was over 70 pages in length and the contents gave Treffry ample scope regards routeing. A summary of some of the more interesting items follow. The main routes mentioned in the Act were from Newquay Harbour to St Dennis, via the Parishes of Saint Columb Major and Minor and ending up in a field marked No. 76 on the plans, near Gonnamaroes in the Parish of St Stephen's (beyond Hendra) in the heart of china clay country. There was to be a major branch line from Groze (near the site of [what later became] Tolcarn Junction, just outside of Newquay) to East Wheal Rose Mine, in the Parish of Newlyn, out of which there would be yet another branch commencing in the village of Summercourt, in the Parish of St Enoder, and terminating at or near the village of Ladock, in the Parish of Ladock. The latter was never built. Treffry was given the authority to purchase all necessary lands. It stated that the Tram Road [sic] would be of great public advantage by opening a cheap, easy and expeditious means of conveying mining, agricultural, and other produce between the places aforesaid and the intermediate Districts.

One of the most remarkable structures on the original 1849 Newquay Tramway was this spindly viaduct across the Trenance valley just outside Newquay. A more robust structure was considered but it would have been far more expensive and have taken three times as long to build. Locally known as the 'Trenance Spider' the viaduct was in use between 1849 and 1872/3. It was not strong enough for locomotive use. *Woolf/Greenham Collection*

Although there is much to criticise regarding the actions of the local town council, especially for the demolition of historic buildings, such as the original CMR railway station, the girl's grammar school, the old Post Office, the old whim engine house, the fish cellars, the Mount etc., one must give credit where it is due. The old tramway route from Newquay station to the bottom of Marcus Hill has been made a pedestrian/cyclists path, which is paved in such a way that is resembles the tramway track, seen here in 2003. *Author*

The entire Act was riddled with legal provisions pertaining to all manner of things, including acquisition, damage to lands, access to the tramway, rights to cross the tramway, the valuation of land and making it clear that while Treffry had authority to purchase and build upon lands, he did not have the legal right to any adjacent mines and minerals. Perhaps the most surprising aspect of the Act, and a previously unpublished fact, was that the tramway allowed Treffry and his Heirs and Assigns to purchase land adjoining the Tram Road for the purpose of making 'additional Stations, Yards, Wharfs, and Places for the *Accommodation of Passengers*, and for receiving, depositing, and for loading or unloading Goods or Cattle to be conveyed upon the Tram Road, and for the erection of Weighing Machines, Toll Houses, Offices, warehouses, and other Buildings and Conveniences'. He was also given the right to acquire land for access roads.

The width of the required land for construction of the Tram Road was 10 yards except for passing loops or where embankments had to be raised or cuttings made, or where buildings were erected, in which case the maximum breadth could be 50 yards. Where the Tram Road crossed another Road or Turnpike by bridge a clear space of 35 feet had to be provided for road users. Provided any facility did not cause inconvenience to the Tram Road or cause injury thereto it was stipulated that any adjoining landowner could, at his own expense, lay down a collateral branch line (siding) for the purpose of bringing carriages to or from the Tram Road! A five pound fine would imposed upon anybody wilfully obstructing the Tram Road or pulling up or removing stakes driven into the ground to set out the line of the Tram Road.

The section of the Act dealing with charges gave Joseph Thomas Treffry and his Heirs and Assigns the right to demand, receive and recover a series of Tolls. The list of charges and commodities was very comprehensive covering every type of commodity imaginable. In order to calculate such charges Treffry had to provide mileposts along the routes of the Tram Road and all tolls had to be published and also painted onto a Toll Board with 'distinct black letters on a white background'. Tolls had to be charged equally to all customers. A weight limit of four tons was placed on any carriage but this was increased to eight tons for a boiler or piece of machinery. The Act also addressed the matter of Newquay Harbour dues, which, where relevant, were additionally charged to Tram Road dues. It is interesting to note that except where reciprocal arrangements were in existence with foreign countries, all foreign ships and all commodities and merchandise transported by the Tram Road that had either originated on or were destined for foreign ships were charged double the standard rate.

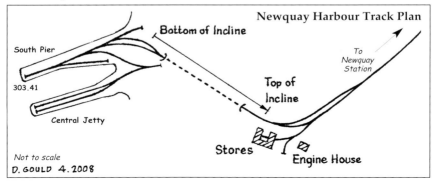

Newquay Harbour Track Plan

South Pier

Bottom of Incline

To Newquay Station

303.41

Top of Incline

Central Jetty

Stores

Engine House

Not to scale

D. GOULD 4.2008

After over 30 years of picture research that included all the major collections, this is the only photograph to come to light of a horse-drawn 'tram' working through the streets of Newquay (as distinct from the harbour area). Seen in about 1900 at the bottom of Marcus Hill, where Bank Street meets East Street, at least two horses head five wagons, while a single member of staff covered in china clay looks on.   *Newquay Old Cornwall Society*

In this 'before and after' comparison the old tramway route can be seen *centre left*, while the road traffic, mobile ice cream vendor, Fat Willy's Surf Shack and a slot machine entertainment establishment are manifestations of a later age! The tramway was lifted in 1928 and this later photograph was taken in September 2006.   *Author*

The Act gave Treffry the legal authority to appoint or remove the Harbour Master, a 19th century 'hire or fire' role. This was a powerful post as the Harbour Master could stipulate which vessels could enter, or not enter the harbour, whether it could be moored and the location of such mooring, determine priorities and oversee all commodities, with special emphasis on combustible and flammable items. He had the authority to impose fines on those breaking any regulations and furthermore Treffry and his agents could make any Bye Laws or regulations that they saw fit. The Act was a substantial document that gave Treffry the authority to proceed with his plans.

As regards Newquay, as detailed in the History chapter, there was a small wooden quay in the area back in the 14th century and by the latter part of the 16th century the surrounding hamlet was known as 'Newe Kaye'. The hamlet comprised just a few fishermen's cottages but it featured in Carew's 1602 survey of Cornwall. A primitive harbour was built to protect vessels, in addition to the natural protection afforded by the headland to the north-west known as Towan Head. The first significant change occurred in 1770 when Richard Lomax, Lord of the Manor of Towan Blistra, purchased the harbour and surrounding area. By this time there were signs of growth not only from the pilchard industry but also from sheep farming and in particular lead, iron, tin and silver mining. The discovery of rich deposits of lead in the East Wheal Rose area in 1811 added to the potential traffic. Suddenly the harbour was not only handling fish but also corn, sand, manure, salt, limestone, coal, iron ore and lead ore and in such volumes that in 1832 Lomax embarked on a £10,000 harbour expansion scheme. A total of 250 men were employed building a new south quay and extending the north quay. The new enlarged harbour was ready for service in 1833 (the same year as Par).

As already stated, following Lomax's death in 1838 Treffry purchased the harbour and surrounding land at auction and progressed his plans for the northern end of his north/south tramway. An Act of Parliament for all necessary works was passed in November 1843 and work commenced on the harbour section the following year. One of the problems was transporting wagons from the quayside up to street level, effectively at the top of the coastal cliffs. In order to achieve this it was necessary to build an incline but such was the topography that much of this had to be enclosed in a tunnel. Accordingly a tunnel that was 80 yds in length, 17 ft high and 14 ft 6 in. wide, ample to accommodate a single standard gauge railway line, was built. The average gradient was 1 in $4\frac{1}{2}$. Cornish miners who were deemed to be well qualified for the job undertook the excavations. While excavating the tunnel site miners came across some 16th century mine workings. Initially a rope was connected to a whim, powered by horses, which was used to lift wagons up the incline. However, this was soon replaced by stationary steam engine whims that raised and lowered wagons via a steel cable. To provide a good draft for the fires the engines had very tall chimneys. The engine house was located behind Fore Street, now in the area occupied by Somerfields supermarket. At the harbour end of the tunnel there was a simple loop and a short siding leading onto the south quay. There was also a refuge siding. There was no tramway on the north quay and the central jetty was not built until 1872. Wagon movements on the quay were also horse-powered.

The tramway through the streets of Newquay was just over a mile in length. There were five recognised road crossings and it is said that a boy with a red flag preceded the trams at these locations. Reports indicate that these crossings were ungated, however, in this Victorian scene there is clearly a gate across the track. For the benefit of local historians, the house is that of Dr Boyle, the gas for the lamp came from the 1886 local gas works and the tracks in the snow (a rare event) in Bank Street have been made by horse and cart. *Newquay Old Cornwall Society*

Photographs of even just the tramway tracks in the town are hard to find but in this pre-World War I scene buildings have appeared in Dr Boyle's garden. The shops are H. Westlake for shoes, Carne & Sons for gentlemen's outfitting and T. Jarvis for fine china. The street lamp is electric and cobbles protect the tramway from the wheels of road traffic. *Newquay Old Cornwall Society*

This 2006 scene in downtown Newquay is just recognisable from those on the previous page. Bank Street is 'one-way' only and clogged with traffic but the old tramway alignment is still obvious and much used by buses from the local bus station. I wonder what the Victorians would make of the 'printed T-shirt' shop? *Author*

At the top of the incline adjacent to the whim building there was a passing loop where the horses were attached/detached. Next to the whim engine house was a tramway-served stores building operated by the Union Company (later Messrs Pollard & Co.) under a private siding agreement, between November 1877 and 1902. As an early example of 'outsourcing' the horses were provided under contract by the Hoytes family, who also operated early coaches and horse buses and in future decades they also made deliveries for the Great Western Railway. The single line tramway then ran through the streets of the growing Newquay past the bottom of Marcus Hill via Crantock Street, Manor Road and Island Crescent behind the Victoria Hotel and Cliff Road to what was to become, from 1874, Newquay goods yard. In official parlance the line ran from milepost 302.31 to 303.41, in miles and chains from Paddington via Bristol; a total length of 1 mile and 10 chains. There were five recognised level crossings at; Station Road (302.52), East Street (302.74), Crantock Street (303.15), Wesley Hill (303.19) and Treverne Terrace (303.23).

From the eventual station site the lightly-laid single-track tramway crossed the incredibly spindly Trenance viaduct, locally known at the time as 'The Spider' or, in some early documents, 'The Trenance Spider'. The viaduct should not be confused with St Austell viaduct over the Trenance Valley on the Cornish main line, just to the west of St Austell. There was great debate between Treffry and his steward Pease over the cost and time-scale for building the viaduct. On this occasion Treffry went for the 'cheap and cheerful' option, which required 18 granite pillars but a complex wooden superstructure. There were to be 18 arches, each with a 25 ft span and the maximum height of the viaduct was 98 ft. The alternative would have been a much more substantial and expensive structure and one that would have taken three times as long to build. East of the viaduct was Treloggan Junction, later known as Newquay Junction and finally Tolcarn Junction, where from 1857 the tramway took two routes; the first in a

MANOR ROAD

KNOWN AS THE TRAMTRACK IT WAS OPENED IN 1849. IT RAN FROM THE RAILWAY STATION ALONG WHAT IS NOW MANOR ROAD TO THE WHIM YARD.

IN 1874 HORSES WERE REPLACED BY A STEAM ENGINE TO PULL THE WAGONS.

1921 SAW THE LAST LOAD OF CHINA CLAY LEAVE THE HARBOUR BY SCHOONER.

THE FINAL FISH TRAIN TO LEAVE WAS IN 1926. THE RAILS WERE TAKEN UP IN 1928.

JOHN COTTON'S CHAPEL NOW THE SALVATION ARMY HALL WAS BUILT IN 1833. THIS IS THE OLDEST PLACE OF WORSHIP IN NEWQUAY.

THE MUSEUM, BUILT IN 1862. WAS ALSO A CHAPEL, LATER, IT WAS USED AS A KNITTING FACTORY FROM 1912 - 1968.

NEWQUAY TOWN COUNCIL

CLLR DEREK JAMES
TOWN MAYOR 1987 - 89
1993 - 94

This Newquay Town Council cast-iron sign can be found in Manor Road, on the route of the Newquay Tramway. As with other similar signs it contains inaccuracies. Steam engines did in fact replace horses on the tramway in 1874, but not through the streets of the town! The last load of china clay *was* shipped from the harbour in 1921 but there were certainly no 'fish trains' in 1926, or at any other time for that matter. As a matter of interest evidence from scores of photographs show that nothing but open 4-wheeled wagons worked down to the harbour. The 1925 Ward Lock Guide states, 'The Harbour is connected with the railway by a mineral line. From here china clay is occasionally shipped, the vessels returning with coal and other merchandise, but the business is not very extensive' - the text obviously having been written sometime earlier.   *Author*

southerly direction to East Wheal Rose mine and the second easterly but curving towards Trencreek on its way to St Dennis and Hendra. Work progressed steadily and the first wagon ran across the viaduct and down to the harbour in January 1849.

However, before the line had been fully opened to East Wheal Rose there was a terrible disaster at the mine. Especially at lower levels the mine was very wet and over the years many hundreds of gallons of water per minute were pumped out of the mine. Between 1842 and 1850 water removal increased from 734 to 1,102 gallons *per minute*. Shafts were sunk below the 160 fathom (nearly 1,000 ft) level in search for better lodes. In the year 1846 no fewer than 1,200 men, women and children worked in the mine. One day there had been heavy rain storms and flash floods had entered the mine. Even at maximum revolutions the pumps simply couldn't cope and as a result 39 miners were drowned. It is said that the tramway proved of some use in taking materials from the mine at this time, even though it had not formally opened.

The *Royal Cornwall Gazette* of 2nd February, 1849 gave a wonderful description of the completion of the tramway. Under the headline 'Newquay and Par Railway' the paper reported:

On Monday last, the Newquay Viaduct [Trenance viaduct] on this line was opened by J.T. Treffry Esq. riding over it, and afterwards sending his loaded waggons [*sic*] across with supplies for the line beyond it. At a later period of the day, Barley was sent over it for shipment at Newquay. The viaduct, an exceedingly light, yet very strong structure, is 98 feet high from the base of the piers, and 630 feet long [in fact it was just over 430 feet long]. The line will be opened as far as East Wheal Rose Mine in the course of February.

It may be of interest to know that the barley referred to was in fact corn that had originated on the farms of Trerice and Tredinnick.

The article continued to discuss the 'railway' and not the 'tramway'.

The Newquay and Par Railway will afford very great advantage to the trade and agriculture of Cornwall. It will connect the two channels (north and south coasts), and thereby obviate the inconvenience felt more or less every winter, when coasters cannot safely come round Land's End, not to speak of other benefits resulting from Railway connection between ports on opposite sides of the County. Traversing a valuable minerals district, it will enable the lead and iron mines in its course to ship their ores, and receive their coals and timber, in the easiest and cheapest way. The China Stone and China Clay from St Dennis and St Stephens can be sent direct to the Potteries by a route more than a hundred miles shorter than that round Land's End. To the agriculturists it will convey the necessary supplies of shell sand, and it may not be out of place to add, that the dues sought and conferred by the Act for the carriage of sand are only two thirds of the amount of those authorised by the Rock and Delabole Railway Act (a scheme that never came to fruition), which passed in the same session. Crossing the entire County, with facilities for branching on either side, it may be extended in every direction, as required, and we believe that if it should be thought desirable, there would be no difficulty in communicating with Falmouth harbour.

After criticising certain government policies, the newspaper is incredibly flattering to Treffry with, some would say, ample justification.

Under the difficulties with which the agriculturalist must now contend, every convenience like that afforded by the Newquay and Par railway, for bringing manure to the farm and taking his produce to a port or market, becomes doubly valuable; and when better times shall return, and wisdom shall once more guide the Councils of the Realm, undertakings like this shall share the prosperity. The interest taken in this work would be imperfect, if it is not remembered that the undertaking is not created by a Company, but owes its whole existence to the judgement, engineering skill, and enterprise of one man. Mr Treffry himself laid out the line, and with no assistance but with that of his own agents, levelled it, completed all the preliminaries which the Standing Orders of Parliament require, and obtained the Act, at a cost, for the Act and all previous arrangements and preparations, not of tens of thousands, but, of less than a single thousand pounds! The work has been carried on under his own directions and eye, and the funds for effecting it are supplied from his own resources.

The article ends by calling Treffry a 'true patriot'.

With the full support of Sir Christopher Hawkins, the East Wheal Rose Mine owner, who also owned Pentewan Harbour, the very first load comprising 30 tons of lead ore left the mine for shipment at Newquay Harbour on 26th February, 1849. However on the other Newquay Tramway line to St Dennis, although much work had been undertaken there remained much to do. Although the harbour tunnel had been completed other tunnels at Coswarth, 33 yds, and Toldish, near Ruthvoes, 530

Having run through the streets of Newquay town the Newquay Tramway wagons had to gain access to the harbour at the foot of the cliffs. To achieve this objective an 80 yds-long tunnel was built at an average gradient of 1 in 4½. Wagons were raised and lowered by a cable powered by stationary steam engines, originally supplied by William West of St Blazey and later by Swindon works. This view shows the now demolished engine house about 1923. Horses were attached/detached at this point.   *Woolf/Greenham Collection*

Most of the upper tunnel entrance and whim engine house area is now under Somerfields supermarket, its car park and a warehouse. The tunnel was exposed during excavations in November 1987 and the Mayor and Mayoress of Newquay were on hand for a press shot before burying a bottle containing relevant names. Note the stacked materials for imminent use in reinforced concrete in the background.   *B.S.J. Press Photography/Courtesy M. Dart*

yds, still needed work done. Nearby there were a number of mines including Gaverigan United, Halloon, Indian Queens Consuls, Park of Mines, Ruthvoes, Toldish and Trevarrene, the ore from which all travelled by crude roads to Newquay. Treffry also had a grand plan to build a vast 'Harbour of Refuge' across Towan Head (way beyond the existing harbour) with large protective walls and a deep channel for vessels of every kind to shelter during the frequent storms.

Considerable work was taking place and a report published in the *Royal Cornwall Gazette* of 30th November, 1849 included extracts from the journal of Mr C.W. Peach, who travelled from Fowey to Newquay in the company of Treffry himself:

> Passing between St Austell and Roche, he observed that between the latter place and Newquay, Mr Treffry's railroad, for more than a mile in length, was on an embankment, the utmost height of which was 30 feet. Not far distant from this is a tunnel about half a mile in length (Toldish), which though cut through, is not arched. In cutting this tunnel, they had to pass through a lode of iron, about seven fathoms in thickness, which will ultimately be worked, and being so convenient to the railroad, the transit of the ore to the sea side will be comparatively easy. Before reaching Newquay the railroad passes through banks of sand, which being of excellent quality for manure, may be conveyed by rail far inland at a cheap rate, and thus bring in a good revenue to the proprietor and give the farmer the opportunity of putting double the quantity on his land, not only thus benefiting his land and his pocket, but as well preventing the tearing up of the parish roads, and thus again saving expense, from less labour and materials being required, giving an advantage even in this respect.

The writer then gives a very long-winded description of the improvements Treffry was making to the harbour and describes a large breakwater to provide shelter for a considerable amount of shipping in the often hostile waters (I should at this stage point out that these comments relate to Treffry's 'Harbour of Refuge' plan and not the existing Newquay Harbour already referred to). He speculates that if successful it could even become a replacement for 'the dangerous and exposed pier at Newquay'. The new harbour (which was never finished mainly due to Treffry's death in 1850) on the west side of the Headland (Towan Head) would be 'secure from surf' and vessels can run to it 'whichever way the wind may blow'. He continued claiming that 'the new harbour is to be communicated by a branch rail from that which passes to Newquay. A water supply would be brought down to replenish shipping and for the use of the population which will, no doubt, be gathered around the new harbour'.

Peach stated that the water would also supply the steam engine at the mine and may be used to drive stamps for crushing the lead ore and also for washing the ore. He then went on to explain Treffry's plans to build another wall of refuge on the eastern side of Towan Head that would contain some 700 acres of water of sufficient depth for ships of any size, a thing greatly required on this exceedingly dangerous coast. As regards the original 'Harbour of Refuge', for some decades all that has remained has been some pieces of solid masonry. An old resident of Newquay remembered men 'pushing little waggons [*sic*] along the railway under the bridge from the rocks on the Newquay side of the isthmus'. Apparently staging was erected across the new harbour to form a temporary viaduct for the waggons to run onto the new pier.

These past and present shots show the harbour end of the tramway tunnel in about 1907 and 2007. Although this view has been published before it is quite unique and shows not only two small GWR goods wagons waiting to be hauled up the 1 in 4½ incline but the view through the 80 yds-long tunnel. Wagon No. 31076 is full of imported coal and it has a tare of 4 tons 11 cwt., a wooden frame and a metal body. Note that the actual point is just inside the tunnel to save space on the harbour lines.   *Woolf/Greenham Collection*

After being used for storage and then as an aquarium the old tunnel is now fenced off and back to a storage role. The surroundings are decidedly nautical. *Upper right* is one of the old pre-tunnel chute apertures where various commodities were tipped onto the harbour for shipment.   *Author*

The huge blocks of granite were brought down from the Luxulyan area by tramway to Par and then shipped on flat-bottomed boats. These were then rowed across the Gazel to the rocks where the granite was then hoisted into the waggons by a derrick. Peach had indicated that the 'crane' on the site was 70 feet tall. Once the wall was complete men were engaged in blasting rocks in the centre of the harbour-to-be as well as on the Little Fistral side of the area to be enclosed to provide sufficient draft for visiting ships.

The *Royal Cornwall Gazette* of 31st August, 1849 reported that a dinner had been enjoyed at Clemens Hotel in Newquay for 50 invited guests and shareholders who were given a guided tour of the tramway to East Wheal Rose and the harbour area as well as the Harbour of Refuge which, as mentioned above, was being built by Treffry but was never finished.

At the end of 1849 Treffry had been a signatory to the creation of a substantial new clay company, known as the West of England Clay Company. Treffry attended a ceremony in December 1849 at Toldish tunnel to lay the last few bricks of the tunnel lining. The single line tunnel was 530 yds long, over 8 feet high and wide enough to accommodate a single standard gauge track. The trackbed was almost level falling at 1 in 497 towards Newquay. This was to be his last act on the tramway because in January 1850 Treffry caught pneumonia and died at his home in Fowey. He was 68 years of age. His death was a disaster in terms of early and meaningful progress on the tramway, transport and harbour front.

Treffry had never found the time to get married and he left the great Treffry Estate to his cousin the 41-year-old Reverend Edward John Willcocks, with the proviso that he should change his name by deed poll to Treffry. He was generally known as Revd Treffry. Apparently Treffry, alias Willcocks, was far from dynamic and compared with the pace of events under the recently deceased, progress from 1850 onwards was positively pedestrian. Nevertheless the 'new' Treffry must also have been involved in the extension of the original Treffry Tramway from Ponts Mill down to Par Harbour, thereby obviating the continuing need for the canal. Also further work was completed at Domellick and Hendra beyond St Dennis (Junction) where two inclines continued from the terminus of the tramway at a point called Gullies Wharf up towards Hendra Pit and other china clay works, as well as Quarry Close stone quarry. The main traffic would be inbound coal for the drying kilns and outbound china clay and stone for shipment from Newquay Harbour. It is thought that some problems encountered in incline operation were overcome by 1852 under the auspices of Revd Treffry but as mentioned below it would be 1857 before the tramway was opened throughout to Newquay. As an aside, although a stationary steam engine worked at Hendra until 1926 it is thought that the incline was abandoned by 1913, if not before. So clearly the years following Treffry's death were not completely devoid of progress.

After Treffry's death, and to be fair to the Revd Willcocks, certain estate affairs were much delayed because William Pease the key administrator had resigned and left for the Boconnoc Estate. There was clearly chaos in the Treffry Estates office at this time. Historian Roger Lacy states that the Treffry Papers in the County Records Office at Truro confirm that much of the paperwork regarding property ownership (and very much more) was incomplete. Matters were delayed in the High Court of Chancery for several years and certain administrative matters were dealt with by appointed Trustees. In 1853 the court had appointed one James Henry Meredith to help execute the affairs of the estate but he died in 1857. It was not known precisely what land had been acquired for the Hendra to Newquay section of the tramway and as late as 29th April, 1854 the Trustees were writing to Sir John Buller about land on his estate near Trencreek to clarify outstanding ownership matters. Also on 3rd July, 1857 the Trustees let it be known that although the tramway was open a total of £3,500 still needed to be paid to secure the final 77 acres of land. In April 1857 an Act of Parliament was submitted addressing a number of issues concerning the tramway and abandoning those sections that clearly would not now be built, the Bill appearing in July of that year.

The 12 miles, 3 furlongs, 7 chains Newquay-St Dennis-Hendra line was finally completed and issues resolved, resulting in a grand opening on 22nd April, 1857. The *West Briton and Cornwall Advertiser* of Friday 1st May, 1857 provided a full report. Under the heading 'Treffry Estate' the newspaper reported:

On 22nd instant, the Rev. Edward John Treffry, of Place, Fowey, also his fourth son (Master Harry Treffry), together with two newly elected Trustees of the estate, Mr Robert Thomas Head, of Exeter, and Mr Edward Lambert, of London, accompanied by the principal agents of the estate, opened for general merchandise the portion of the Newquay railway extending from Newquay to St Dennis, a distance of about 12 miles. The party met at St Dennis, where a great many persons, including the vicar of the parish, (the Rev. John Childs) assembled to witness the opening. Various flags waved in the air, the railway carriages (each also containing a flag) were on the line in readiness for their first start for public traffic. The foremost carriage was quickly occupied by the Rev. Mr Treffry and his son, the Rev. Mr Childs, the Trustees of the estate, &c., and amidst very hearty cheers of the inhabitants of the district, off started the carriages (drawn by single horses) for Newquay, two of which were filled with china stone, as a portion of cargo for exportation. From there being a trifling descent on a long portion of the line, the horses were unconnected at different parts, and the carriages went on their course at almost locomotive speed. [This account poses some interesting questions such as the number of wagons, which would appear to amount to three in total, whether horses were waiting at predetermined parts of the line to provide power on any upgrade, where did the horses go that were detached etc.?] The party quickly arrived at Newquay, and were ushered in by the firing of a cannon; and the town presented a very animated appearance, flags having been hoisted in different parts. On arrival, the party soon made their first official survey of this interesting and much frequented watering place; first visiting the partly constructed refuge harbour on the north part of Newquay, and then returning to the inner wharf, and after a general inspection of the port &c., partook of a substantial dinner at Prout's Hotel (now, and originally, the Red Lion Inn). After the removal of the cloth appropriate toasts were drunk, and leaving at an early hour, the party returned by the same route as they arrived in the morning, the Trustees accompanying Mr Treffry to Place. It may be added that Mr Ellery, of St Dennis Consuls Mine and Clay Works, attended at the terminus for the purpose of making arrangements for immediately availing himself of the railway, when it was arranged, that on the following day a cargo of coals (which had been imported at Newquay) should be conveyed over the line to St Dennis, the advantage of which will at once be felt by both parties. Credit is due to the musicians of the St Dennis brass band for the manner in which they performed on the occasion. [Another interesting question would be how did the band travel from St Dennis to Newquay and back?]

At this point I would like to mention the past confusion that has prevailed over the opening dates of the St Dennis line. There are textual references that could imply that the opening date was 1849, the same year as the East Wheal Rose branch. The highly respected historian, the late C.R. Clinker in his *Great Western Chronology* (1963) states that 'Newquay Harbour to Hendra opened in short sections from 1846 onwards; final section to Hendra, November 1849'. There could have been short stretches of the line opened before the 1857 'grand opening' described above, but nevertheless his statements are clearly inaccurate. John Keast, who has written on Treffry, also states 1849 as the opening date and Maurice Dart repeats the Clinker data in his *West Cornwall Minerals Railway* book of 2005. In the past I too have been guilty of perpetuating this error, the last occasion being in *Branches & Byways: Cornwall* 2002, influenced by the equally respected historian, the late John Penderill-Church. He has stated that the St Dennis line was complete as far as Ruthvoes in 1846 and that June 1849 saw Treffry's Newquay line finished as far as St Dennis. The former statement is clearly inaccurate because the viaduct across the Trenance Valley was not opened until the end of January 1849. He quotes Treffry, who in a letter to his friend F. Bodger states,

> My Newquay line is in full work at last, after five years of effort. On this day I am going to see the finishing part of the embankment over the Goss Moor, at a place where the last bridge is building. When it is finished the wagons can then go over it. The stone will then be conveyed to arch the tunnel, which cuts through the hill north of Gaverigan Gate [in other words Toldish tunnel at Ruthvoes].

Although of dubious quality this exceptionally rare photograph pre-dates the CMR-constructed 1872 central jetty. The tunnel mouth can just be detected and there are railway wagons along the south quay. The quayside capacity is obviously very limited. In the foreground is a fascinating wooden gantry used for loading pilchards direct from wooden ships at the north quay to the 'Active' fish cellar. *Newquay Old Cornwall Society*

In this remarkable photograph, recorded about 1880 on an old plate camera, no fewer than six tramway wagons are seen on the south quay of Newquay Harbour. Two have been loaded with coal and four empties wait to be loaded from the wooden ship at the quay. The damaged glass plate still shows plenty of detail including the growing town of Newquay in the background.

Newquay Old Cornwall Society

This very unusual viewpoint is looking inland from the south quay across the 1872 CMR central jetty. Three primitive clay wagons have discharged their loads. The ship on the left is the *Alfred* of Padstow, an 84 tonner built in 1865. It was converted from a schooner to a ketch in 1904 but was lost on 11th September, 1910 when it was in collision with the SS *Pink Rose* three miles south east of Runnelstone while working from Cardiff to Plymouth with a load of coal.

Cornish Studies Library

This letter would seem to at least part relate to the earthwork on the 'missing' (until 1874) section of the tramway, as originally planned, between Mollinis (Bugle) and St Dennis Junction. Also, in his letter Treffry was going to see an unfinished bridge, so how could the line have been 'in full work at last', especially as Toldish tunnel was in an incomplete state? In his 'at full work' statement he was probably referring to the East Wheal Rose line but we will never know. It is possible that short sections of the tramway were in use prior to 1857, especially at the Newquay end, because a general siding and other sidings for coal traffic (run by Messrs Edward Albert Martyn and Nicholas Lewarne) had been opened at Halloon, near to the present St Columb Road station.

Roger Lacy has studied this subject in depth and holds the opinion that in view of the problems encountered after Treffry's death and in view of the 1857 newspaper 'grand opening' report there is no doubt that the St Dennis line opened on 22nd April, 1857, just under eight years after the East Wheal Rose Mine section. Significant parts of the St Dennis route were ready for service years in advance of the last completed sections but having fully considered all facts and opinions the author supports Mr Lacy's view. He has also pointed out that a letter from the Treffry estates office at Par dated 23rd April, 1857 to the Harbour Master at Newquay instructs him to 'make every effort to secure vessels at Newquay now that the line is open for traffic'. On the other hand why would so much time and effort be exercised on the Hendra inclines in 1852 if there was no outlet for the traffic generated? The answer seems to be that shortly after being made ready for service a dispute followed about various responsibilities and the High Court adjudicated on 17th March, 1859 that Edward Stocker and William West, the owners of the stationary whim engine at Hendra, were responsible for its operation but that the Treffry Estate was responsible for supplying the cable and for keeping the cable drum in good repair. It is healthy that there may still be some facts for future authors and historians to glean!

Returning to the Newquay Tramway, since the opening of the tramway in 1849 traffic had slowly but steadily been building. During the week ending 18th May, 1849 four ships arrived at Newquay and seven sailed. If these figures were typical and the figures are extrapolated then traffic would have been approximately 300 ship movements per annum. In later years Messrs Martyn and Lewarne opened a coal yard at Fiddlers Green at St Newlyn East on the East Wheal Rose line. To serve the local agricultural community there were other sidings at Trevemper and Benny. However there followed another depression in the mining and china clay industries giving little incentive to complete the 'missing' section of tramway from Bugle to St Dennis Junction.

In the year 1858, the first full year of operation of the St Dennis line into china clay country, horses conveyed a total of 2,788 tons of china clay down to Newquay Harbour for shipment, fourth only to Charlestown, Par and Pentewan. Each wagon conveyed about four tons of clay and in broad-brush terms a total of 700 wagons would have traversed the streets of the town in each direction during the year, about three or four wagons per working day. However, the above tonnage figure does not include any other commodities,

One of Treffry's greatest unfinished projects was to build a massive 'Harbour of Refuge' at Newquay. This project was to incorporate Towan Head, which would effectively be cut through and in conjunction with a truly massive sea wall would offer protection to north coast shipping. The vast wall was part-built but never finished and after work ceased in the 1850s, after Treffry's death, the structure was left to the ravages of 150 years of Atlantic storms. In 2007 this fragment was all that remained (*see page 16*). *Author*

This panorama shows the Newquay headland. There were local riots when hotels started to be built on this beauty spot culminating in the 'Headland Riots' of 1897. On the left is the Headland Hotel and the white building is the lifeboat house. The 'Harbour of Refuge' was to cut through the headland in the dip beyond the house, in addition to vast protecting walls either side. *Author*

especially incoming coal traffic. There would have been much activity on the single quay at the harbour as wagons were shunted by horse backwards and forwards in order to reach the right vessels on the very restricted track layout. It was unfortunate for the Treffry estate and the viability of the Newquay Tramway that almost from the date of opening East Wheal Rose lead mine was in terminal decline. In order to find more lead, shafts were going deeper and deeper but at these levels both the quantity and quality of ore was diminishing while costs were rising. By 1853 production was a mere 20 per cent of the peak output of 1845. Water ingress at lower levels was colossal and, as mentioned before, four huge steam-driven pumping engines were removing 1,102 gallons per minute! One can but imagine the volumes of coal that were being consumed. The lines soldiered on and there was a suggestion by powerful clay producers that locomotives should be used on the tramways but with light 42 lb./yd track it was in no fit state for use by anything other than horses. Also the restricted dimensions of Toldish tunnel would preclude the use of locomotives. As an aside, by 1870 the Treffry Tramways (including the Newquay Tramway) and the Pentewan Railway were the only lines of any length in Cornwall that remained horse-worked and it was not until the arrival in 1870 of William Richardson Roebuck, a London businessman, that change was likely to occur.

By 1874 the CMR was in charge and locomotives worked the lines, except for the town tramway and on the harbour quays. In 1876 7,200 tons of china clay and china stone were exported through Newquay to both home and foreign ports out of a West Country annual total of 232,000. This small 3 per cent figure decreased to 4,125 tons in 1885 as traffic on the Cornwall Minerals Railway was largely taken to Par on the south coast. This was not surprising as from 1874 the CMR imposed a surcharge of 2d. per ton for all loads using the incline and harbour! The anticipated iron ore traffic failed to materialise and the capacity provided by the new central harbour jetty was used but never fully exploited. After a period of dwindling and erratic output the once huge East Wheal Rose lead mine finally closed in August 1885. During 1889 the south quay was severely damaged by a tremendous storm, only 107 commercial ships sailed into and out of Newquay Harbour with imports (all commodities) amounting to 9,000 tons and exports of 5,500 tons. Even though the ships were larger in 1889 compared with 1849, this compares unfavourably with the scene 40 years earlier and shows a dramatic downturn that would continue for a further 30 years, before complete closure. The line from the station to the top of the harbour incline and on the actual quays remained horse drawn for the entire 73 year life of Treffry's old tramway. The last days of the tramway and details of its demise appear in Chapter Seven.

Joseph Austen Treffry was a man of exceptional energy and imagination. His business interests were widespread and he was a true pillar of the community. He was a man before his time but sadly he never saw the gap in his tramways between the Bugle area and St Dennis completed in his lifetime. At his funeral in 1850 it is said that virtually every man, woman and child from miles around attended the funeral. His successor Edward Treffry died in 1880 aged 71 and from that time the Treffry Estates Company took over the family business.

The headquarters of the CMR was strategically located at St Blazey. Unusually for the area, the building was entirely brick built, with the bricks being imported from Devon. The commodious structure included offices, works, repair shops, a roundhouse running shed and many ancillary buildings. Opened in 1873/4 the building is still part-used and grade II listed, ensuring its survival. *M. Dart Collection*

This is another example of an extreme photographic rarity, the CMR in the course of construction in the Luxulyan Valley north of St Blazey during 1872. The 1868/70 valley floor tramway from Ponts Mill is being used to supply construction materials and a horse-powered single wagon has just arrived at the site of Rock Mill viaduct. Note the men on one of the piers and the wooden crane for lifting the granite blocks. In the background an embankment is being in-filled. *Charlie Saundercock*

Chapter Six

The Cornwall Minerals Railway

Origins and Construction

In broad brush terms William Richardson Roebuck's business objectives were to take over the Treffry Tramway network, to convert all of the lines for locomotive haulage, thereby carrying far bigger payloads, to provide the missing link between Mollinis (Bugle) and St Dennis (Junction) and to construct additional branch lines to serve the china clay / stone and the iron ore industries. He had substantial investment capital and he started negotiations with the trustees of the Treffry Estates to lease the tramways and acquire other lands. In order to do this he needed to contact all of the significant land, pit and mine owning families in central Cornwall. This included the Treffry, Hawkins, Rashleigh, Carlyon, Robartes, Fortesque, Edgecumbe, Falmouth and Arundell families and also a significant group of independent mine owners. They all realised the potential benefits of a railway network serving their various industries, especially as Roebuck was supplying a common service with standard rates of carriage and particularly as they were not stumping-up the capital required. Roebuck also had to consider who to appoint as engineer, which company of contractors to hire, estimate the full cost of construction, the cost and supply of locomotives and stock as well as a plethora of infrastructure items.

After securing their general agreement to his proposals, but particularly agreement to a 60 year lease between him and the Trustees of the Treffry Estates, in the shape of Edward John Treffry and his son Charles Ebenezer Treffry, he formed the Cornwall Minerals Railway. This was incorporated by an Act of Parliament on 21st July, 1873. The proposal had to go before Parliament because Roebuck had previously formed a limited company under the Railways Construction Facilities Act of 1864 and obtained a Board of Trade certificate but this was rejected by the House of Lords. The Act also called for the amalgamation therewith of the New Quay & Cornwall Junction Railway. Roebuck had acquired interests in several pits and mines and in 1872 he had invested heavily in the Cornish Consolidated Iron Mines Corporation that operated the Perran Lode. The company purchased large tracts of land in order to extend the tramway. The CMR launched major construction works including a heavily-engineered railway line from Fowey to Par and St Blazey. They built a new alignment up the Luxulyan Valley, avoiding the Camears incline and the Treffry viaduct completely. The company linked the Bugle area with the St Dennis area (the missing link), now part of the Newquay branch line alignment. On the New Quay & Cornwall Junction Railway they were also to link the broad gauge Cornwall Railway at Burngullow with the standard gauge line down from St Dennis Junction to Hendra, and at least theoretically, provide dual gauge track. They built branches to Carbis Wharf (from Bugle), from East Wheal Rose to Treamble and Gravel Hill (latterly from Shepherds) and eventually in 1893, the Goonbarrow branch to Gunheath and Carbean and the Wheal Rose branch, near Bugle. The existing tramway was completely upgraded and several overbridges needed to be built. Many viaducts were constructed, especially in the Luxulyan Valley, but also across the Trenance Valley at Newquay. An ancient wooden structure (*see Chapter Five*) was replaced with a masonry and iron structure. The CMR also built a stone jetty in the middle of Newquay Harbour to increase handling capacity. The old narrow Toldish tunnel at Ruthvoes on the Newquay Tramway, near St Dennis, was also to be avoided by a detour from the original alignment. The Fowey line included boring the longest tunnel in Cornwall, the 1,173 yds-long Pinnock tunnel and a 50 yd tunnel at Luxulyan. Locomotives were to be introduced and a large brick roundhouse and turntable, depot and works was built at St Blazey, the CMR's Headquarters.

The appointed engineer was W.H. Thomas, the contractor Sir Morton Peto in association with William West of St Blazey, who had a significant foundry in the town. Progress was swift and the best way to describe the scenes in 1873 is to quote, at length, from the *West Briton* of 4th September, 1873:

Since the autumn of last year we have occasionally heard that a company, which has assumed the name of the Cornwall Minerals Railway Company, meant to open up the northern portion of Cornwall, particularly the iron and china clay districts, by a series of narrow gauge lines [standard gauge in today's terminology] with outlets for shipping purposes at Fowey and Newquay.

The capital of the company was advertised as one million sterling and Sir Morton Peto was said to have taken the contract, but beyond these statements, which have appeared from time to time in the newspapers, and the establishment of a certain number of officials at Truro, Newquay and Fowey, very little has been known in Cornwall of the doings of the company, and Cornishmen generally have been somewhat incredulous respecting the work which it was reported to be carrying out, especially as the Act of Parliament authorising the construction of the lines in question had not received Royal Assent till the conclusion of the past session. However, about three weeks ago a meeting of the company was held in London, when the Chairman, A.C. Sherriff MP, made a statement to the effect that although the Royal Assent to the Act of Parliament had only just been obtained, two-thirds of lines - 50 miles in length - had actually been completed. This Mr Sherriff fairly characterised as unprecedented in the history of railway enterprise. The statement certainly somewhat staggered a great many people in Cornwall, who have been in the habit of pooh-poohing the whole scheme and has caused many enquiries to be made as to what the company is really doing.

It should be explained at the outset that the Cornwall Minerals Railway entered into an arrangement with the trustees of the Treffry estate, by which they became possessed of the three tramways belonging to that estate, and which were constructed at great cost by the late Mr Treffry. These trams, namely from Newquay to East Wheal Rose, from Newquay to St Dennis, and from Par to Bugle, have formed the base of the company's operations, and we propose to show how far they have been utilised by reconstruction and improvement, where abandoned altogether for the sake of better gradients and greater convenience for traffic, and where new lines have been made or are now in the process of construction.

Taking first that portion of line upon which the work is in the most advanced stage, the East Wheal Rose tram, and its extension to Treamble, we may state that comparatively little remains to be done in this section to complete the line from Treamble to Newquay, a distance of 9¾ miles. The present terminus at Treamble iron mine, near the celebrated Duchy and Peru mines, is in the parish of Perranzabuloe, and about two miles from Perranporth. A high level and a low level tram run from the railway into the mine, from which large quantities of valuable brown haematite are being taken by quarrying. The position of the mine is strikingly picturesque, and contrasts remarkably with the ordinary Cornish tin or copper mine. Devoid of ghostly engine houses and dilapidated stacks, it lies at the foot of a bush-covered hill with Treamble Mill nestling amid a cluster of trees in the valley, at the opposite side of which are thick copses and gently inclining green slopes leading away to the Perran cliffs and sand-hills on the west. From this point the line passes over an embankment of about 400 yards to Treworten, where it crosses the Rescurra and Perran road by a girder bridge, 25 feet above the level of the road. About 160 yards of this embankment, varying from 25 feet to 11 feet in height has been done and the remainder, gradually running down to two feet high, will be quickly finished.

A curious difficulty was met with in the construction of Treworthen bridge. A creek comes up here from the sea, and there is a tradition in the neighbourhood that there is 'no bottom' to be found. But engineers, not having much faith in traditions, went to work to find a foundation for the bridge abutments. However, they soon discovered that the 'natives' were not far from the mark in their traditional knowledge. About five feet from the surface they came upon hard ground, but further trial proved it to be merely a crust or layer about three feet thick, formed of loose stones which had been worked together into a kind of concrete, and beneath which there was literally no bottom, for continuous boring failed to find anything but sand. The crust, however, was considered to be sufficiently firm, and the footing of the bridge was placed upon it.

We should mention here that it is in contemplation to make a light line of two miles from Treworten bridge along the valley by the Mount (Agra Bank) iron mines to Ligger Point, at the northern extremity of Perran Beach, where the Cornwall and Devon Incorporated Mines Company have the Gravel Hill iron mine.

The Treamble and Treworten bridge embankment is succeeded by a cutting of about 380 yards long, and 40 feet deep at the highest point, the stuff from which has been used for the embankment. This cutting is completely taken out. The remainder of the work proceeds in the same order, embankment being followed by cutting and cutting by embankment in regular succession. There is hardly any level work, and the same remark applies to the whole of the lines in course of construction by the company, a piece of line running across the Goss Moors alone excepted, but on this section of the line the stuff is not generally speaking hard, the rock being principally killas. There are however, two or three exceptions where the cutting passes through ironstone and hard killas with veins of spar. Passing through the cutting last named, we come to an embankment of 220 yards and an average height of 12 feet, of which 140 yards are completed, then to a cutting of the former description - killas and ironstone - a heavy piece of work which is all done with the exception of finishing off the sides. The line passes along by Treworthen Farm and Greenland or 'Mexico' Mill to Rescurra, in which distance there are four embankments and four cuttings varying in height from 40 feet downwards, nearly completed, close to the Duchy and Peru old shaft there is a very heavy cutting through killas and spar. We then come to the long cutting at Rescurra, which is 700 yards long, and of which 440 yards of the heaviest work is done, being 20 feet deep; the remaining portion has an average depth of 11 feet. Now, bearing more to the south east, an easy sidelong bank, a cutting of 20 feet deep and an embankment of 25 feet average depth for 130 yards, all the work on which is completed, bring us to Deer Park iron mines (Mr Barton's), where there is a bridge and a double culvert erected for accommodation road and drainage purposes. The line will be exceedingly convenient and valuable for these mines, passing, as it does, through the sett.

Another mile in the same direction, the work on which is comparatively light, and nearly all done, brings us to Shepherds. A cutting of 350 yards and an average depth of

12 feet is all out; a sidelong shallow bank of 550 yards is nearly finished, and the remainder of the work, which is still lighter, is completed, including three occupation road bridges. Next comes the heaviest cutting on the line - the Fiddler's Green cutting - which is 1,060 yards, or nearly five furlongs long, and varying from 27 feet to 10 feet in depth; this is cut through and very nearly ready for laying down the permanent way.

From Fiddler's Green to the junction with the East Wheal Rose tramway, near Metha, a distance of a mile and a half across Newlyn Downs, and by Nanbellan, the line takes a northerly direction. A mile of this is embankment, with an average elevation of 12 feet and 16 feet at the highest part, and there is a bridge over the parish road at Ilgram. The line here is ballasted and complete in every way, and an engine runs over it daily conveying trucks, material and workmen to and fro [there were reports of a contractor's engine being landed at Newquay]. The rails are laid entirely on cross-sleepers nine feet long and about two feet apart, and the work has been very substantially done and neatly finished.

The permanent way continues from the junction over the tram as far as Gwills, a distance of 2½ miles, the old rails having been taken up, the line widened, and otherwise improved, the permanent rails laid and ballasted, and everything completed excepting three road bridges. The engine runs without stoppage from Fiddler's Green to Gwills - four miles - and having mounted the fiery steed and ridden over the new line we can vouch for its being as smooth and evenly laid a bit of rail as ever an engine passed over.

Gwills is distant from Trevemper about a mile, and from Newquay two miles and a half, all of which is over the old tramway, which only requires relaying to complete the whole line from Fiddler's Green to Newquay, but there is a serious difficulty in the way.

This is the great work upon the Newquay section of the Cornwall Minerals Railway lines. Although it is but an alteration of the old viaduct which carried the tram rails, it is estimated to cost about £10,000. Many of our readers who have visited Newquay will have a vivid recollection of this frail thread-like erection poised in mid-air, with its network of wooden trestles and its seventeen attenuated 'feelers' descending some 90 ft into the valley below. It has been not inaptly dubbed by some Newquay wag as the 'Tolcarne Spider' and its proportions are certainly 'Preadamite'. The 'spider', which is half a mile from the proposed Newquay terminus, has been shorn of more than half its legs, and the trestle work at the top has entirely disappeared. Nine of the seventeen piers have been taken down, and the remaining eight, which were only five feet thick at the bottom, have been strengthened by the erection of two buttresses at each side of solid masonry, four feet thick at the bottom and tapering up to three feet at a height of 50 feet from the ground. The masonry of the old piers only extended to a height of 45 feet, the remainder being composed of timber work, so that the piers have all had to be raised considerably, the centre pier being carried to a height of 85 feet, which leaves the viaduct about five feet lower than the old one. The viaduct is 450 feet long from abutment to abutment; and the span from pier to pier is 45 feet. The whole of the piers are finished, and immense wrought-iron longitudinal girders have already been thrown across four of the piers. These girders are 50 feet long, and support, at two feet apart, cross girders which will carry the rails, and which project over the sides of longitudinal girders sufficiently far to form a pathway on each side of the viaduct. This pathway will be protected by iron railings attached to uprights, which form part of the cross girders. The remainder of the girders have only now to be fixed to complete the viaduct, which will be a very imposing structure. There is a charming view from the top along the Tolcarne Valley, and the picturesque appearance and symmetry of the viaduct itself gains by its restoration. The remaining half mile of railway will be over the old tram but improved and relaid.

The passenger and general goods station will be above Tolcarne Road. Here will be a large platform, about 300 feet long, covered in, including two lines of rails, in the manner forming protection for trains, which may wait here overnight, and for arriving and departing excursionists. The commodious waiting room, of course, is calculated on the general traffic only.

The heavy goods for shipment go down an incline through a tunnel for 80 yards under the town and open out on the harbour, where considerable improvements have been made by the company, at a cost of £2,000.

Newquay Harbour is formed by two breakwaters enclosing a piece of the beach. Only the southern breakwater, or quay as it is usually called, can be used for discharging vessels, there being room for two at a time, and lines of rails laid along the quay. But in 1872 the Cornwall Minerals Railway constructed a stone jetty 100 feet long and 20 feet wide inside the harbour, with wharf room for a vessel on each side. This jetty has two lines of rails along the top, and is through 150 feet of heavy timber trestle work, or stays connected with the land, so that the accommodation for exporting and importing heavy materials has been much increased.

We are glad to find the Newquay people appreciate the future which is in store for their already rapidly increasing town, and that they are preparing to accommodate the hosts of visitors which the railway will convey to them. Close to the station on Tolcarne Head, a site has been purchased for an hotel, and the company, by which it is to be erected, intends, as far as possible, not to spend its capital in bricks and mortar, but in providing a comfortably arranged building in which families or single visitors can be accommodated according to their requirements.

The total length of railway from Treamble to Newquay is 9¾ miles, of which 4¾ miles are new line, and five miles altered and improved tram. The bridges over parish and occupation roads and water courses are very numerous and nearly all completed. They are substantially built with elvan stone, the smaller ones being arched over, and the larger ones spanned by iron girders.

The number of bridges which are found necessary in a county so cut up as Cornwall is by parish and accommodation roads, adds considerably to the cost of making a line of railway. From Treamble to East Wheal Rose Junction - 4¾ miles - no fewer than fourteen bridges have to be built over public roads, besides several culverts and cattle arches, whilst on the tramway between East Wheal Rose and Newquay four new bridges over public roads have to be built in order to avoid the present level crossings.

On the new portions of the line the company have been put to considerable expense by the erection of substantial dry stone fences, five feet high, on each side of the railway, for the protection of cattle. The erection of these fences is, we understand, enforced by the Board of Trade; they are no doubt very effective, but as they are costly and of a much more substantial character than usually thought necessary, for the purpose, the company may be excused for feeling a little aggrieved.

A station is contemplated at Shepherds, near Fiddler's Green, about 6½ miles from Truro, where the junction with the Truro and Perran line will take place; and there will be sidings for the accommodation of goods traffic at Treamble, Duchy and Peru, Shepherds, East Wheal Rose Junction, Gwills and Trevemper bridge.

This branch [the 1857 line to St Dennis and the 'missing link' to Bugle and beyond], on leaving Newquay, passes over the same line as the Perran and Newquay branch, which we have just described, as far as the junction a little to the west of the Tolcarne viaduct (Trenance), whence it branches off almost due east, and runs a pretty straight course through the parishes of St Columb Minor, Colan to Halloon, in the parish of St Columb Major, and within about two miles and a quarter of the town of St Columb, which will be accommodated here with a passenger and goods station. This portion of the line is all upon the old tramway, but there is, nevertheless, some heavy work already done and in the process of completion. The first difficulty encountered was at Quintrel Downs, on the Newquay to Bodmin road, where, in order to avoid a level crossing, a skew bridge has had to be constructed, and the road raised for a distance of 170 yards on one side of the bridge and 60 yards on the other; a temporary deviation has been made; the work of raising the road is progressing rapidly, and the seven iron girders which carry the road across the line are fixed, but cross arches are still to be erected between the girders before the macadam for the road is laid on. A very long cutting on the old tram brings the line to Coswarth tunnel, which has had to be widened and heightened; in fact, the whole of the old masonry has been taken down, and the tunnel, which is 33 yards long, has been entirely rebuilt with elvan, and is now a very fine piece of work. The rails in the cutting have also been taken up and the cutting widened, but the permanent way not yet laid. From this point to the Toldish tunnel, a little to the west of Halloon, the work will consist entirely of improving and relaying the old tramway, but at Toldish there is a deviation of a little over a mile in length, in order to avoid the tunnel. The whole of this deviation, the earthworks on which are easy, is ready for the permanent way. The tunnel will be abandoned by the railway, but as it runs under Ruthvoes iron mines, where there is said to be a large deposit of red haematite, it will be used for conveying ore from the mine to the railway siding.

From Toldish to St Dennis the line again continues on the tram, which has not yet been altered. Here the tramway enters the heart of the china clay district, and proceeds close to St Dennis churchtown up a very steep incline to the Hendra clay works, belonging to the Treffry Estate, the incline being worked by a stationary engine.

We have next a piece of new line 2½ miles long, branching off from the tramway at St Dennis, and proceeding through a series of clay works to Drinnock [sic] Mill, where a junction will be formed with the Newquay and Cornwall Junction broad gauge line, along which Burngullow station, on the Cornwall Railway, is reached in 2¾ miles.

The St Dennis and Drinnock Mill junction, although but 2½ miles long, involves some very heavy work. Nothing has yet been done at the St Dennis end, but the cuttings for a mile and a half will be light - not in any place more than 10 feet deep. About half a mile from St Dennis a commencement has been made with a short piece of shallow cutting; about 180 yards of cutting have been done and 80 yards of an embankment. The line is 'pegged' out across the fields, and a little further on in the direction of St Stephens – the course of the line here being south-east - there is a stiff piece of work through a very peculiar formation, immense granite 'boulders' or separate rounded rocks lying close together some five or six feet below the surface, About 80 yards of this cutting, of an average depth of eight feet, have been taken out, and an embankment of the same length and height formed, but there are still nearly a hundred yards to cut through. It is said that, although they are so near the china stone, yet some of the hardest granite is to be found in the neighbourhood, as proof of which the fact is adduced that a quarry close to the cutting just named supplied stone for the building of Trevose lighthouse, north east of Newquay.

Some distance south-east of the above cutting another start is made with the work, at that point where two parish roads cross the line within 200 yards of each other. In order to avoid the expense of two bridges, it has been arranged that at a point equidistant from each road a bridge shall be built, and both roads thrown into one, a new connecting road being considered for the purpose. A short distance further the Treviscoe clay works, belonging to Messrs Martin, are reached, the line coming into the works by an embankment 16 to 18 feet high and 140 yards long, which is not yet touched; but there are immense piles of clay waste at the disposal of the contractor, which can be easily removed for embankment purposes and for filling up the various old clay pits through which the line passes.

The only difficulty in this portion of line is with regard to the drainage of the clay works, the contractor having to take care that the culverts are not stopped up. Unfortunately, however, nobody seems to know where the culverts are, and shafts have had to be sunk and cross-cut driven in order to find them. One culvert was discovered six feet beneath the bottom of a pit, which is itself nearly 60 feet deep. These culverts, when found, have to be strengthened so as to bear the weight of the line.

After crossing the Treviscoe works the line comes into the Conversant Company's works, where a pit of 58 feet deep and 140 yards span has to be crossed, and a little further another pit 30 feet deep and 50 yards across; but the depth to be filled up is lessened by the cutting which passes through at a depth of 25 feet. The rock to be cut through here is all decomposed granite, or china stone, so that the work will not be heavy, but the stone will have to be handed over to the owners of the pits.

On leaving the clay pits the work becomes heavier, one cutting being 30 yards long and 20 to 40 feet deep, the greater part of it being 40 feet, and a short distance further on another cutting 260 yards long and an average depth of 15 feet through solid granite. Of this only about 25 yards remains to be done. From the cutting an embankment has been formed 60 yards long, which brings the line to the Drinnock Valley, where a public road, a leat, and a tramway belonging to the West of England Clay Works will be crossed by a bridge of 65 feet span. The bridge is in the process of construction, but an embankment of about 35 yards has still to be made to complete the communication with the Cornwall and Newquay Junction line.

This line, like than at Perran, has no lack of bridges to cross. On the tramway portion there are no fewer than three new bridges over public roads, 20 to 25 small arched bridges over accommodation roads, &c.; and on the St Dennis extension of 2½ miles there are eight bridges over public roads, and several accommodation bridges. The whole distance from Newquay to Burngullow is 16 miles; of which 11 miles - from Newquay to St Dennis - is tramway (excepting the mile of deviation line at Toldish); 2½ miles from St Dennis to Drinnock Mill is new line; and the remainder (2¾ miles) is over the Newquay and Cornwall Junction line, where a third rail will have to be laid down, and continued over the new portion of line, making a mixed gauge as far as the Act of the Newquay and Cornwall Junction Railway authorised the construction of that line.

It will be seen that there is a good deal of work still to be done on the St Dennis extension, but on the termination of harvest work, which has interfered considerably with the progress of the line, additional men will be engaged, and judging from the rapidity with which very much heavier work has been accomplished on other portions of the group of lines that Sir Moreton Peto is constructing there should not be any difficulty in completing this section by the end of February next. Stations are contemplated at St Dennis and Halloon (for St Columb) and a siding at Quintrel Downs.

Unfortunately the comprehensive report did not include a progress report on the Fowey to St Dennis Junction section, including the Luxulyan Valley deviation, or the Retew branch from St Dennis Junction down to Melangoose Mill. However, some five months later, in February 1874, it was reported to the second annual general meeting of the CMR that progress during the past six months had been very satisfactory. Roebuck had been able to employ considerable manpower on constructing the CMR and his task force were organized into three large groups. He was winning the battle with the major obstacles of the 1,173 yard Pinnock tunnel between Par and Fowey, which was to become the longest in Cornwall, and the sheer granite cutting and 50 yard tunnel near Luxulyan, not to mention the large St Blazey headquarters complex. By February it was reported that the wharves and jetties at Fowey were in a 'forward state' and the earthworks between Fowey and Pinnock tunnel were almost complete, with ballasting and the permanent way commenced. At the western end of Pinnock tunnel down to Polmear, at Par sands, had been completed and the track laid. Some girders were required for a bridge over a road at Polmear. The crossing of the old canal and the river at Par had been completed but brick delivery problems had resulted in the St Blazey complex being delayed.

The most difficult section from Ponts Mill and up the lush Luxulyan Valley to Luxulyan was presenting something of a challenge but it was anticipated that two granite cuttings above Ponts Mill would take a further five to six weeks to complete and further up the valley there was still much work to do on the viaducts, including riveting the girders. Between Ponts Mill and Rock Mill viaducts there was a 40 ft deep gap in an embankment that would take an estimated six weeks to fill. A further granite cutting at Rock Mill would take three to four weeks to complete as would another cutting at Luxulyan.

From Luxulyan to Bugle the original tramway had been reconstructed and the permanent way had been laid and ballasted. The two public overbridges at Luxulyan and Bowling Green were behind schedule but Sir Morton Peto was confident they would be finished on time. The long stretch of line between Bugle and St Dennis Junction (then known as Bodmin Road Junction) was progressing well except the sizeable embankment that carried the railway over what was to become the main A30 road across Goss Moor, which still required a massive 13,000 cubic yards of material to complete the same. Much of the permanent way between Newquay and St Dennis Junction and from Treamble to Newquay had been laid but a number of overbridges were running behind schedule, including those at White Cross, Halloon (St Columb Road), on Goss Moor, Benny Mill and Matha. Also cuttings at Fiddler's Green and Rejourra on the Treamble line had still not been completed.

This unusual scene from May 1922 depicts three branch lines in the depths of the Luxulyan Valley. Running across this section of the valley is Rock Mill viaduct, which still carries the Newquay branch line. On the left is the tramway to Orchard Quarry and on the right is the branch to Rock Mill Quarry. The old Carmears Incline was located on the hillside in the background. The quarry lines closed in the 1920s and 1930s.   *Author's Collection*

Of the remaining sections of line the situation was mixed. The link-up to the Newquay and Cornwall Junction Railway, between Hendra and Drinnick Mill, was 'rapidly approaching completion' but due to the late acquisition of property, work on the Retew branch, down to Melangoose Mill, was not progressing well. No work had started on the mile long Carbis Wharf branch, but this would present few construction problems and the ground could be prepared very quickly indeed. However Roebuck was working the navvies hard and the company came in for some criticism from the Methodist Church for allowing work to be undertaken on the Sabbath! Many of these navvies were, in the best traditions of the railway builders, Irish or of Irish descent.

Locomotives

The locomotive engineer of the Cornwall Minerals Railway was Francis Trevithick and he was based at the CMR headquarters at St Blazey, where both the main running shed and the locomotive works were located. He designed a 30-ton 0-6-0 tank locomotive with two outside cylinders specifically for the CMR. The traffic forecasts were hugely optimistic and an order for no fewer than 18 locomotives based on his design was placed with the engineering firm of Sharp, Stewart & Company at a cost of £43,200. The builder's works numbers were 2350 to 2361 and 2368 to 2373 but the CMR's running number sequence of 1 to 18 did not follow the order of build. Four locomotives were named; No. 1 *Treffrey* (the name was misspelt and it should of course have been Treffry), No. 2 *Lord Robartes*, No. 5 *Fowey* and No. 6 *Newquay*.

The locomotives were not particularly powerful but in normal operation they were designed to work in pairs, back-to-back. There were no coal bunkers and coal was, inconveniently, carried on the top of the side water tanks. The backplate to the footplate had a gap in the middle, which was designed to enable the footplate crew to easily move from one locomotive to the other! In this context the locomotives loosely resembled a 'Fairlie' type of operation when paired normally. The links between the locomotive order and the structure of the engine shed was remarkable. If 18 locomotives were scheduled to work back-to-back then there would obviously be nine 'pairs'. The brick built CMR locomotive roundhouse at St Blazey had nine tracks leading to nine bays each capable of taking a pair of locomotives! The building is now listed and it survives, and the turntable is still in occasional use.

The CMR livery was said to be a dark reddish brown with yellow and black lining, although one reference suggests some of the locomotives were just plain black. All of the locomotives had Allan straight link motion, this being standard Crewe practice and reflected the fact that Trevithick was the retired locomotive superintendent of the northern division of the London & North Western Railway. Unfortunately because of the downturn in traffic in the mid-1870s, 18 locomotives were never required and it is said that when the GWR took over operation of the CMR in 1877 some of the locomotives had never been steamed. Consequently half of the new locomotive stock was returned to the manufacturers for resale. Apparently the CMR still owed Sharp, Stewart &

The CMR ordered 18 locomotives from Sharp, Stewart & Company. They were all 30 ton 16 cwt 0-6-0 tank locomotives with outside cylinders. They were designed to work back-to-back in pairs. Four of the locomotives were named but to the huge embarrassment of the manufacturers No. 1 *Treffry* emerged from works with a misspelt nameplate, which showed *Treffrey*, as seen here. Half of the locomotives were returned unused to pay-off debts.   *P.Q. Treloar Collection*

Of the surviving CMR tank locomotives all were rebuilt by the GWR in 1883/4 with saddle tanks, increased water capacity, coal bunkers and extended frames. They were reboilered in 1895 and transferred away from Cornwall. They could normally be found shunting at Swindon, one example surviving until 1936. Here No. 1395 is seen at Swindon on 11th September, 1932.

Author's Collection

Company money and the credit for the returned locomotives cleared the debt. Nos. 1 to 9 were taken into GWR stock and renumbered 1392 to 1400 and therefore these locomotives carried CMR numbers for only three years. Nos. 10 to 18 were sold to other railway companies based mainly in East Anglia and No. 10, which was sold to the Colne Valley & Halstead Railway, unbelievably survived until 1948, by then working at South Hetton Colliery.

Nos. 1 to 9 were rebuilt by the GWR in 1883/1884 as saddle tanks with extended frames. The water capacity increased from 780 to 840 gallons and the overall weight increased by two tons. They then had rear bunkers for carrying coal and the crew were afforded better protection by the provision of a slightly extended cab. No. 1398 was sold to the Sharpness Dock Company as early as 1883 and in December 1912 No. 1400 took the number 1398. Of the remaining eight locomotives six had new boilers fitted by Swindon works in 1895 with a working pressure of 150 lb. per square inch. After absorption these locomotives were reallocated away from St Blazey, with but a single short term exception. By 1882 the GWR had imported four of its '850' class 0-6-0STs to St Blazey for CMR use; Nos. 1909, 1915, 1918 and 1919. Most of the ex-CMR class could be found shunting at Swindon works and Nos. 1393 to 1398 lasted there until 1936 when they were withdrawn from service. It is interesting to relate that in 1910 and 1934 locomotives of the 1361 and 1366 classes of the GWR, built to replace the ageing CMR locomotives, were in many respects almost identical in terms of specification to their rebuilt predecessors.

The only other locomotives owned by the CMR was the example they used exclusively on the Goonbarrow branch. To work the 1893 branch line they acquired a 27 ton saddle tank from Peckett & Sons of Bristol. The locomotive was appropriately named *Goonbarrow* and it had coal and water capacities of 1½ tons and 780 gallons. It had two outside cylinders, 14 in. by 20 in., and 3 ft 7 in. driving wheels. It too was absorbed by the GWR in 1896 and rather surprisingly taken into stock and numbered No. 1388. It was sold in 1911 to Cwm Ciwe Colliery, Llanharan, South Wales. The colliery closed in 1921 and the locomotive was 'lost' from all known records.

Opening for Goods

In the early months of 1874 building work at Newquay was being completed, including an engine shed and turntable, and the fine West & Son of St Blazey iron girders had been positioned on the new Trenance viaduct in readiness for the locomotives and trains that would soon be running over them. In the meantime part of the huge order for 18 new build 0-6-0 tank locomotives from the Sharp, Stewart Company of Manchester had arrived, in addition to the first few dozen of the 400 goods vehicles on order. A light locomotive traversed the entire line from Fowey to Newquay on 27th April, 1874 and a Board of Trade inspection took place on 15th May, 1874. An operating certificate was not granted and additional works were required. This included point detection work, the line having been provided with Russell's instruments, block telegraph and semaphore signals. Stevens's facing points indicators were used and the signalling was largely controlled from a series of CMR-designed signal boxes.

In order for locomotives to operate between Fowey, St Dennis, East Wheal Rose and Treamble to Newquay the old Newquay Tramway 'Trenance Spider' viaduct had to be replaced. A number of the old piers were used in the new structure (seen here in CMR days) suitably heightened and strengthened. The metal girders were manufactured by William West of St Blazey and the single track structure was ready for service in 1874. It lasted until 1939.

Woolf/Greenham Collection

In this period piece what was originally thought to be a CMR 0-6-0T is seen crossing Trenance viaduct with a goods train from Newquay in Victorian times. However contributor Max Birchenough has more accurately identified the locomotive as a GWR 2-4-0 'Metro' tank locomotive. Some of the loads may have been imported through Newquay Harbour. The pier strengthening can clearly be seen.

Woolf/Greenham Collection

Work continued on all seven days of the week and again there were complaints from the local community about Sunday working as up to 60 navvies worked between Goss Moor and Halloon (St Columb Road) with a steam locomotive 'constantly running' bringing in ballast to assist with track-laying. Finally after all outstanding issues had been addressed and the last piece of ballast had been tamped into the trackbed the CMR formally opened for goods and freight on 1st June, 1874, just 11 months after the CMR Act had been passed. The only non-compliance with the terms of the Act had been the CMR's failure to lay dual gauge track between St Dennis Junction and Drinnick Mill to complete the link-up with the Newquay & Cornwall Junction Railway. The Cornwall Railway was aware of this fact and it eventually instituted legal proceeding against the CMR. This came to a head in 1875 when the CMR was ordered to lay the rails, which it promptly did but in such a fashion that the broad gauge element was deemed to be unusable!

No reference has been found to the impact the closure of the Treffry and Newquay Tramways (approximately between 1st June, 1873 and 1st June, 1874) had on the customers of the tramway or how the various commodities were alternatively transported during the construction of the CMR. The CMR published a detailed list of tolls for a huge variety of commodities but the most interesting note was that, 'For goods which pass over or along, or use any inclined plane connecting the railway with the Harbour of Newquay, or the pier, wharves or works adjoining the same, shall pay *in addition* to standard tolls, two pence per ton'.

Mr J.C. Richardson, the CMR's General Manager, flagged away the first train from the railway's Par station (St Blazey). The guard on the occasion was former Bristol & Exeter Railway employee John Rice, who had also worked on the Treffry Tramway. Station masters had been appointed, despite the absence of passenger trains. These managers were located at Fowey, St Blazey, Luxulyan (then know as Bridges), Bugle, Roche (then Holywell and later Victoria), St Columb Road (then Halloon) and Newquay, in fact at every site that would within two years boast a passenger station, except for Quintrel Downs. There were also CMR freight representatives at Retew and Treamble. In addition the CMR was a major employer in the area with drivers, firemen, guards, shunters, fitters, cleaners, porters and crossing keepers on their books. Staff were also located at Fowey, Par and Newquay Harbours. As far as can be ascertained the Carbis, Retew, East Wheal Rose/Treamble branches opened or, in the case of the old tramway lines, reopened at the same time as the 'main' Newquay branch. Except for the Newquay Tramway lines through the streets of Newquay and at Newquay Harbour the age of the horse had gone.

Roebuck had spent vast sums of money on the CMR but he made one near calamitous mistake. He had failed to forecast a major downturn in all of the industries his railways were built to serve. By the time of opening in 1874 the iron ore boom was over as cheaper sources from southern Europe and South America began to flood world markets, drastically affecting commodity prices. In fact 17 out of 25 iron ore mines had closed by 1874 and bankruptcy ensued. There had been over-production in the china clay industry between 1870 and 1873 and by mutual consent between the pit owners output was severely restricted, which had an impact on freight tonnages. The CMR sued the Cornish Consolidated Iron Mines Corporation for failing to honour their contractual obligations but predictably the latter company went into liquidation. The contractor of the CMR,

An unusual close-up of a wooden sailing ship actually being loaded with china clay at Newquay Harbour. China clay is shovelled down the wooden loading chute, an activity normally undertaken only in dry weather. The exact positioning of ships in the tight confines of the harbour were determined by the Harbour Master.

Woolf/Greenham Collection

Sir Morton Peto, also 'went bust', allegedly even selling his wife's jewellery in a failed attempt to stay afloat! The Treffry Estate was unloading clay works leases like there was no tomorrow. The CMR struggled on but china clay production continued to decline resulting in a slump during 1875 and 1876.

Opening for Passengers

Although the CMR had from the start planned to implement a passenger service, in a despairing attempt to augment its income the CMR instigated such a service between Fowey and Newquay on Tuesday 20th June, 1876, using small four-wheeled coaches that came from Bristol and seemed to have their origins on the Midland Railway. The entire passenger rolling stock ever owned by the CMR (as distinct from the GWR that was shortly to take over operations) comprised three composite coaches and three third class coaches. The initial timetable showed trains leaving Newquay at 6.45 am and 4.15 pm, arriving at Fowey, some 26 miles distant, at 8.20 am and 5.50 pm, an average speed of about 17 mph. Return workings left Fowey at 10.20 am and 7.30 pm. Horse-drawn coach connections were provided at St Blazey to transfer passengers from Par (CMR) station to Par (Cornwall Railway) and vice versa. Another was provided from Halloon (St Columb Road) to Wadebridge. There was a wonderful and comprehensive account of the inaugural passenger train in the *West Briton and Cornwall Advertiser* of Thursday 22nd June, 1876, even though today the language seems a trifle strange, if not cumbersome. The report that follows is verbatim.

When the CMR opened to passengers in 1876 local dignitaries and railway officials gave speeches at Holywell station, later renamed Victoria and eventually, in 1904, Roche. In those speeches they anticipated large numbers of people using the train to visit the famous Roche Rock, seen here. With only two trains per day opportunities for visits were somewhat limited! The building on the top is the 15th century chapel of St Michael, which includes a small hermit's cell, as seen in 1989.   *Author*

The Cornwall Minerals Railway Company did not receive a very cordial welcome in the county when the line was first projected, nor, indeed, up to this time has there been much Cornish capital subscribed towards it; but the people along the district which it touches seem to have suddenly woken up to an appreciation of its value and importance. There was very much doubt as to the success of the line, and the falling off in, or rather the entire disappointment as to the anticipated heavy ore traffic, helped to support the gloomy forebodings. The men at the head of the company, Mr Roebuck as chief promoter, and afterwards Mr Richardson as manager of the line, were not men to be discouraged by ordinary difficulties, and they pressed onwards. The line was commenced about four years ago, and was opened for mineral traffic about two years since. Since then the company has been paying attention particularly to the china clay and china stone traffic, which seems to be ever increasing, and this, up to the present time, has been more than realised the most sanguine exportations formed by the company. There is still much hope that by revival of trade and an improvement in the price of iron, the extensive iron mines of the Perran district will be extensively worked, employ a large amount of labour, and give a heavy traffic to the Cornwall Minerals Railway. There has been some delay in the opening of the line for passenger traffic, owing to the difficulties with which the company has had to contend, and to the fact that much of the finishing work had to be done out of revenue. The important event came off on Tuesday last with great success, and with much promise for the future. We have had much pleasure in previously travelling over the line, and in bearing testimony to the excellent manner in which the permanent way has been laid, and we need say little more on this point now, seeing that the Government inspector has no fault to find with it. Everything has been well done. These notes were written while travelling on the line, so that passengers may feel assured of comfort whilst travelling, especially as the carriages are very nicely built. The stations are not yet all finished, and, though some of them have not much pretension to architectural beauty, they are all that is required at present. The station at Newquay will be a fine substantial structure. All the appointments connected with the running are of the best. The line is fitted with an inter-locking signal apparatus by Messrs, Stevens and Son, all the points being double locked; there are upwards of four miles of guard rail in connection with the various curves, and the trains are all fitted with vacuum brakes, worked from the engine, of sufficient power to pull up a train going at the rate of fifty miles an hour in a little over twenty yards [a remarkable claim]. The carriages are upon the Midland plan, first and third class, new and comfortable, and, in fact, everything that could be done for the convenience of passengers has been carried out. There has now been thoroughly and well carried out the idea which originated with Mr J.T. Treffry, of Fowey, many years ago, and who did much towards carrying his plan into execution. The Cornwall Minerals Railway Company utilised what they could of his work, and now we have excellent passenger accommodation from coast to coast, from the north to the south, and let us hope that the company will one day be fully rewarded for their pluck and enterprise. That they have conferred an immense boon on the county no one will doubt, and the benefit will continue to grow and increase. The first train started from Fowey on Tuesday morning amidst the cheers of a large crowd, and these were only the commencement of a series of cheers and demonstrations as the train proceeded all along the line till Newquay was reached, where there was a perfect ovation. The company were represented by Mr. Richardson, the general manager, Mr. Clunes, assistant manager, and Mr. Constantine, the locomotive superintendent, who drove the engine. When the train reached Par station, situated near St Blazey, there was more cheering, and there was a great deal of bunting floating in the breeze. Par station being situated some distance from the Cornwall Railway station, it is intended, we believe, to run a 'bus service' between the two stations. The St Blazey band now joined the party, and went on to Newquay. After leaving Par there is some pretty scenery passed through in the Luxulyan Valley, which has already been described, and the Treffry viaduct will always be an object of interest. We pass on through the deep granite cutting, and arrive at Bugle, in the heart of an important clay district, from which the line draws a very heavy traffic. Bugle is 4½ miles from Bodmin. After some more cheering and taking up some more passengers, we proceed to Victoria for Roche, a station situated within three miles of the Bodmin and Wadebridge line, and it is intended ere long to form a junction with that line here [no such line was ever built]. At Victoria station there was a still larger demonstration, the platform on each side being crowded with children and adults. The school children were placed on one platform and the general public on the other, and that at which the train arrived close to. There was a salute of fog signals [detonators], and when the train stopped and the officials stepped on the platform, there was evidently some proceedings about to take place of a more formal character than cheering.

Mr D. Cock, in introducing a deputation from Roche, congratulated the company on what they had already done for the locality. The residents felt it was a great boon to the entire district, and only the commencement of a great future, and in consequence of that they had invited the juvenile portion of the community to assemble there that day, believing as they did that they were to be the men who would feed and support the railway now being established for the benefit of the neighbourhood.

The Revd R.F. Gardiner, the vicar, then read the following address: 'Gentlemen - The inhabitants of the parish of Roche and the surrounding neighbourhood beg to offer you their hearty congratulations on the successful completion and opening for passenger traffic of the Cornwall Minerals Railway Company. Extending as it does from Fowey, on the south coast of Cornwall, to Newquay, on the north, it will afford immense facilities for the carriage of coal, tin, iron ore, china clay and other products. This will be a great benefit to a large number of people, and a stimulus to the trade of the county. In addition to this, it will be a great boon to travellers who periodically visit the beautiful watering-places of Newquay and Fowey, and other places in the neighbourhood, including the far-famed Roche Rock, and will probably induce many who have not done so to take advantage of your line for that purpose. To our own immediate neighbourhood it will be an inestimable benefit, and we therefore, one and all, congratulate you on the spirited way in which this undertaking has been carried out; and, whilst expressing our sincere thanks for the accommodation provided, wish you every prosperity and good dividends.'

Mr Richardson replied and acknowledged the kind reception accorded the company that day. On behalf of the directors and officers of the line, he reciprocated the kindly expression of feeling, and did not doubt for one moment but what the opening of the line for passenger traffic would be the means of bringing a large accession of tourists to view their incomparable rocks and other objects of interest in the locality. The opening of the line had been effected after immense difficulty, but now that it was accomplished, he felt quite sure that it would lead not only to the development of the various mineral resources of the district, but also to the cultivation of those large tracts of waste land which they had all around them. (Applause). He was surprised even now, considering how long the line had been opened for transmission of manures, &c., that some enterprising gentlemen had not already begun to endeavour to make the wilderness, so to speak, blossom as the rose. (Hear, hear.) He assured them that the interests of the company were the interests of the locality, and they might rest satisfied that so long as he had the management of the line, and so long as the board of directors who at present conducted the affairs existed, everything that could be done would be done to develop this very important district, which the line was designed to serve. (Hear, hear.) He felt glad that in their general rejoicing they had not forgotten the children, for it was his belief that those children in the years to come would reap an immense advantage from the line, and would see realised all the anticipations that had hitherto only been held out. (Applause.)

The train then moved on, amid cheers for the directors and officials.

We should state that the children had been supplied with buns, and the inhabitants did their best to give a most hearty welcome.

From Victoria station to Newquay there is a wider and more pleasant country to look upon. There is not so much of the dreary waste land apparent. The view embraces on

This photograph is allegedly the earliest known photograph of a passenger train at Newquay, supposedly taken on 29th June, 1876, just nine days after the inauguration of a passenger service between Newquay and Fowey. Heading the CMR train of four-wheelers is a GWR '850' class 0-6-0T, one of a class built at Wolverhampton between 1874 and 1892. The locomotives later appeared as saddle tanks with shortened chimneys. Note the large carriage lamp ventilators on the roof of the leading carriage. *Woolf/Greenham Collection*

This pre-1904 photograph shows a GWR Dean 2-4-0T being turned on the original turntable at Newquay station, having just arrived from Par. Major modifications were made during 1905 in readiness for the new branch line service from Chacewater via Perranporth and, for the first time, through trains from London. Although heavily modified the houses in the background still stand in Cliff Road (formerly Station Road). *Woolf/Greenham Collection*

the one hand the hills and moors of Roche, St Dennis and St Enoder, and on the other a succession of hills and vales and moorlands, stretching away from Bodmin Beacon to the twin giants in the blue distance, Brown Willy and Rowtor. Halloon is the next station. Thence to St Columb by road is only a couple of miles, wherefore Halloon ought more properly to be called St Columb-road. Ere long it is probable that there will be a station between Victoria and Halloon, at the junction of the Newquay and Cornwall with the Cornwall Minerals line [effectively St Dennis Junction - but no such station was ever built], and eventually the Newquay and Cornwall itself will be opened for passenger traffic from Burngullow [which it never was]. From Halloon to Newquay is a very pretty run, and long before the terminus is reached, first the invigorating air of the breeze fresh from the Atlantic, and then a glimpse of the glorious blue sea rushing up the sands and dashing in fleecy foam against the long coast line, give token that Newquay is near.

The station at Newquay was gaily decorated with flags, and densely crowded. The Foresters and Oddfellows, in full apparel, and carrying their emblems, were drawn up on the platform, with the coastguardmen, the lifeboat crew, duly belted, and the rocket brigade. The members of the Local Board and of the Demonstration Committee were also in attendance to give due welcome, and, in fact, everybody was keeping holiday. As the train passed into the station it was heartily cheered, and when it came to a standstill the band struck up the 'National Anthem', and the coastguard presented arms.

Mr W.E. Mitchell, Chairman of the Local Board, and chief organiser of the demonstration, then stepped to the front and read the following address. 'To the Directors of the Cornwall Minerals Railway: - Gentlemen, - we, the Local Board of Newquay, on behalf of the inhabitants of the district, have very great pleasure in presenting our hearty congratulations on the opening of your line for passenger traffic. We feel sure that the extension of the railway system to Newquay will attract thousands of visitors to our beautiful beaches and magnificent cliffs, and materially contribute to the prosperity of the neighbourhood, and we trust that your energy and perseverance may be amply remunerated.'

Mr Richardson replied, thanking all for the very hearty and enthusiastic reception which they had accorded the company that day, and the very kind address they had presented, he had, on behalf of the directors of the company and his fellow-officials, to thank them most sincerely. He did hope, seeing how their interests were, in a great measure, identical, that nothing in their future intercourse would disturb the good understanding or alter the good opinion which they had formed of the gentlemen who had so successfully carried out the enterprise of the Cornwall Minerals Railway. (Hear, hear.) He had no doubt but what, as was stated in their address, the opening of the line would very largely contribute to the welfare of Newquay, and when the beauties of the neighbourhood became known, and people got to know that the line was opened to this part of the country, they would have legions of visitors to view the charming scenery. Cornishmen, he knew, were fully alive to their interests, and there was but little occasion, therefore, for him to say that, under their altered circumstances, it would be necessary to provide additional accommodation, not only lodging, but hotel accommodation for those who would visit the ancient port. He had looked around, and he had no doubt in his own mind that in the course of a comparatively short time they would see the whole of their beautiful hills clothed with excellent villas, and with those buildings requisite to make it a great sea-bathing place, and taking its deserved rank of first among the bathing places of the country. The opening of the line not only for passenger, but for goods traffic, would tend greatly to develop the large resources of the locality. He had been pained again and again, during the past few months, to see those born in the locality, and employed in it all their life-time, leaving the county in consequence of the depression of trade. The directors of the company were sanguine as ever of the ultimate success of those immense Perran lodes of iron, and as soon as the present commercial cloud, which at present enveloped the whole country, had disappeared, and the iron trade revived, they had no doubt but they would soon be busily engaged in raising the ore for the various markets in Wales and the North of England. (Applause.) So long as he continued to work the line, he should endeavour in every way to study the interests of the public and everything pertaining to the development of their resources.

The procession was then reformed and marched through the town, headed by the St. Blazey band. The procession was in the following order:- Band, coastguard, local board, demonstration committee, Foresters, Oddfellows, lifeboat crew, rocket brigade and general inhabitants. The people of Newquay had evidently determined upon making the day one of general rejoicing, and they succeeded in doing so; the efforts of such a comparatively small population to welcome the advent of that which they recognise as being for their material welfare were of the most satisfactory and praiseworthy character, and the company's officials must have been highly pleased at such a hearty and genuine welcome. The town was decorated with flags, hung from every conceivable point; triumphal arches were erected in various parts, and it is certain that the people must have worked late and early, and with the utmost goodwill, to have made such preparations for the reception in so short a time. The greatest enthusiasm prevailed throughout the town during the entire day, and a regular holiday was kept. The procession after going through the town arrived at Prout's Hotel [the present Red Lion Inn], where it broke up.

About one o'clock the officials of the railway, and several of the leading inhabitants, partook of an excellent luncheon at the hotel named, at which they were entertained through the liberality of the proprietor. Mr Mitchell presided, and in giving the toast of the day, 'Success to the Cornwall Minerals Railway', said for many years past they had been looking forward to this day, a day which he believed would have a most important effect on the prosperity of the neighbourhood. If the reception the officials had met with had not been such as might have been desired, it was only to be attributed to the short notice which had been given them; but he could assure them that not only the inhabitants of the town, but of the district generally, had looked forward with the greatest degree of satisfaction and pleasure to the event of that day. It was impossible for anyone to read over the handbills which had been circulated without being made aware that it savoured somewhat of the South-Western Railway, and it was his hope to see the line still further extended, so that they might have a connection with the narrow gauge route of the country. (Applause.) Locally, however, they must be benefitted by the advent of a passenger traffic; the picturesque beauties of one of the finest spots in all her Majesty's dominions would become known by it; and the facilities afforded for visiting it would most certainly be largely taken advantage of.

Mr Richardson responded, and expressed his surprise at the marvellous reception which had been accorded them on the arrival of the first train. He had been connected with railways for the past thirty years, and he must say that the reception of that day was unequalled in his experience. (Hear, hear) There was no doubt but what the traffic arrangements, so far as Newquay was concerned, was a most important one, and the valuable results likely to accrue were hardly possible to be calculated. He had been connected with districts which, like this, had been locked up for very many years, and at the opening of the railway it was fancied that very little would accrue from it. Yet ultimately, those lines had been made almost the most remunerative in the whole kingdom, and, looking at what they had seen that day, the signs in regard of the Cornwall Minerals Railway were exceedingly hopeful; because, not only might they confidently look forward to a very large passenger traffic, but he thought they might also confidently contemplate the development of a very large mineral traffic - (Hear, hear) - altogether apart from the traffic in iron ore, which gentlemen who understood that business said would ultimately come upon the line. The district in past years had been entirely locked up and so as far as Newquay and other civilised parts of the globe were concerned, there had been a sort of barrier between them. That day, however, they had had a most unmistakeable way of access opened up to Newquay, and it was only necessary that the locality should be known to be highly appreciated and extensively visited by people from all parts of the country. He knew Scarborough, Whitby, Bridlington, and the whole of the leading watering places, but he never met with a finer situation, or a more invigorating climate, than that of Newquay, and, under favourable circumstances, it would become a second Torquay [which it did]. He knew they very much desired to see their own town prosper, and it was equally his own desire, because it must be a source of profit to the company he represented. The shareholders had expended a very large sum of money, and his great desire now was to see them obtain a fair return for the capital ended. (Hear, hear) He pointed out that they could best show their appreciation of the efforts of the company by using their property on every occasion, and concluded by proposing the health of Mr. Mitchell and the committee, referring again to the excellent reception given them.

Mr Mitchell responded, and pledged the town to do all it could to assist the undertaking.

Mr Prout having been thanked for his excellent and liberal entertainment, the proceedings closed with one or two minor toasts.

During the afternoon there were various amusements carried on in the town, and the rocket apparatus was brought out and worked. A tea was provided for about two hundred children, the funds for which came from the town collection for the reception of officials, and in the evening there was a bonfire and display of fireworks on the heights.

We may add that St Columb was not behind hand. Mr Polkinhorn, of the Red Lion Hotel [not to be confused with the Newquay Red Lion], started a conveyance with passengers to Halloon to meet the first up train, and also a second two-horse break to meet the first down train, which was crowded, and which left the Red Lion amid the huzzas of a large assembly. Considering that St Columb is the centre of a large and important agricultural district, it is hoped that ere long the rail will be extended from the Minerals line still nearer [no branch to St Columb town was ever built]. The North Cornwall Coach will continue its route to the station, and Mr Polkinhorn will, in addition to this accommodation, run all necessary conveyances to promote the traffic to and from St Columb.

On reflection, the most remarkable aspect of the various speeches was the boundless optimism expressed by the various dignitaries. There is no doubt that after a very slow start the railway did bring affluence to the already affluent in the Newquay area. The coming of the railway was a major factor in the growth of Newquay and the development of a significant tourist trade, particularly between the late Victorian era and the end of the 1950s. Also the railway served the china clay industry well and over the decades hundreds of thousands of tons of the extracted white material was conveyed by rail from the pits and dries to the ports. However, on the flip side of the coin despite all of the opening day hype the Cornwall Minerals Railway provided for only two round trips between Newquay and Fowey in its inaugural timetable. The income so derived would have been minimal. The envisaged station at St Dennis Junction never materialised in the life of the railway, and proposed extensions to the Bodmin & Wenford Railway and St Columb town were never built. Also the Newquay & Cornwall Junction Railway never carried a passenger service. However, perhaps the greatest disappointment for the CMR would be the failure of the iron ore industry to make the forecast turnaround from its 1870s slump, thus depriving the railway of a potentially significant income.

Featuring prominently in this vintage view at Newquay are the original CMR signal box on the left and the locomotive shed on the right. Neither have very long to 'live' and would be swept away in the radical changes of 1905. Arriving is a museum piece of a train comprising a Dean 2-4-0T and five rattling four-wheelers with double running boards.   *Woolf/Greenham Collection*

This wonderful scene was recorded at Newquay station in 1904, although it could have been made years earlier. The top-hatted coachman is Frank Hicks and in the Hoytes Company landau are Dave Old and Will Pearce. The standing porter has 'Headland Hotel' embroidered on his hat and the name 'Newquay' appears in the glorious station lamp. Note the crude brake block on the rear wheel.   *Newquay Old Cornwall Society*

Chapter Seven

The Great Western Railway

Takeover of the CMR

On 14th July, 1876 the first excursion train was run in connection with the United Methodist Church of St Blazey. Upwards of 200 people availed themselves of the trip which included a public tea at Newquay. Overall there was no evidence of a substantial increase in passenger traffic and during 1877 there were still only two passenger trains per day over the line in each direction. The decline in mineral extraction continued with several major mines and a number of small china clay pits closing. Finances on the CMR were under great pressure and Roebuck, one would think reluctantly, approached the GWR in the early months of 1877 in an attempt to seek a rescue package. It must have been demoralising to have spent nearly five years building the CMR empire just in time to face a financial crash of international proportions.

Roebuck was successful and by an agreement dated 30th April, 1877, sanctioned by Parliament on 10th August, 1877, the GWR undertook to work the line for a term of 999 years from 1st July, 1877, subject to a considerable number of conditions and stipulations. In fact the agreement did not come into operation until 1st October, 1877 owing to certain obligations having to be fulfilled before the agreement was binding upon the GWR. The GWR was to receive 53.11 per cent of the gross receipts, with a guaranteed minimum. The GWR guaranteed to the CMR a minimum net income of £15,000, £16,000 and £17,000 respectively for the first three years, increasing each year by £250 until the sum of £18,500 was reached. Again there were many legal clauses and provisos that the CMR had to adhere to. The lines handed over the GWR operationally were as follows:

	Miles	Chains
The Par & Fowey Railway, from Fowey to the junction with the Newquay Railway	16	39
The Newquay Railway, from St Dennis to Newquay	10	63
The Newquay & Cornwall Junction Railway from Burngullow to the junction with the Newquay Railway	5	25
The Retew Branch from the Newquay Railway	2	5
The Carbis Branch from the Par & Fowey Railway	1	0
The East Wheal Rose and Gravel Hill Branches	9	75
Total	45	47

In 1878 the single round trip Sunday service was withdrawn but by the end of the 1870s there began a slow recovery in local and national industries and there was evidence of an increase in both passenger and goods receipts. China clay and china stone benefitted from this turnaround but the iron ore industry was never to recover. As a direct result of the state of the iron ore industry the Gravel Hill extension, from Treamble, which had been disused for some time, was eventually lifted in 1888. One very positive development was the construction in January 1879 of a double track standard gauge spur between Par

	WEEK DAYS						SUNDAYS	
	1	2	3	4	5	6	1	2
	1 3 A.M.	1 3 A.M.	1 3 P.M.	1 3 P.M.				
NEWQUAY ......de.	7 0	...	4 25	...	...	...	...	...
Halloon (Saint Columb) ...	7 21	...	4 46	...	...	...	...	...
Victoria	7 41	...	5 6	...	...	...	...	...
Bugle	7 51	...	5 16	...	...	...	...	...
Bridges	7 57	...	5 22	...	...	...	...	...
PAR (Saint Blazey) ar.	8 15	...	5 40	...	...	...	...	...
	A.M.	A.M.	P.M.	P.M.				
PAR ....de.	8 20	9 5	5 45	6 20	...	...	...	...
FOWEY ....ar.	8 35	9 25	6 0	6 35	...	...	...	...

	WEEK DAYS						SUNDAYS	
	1	2	3	4	5	6	1	2
	1 3 A.M.	1 3 A.M.	1 3 P.M.	1 3 P.M.				
FOWEY ....de.	8 0	8 45	5 25	7 15	...	...	...	...
PAR ....ar.	8 15	9 0	5 40	7 30	...	...	...	...
PAR (Saint Blazey) ...d.	...	9 5	...	8 15	...	...	...	...
Bridges	...	9 20	...	8 30	...	...	...	...
Bugle	...	9 25	...	8 35	...	...	...	...
Victoria	...	9 35	...	8 45	...	...	...	...
Halloon (Saint Columb)	...	10 0	...	9 10	...	...	...	...
NEWQUAY ......a.	...	10 20	...	9 30	...	...	...	...

CORNWALL MINERALS.—G. W.					[Sec., H. Gibbs.				
Miles from Par.	Paddington Sta.	gov	mrn	mrn	gov	Up.	gov	mrn	aft	gov	gov
33	4 LONDON .dep	9, 0	...	5 30	11½	Newquay .dp	7 20	11 2	...	5 30	....
	13 EXETER .. "	2 40	8 40	1158	4510	St. Columb R.	7 36	1118	....	5 46	....
	13 PLYMOUTH"	6 50	11 0	2	40 6	55	Victoria (for	7 52	1184	....	6 2	....
¼	Par ....dep	8 40	1245	4 23	7 25	Bugle [Roche]	7 55	1141	....	6 9	....
½	St. Blazey	8 45	1250	4 25	7 30	Bridges †	8 5	1147	....	6 15	....
—	St. Blazey .dp	8 46	1251	4 29	7 31	Fowey .dep	8 0	1142	3 50	6 10	8 20
4	Fowey ....arr	8 58	1 3	4 41	7 43	St. Blazey a	8 12	1154	4 2	6 22	8 32
4	Bridges, fr Luxu-	8 56	1 1	....	7 41	St. Blazey ..	8 20	12 2	4 7	6 30	8 40
6½	Bugle .... .[lyan	9 2	1 7	....	7 47	Par 19, 18ar	8 22	12 4	4 9	6 32	8 42
8½	Victoria*	9 9	1 14	....	7 54	19 PLYMTH ar	1018	1 50	6 5	8 10	1026
14½	St. Columb Road	9 23	1 29	....	8 8	19 EXETER . "	1240	3556	9 26	1020	....
20½	Newquay ...arr	9 35	1 42	....	8 21	3 LONDON . "	6 0	5½16	....	4 0	....

b 1&2 class.   * Station for Roche; † for Luxulyan.

Newquay branch timetables from 1878 (*above*), November 1888 (*left*).

(CMR station), which was immediately renamed St Blazey, to Par (GWR/ex-CR station) on the Plymouth to Falmouth and Penzance main line. There seems little doubt that the spur was built as a direct result of GWR influence and from the date of opening it was possible for passengers travelling from CMR lines to book through to any GWR station and vice versa. Between the date of opening in 1879 and 1892 there was of course a difference of gauges between the standard gauge CMR and the broad gauge GWR. All passengers for Newquay had to change trains at Par and all goods had to be transhipped. A large transfer goods shed was provided on the up side of Par station.

In March 1885 the CMR proposed a Scheme of Arrangement with its creditors involving the issue of additional stock. In the CMR's annual report the Directors stated that the scheme would restore control of the affairs of the company to the Board and that the Directors would be able 'to give their attention, with advantage, to all matters relating to the development of traffic'. To provide some scale to the size of activities on the CMR, the accounts for the six months ended 31st December, 1885 showed total gross receipts of £16,406 compared with £15,046 for the previous 6 months, an increase of 9 per cent. Other statistics reflect this upturn, for example between the 1875 low and 1885 china clay and stone production doubled and by 1888 *Bradshaw's* timetable shows that passenger train frequency had grown to four down trains and five up trains between Fowey, St Blazey and Par and three through trains in each direction between Par, St Blazey and Newquay. There were through trains from Newquay to Fowey or vice versa that did not call at Par on the main line.

The GWR broad gauge was abandoned in 1892 and for the first time through running from GWR metals onto CMR lines was possible. By 1893 there were five trains between Par and Newquay, a significant increase in percentage terms. Although referred to elsewhere it should be mentioned that the change of gauge also increased the scope for through traffic at Drinnick Mill on the old Newquay & Cornwall Junction line, where broad gauge track ran up from Burngullow on the main line. These were heady days for the CMR and notwithstanding the heavy GWR influence sufficient revenues were flowing into the company's coffers to provide working capital for further major development schemes.

With a capital requirement of £24,000 construction of a 3½ mile branch line from Roskear Sidings (now Goonbarrow Junction) near Bugle to Carbean, in the heart of clay country, started. The line would serve numerous clay drying installations. Work started in 1890 but over difficult and steeply graded terrain, including the boring of a tunnel at Stenalees, the line was not ready for service until October 1893. The line was to be freight only throughout its life. Strangely the branch was worked independently by the CMR and the company provided its own locomotive until the whole of the CMR was purchased outright by the GWR on 1st July, 1896. A further short line of about ½ mile in length was also built from Bugle station to Martins Goonbarrow, Great Beam and Wheal Rose clay kilns. This was known as the Wheal Rose branch and the name should not be confused with the original Newquay Tramway line to East Wheal Rose lead mine. The third and final CMR financed scheme was taking control of the old abandoned Lostwithiel & Fowey Railway (L&FR). The line had opened in June 1869 as a broad gauge branch from Lostwithiel to Carne Point on the banks of the River Fowey, about a mile short of the town of the same name. The original line suffered from CMR competition once its direct line from St Blazey to Fowey opened in 1874. After a series of price battles between the companies and following a need for heavy repairs to the route, requiring capital the L&FR did not have, the line closed in 1880. The downturn in traffic had been dramatic falling from 27,000 tons in 1874 to less than 8,000 tons in 1879.

The reconstruction included linking the CMR route and the Lostwithiel route and the new network opened for traffic on 16th September, 1895. From this date passengers could travel from Fowey to either St Blazey and Par or alternatively to Lostwithiel. It should be mentioned that during the 1870s and 1880s there were a number of schemes to link the CMR lines to other railways and even rival lines. One previously mentioned was the August 1873 proposal for a connection with the Bodmin & Wadebridge Railway, which envisaged linking Ruthern Bridge, a freight terminus at the end of a branch from the Bodmin to Wadebridge line, with the CMR near to the site of the present Roche station.

GWR Operations

In 1896 the GWR purchased the entire CMR system and the CMR was dissolved. The final takeover was at a time when significant developments were about to take place. The GWR would play a major part in the development of Newquay as a town but more particularly as a holiday resort that would rank amongst the best and most popular in the whole of the United Kingdom.

The mid- to late-1870s was a busy time for the GWR in Cornwall. For years the company had considerable influence on train services in the West Country and particularly on the main line west of Exeter. On 1st February, 1876 the GWR became the absolute owners of the West Cornwall Railway, a company that for years had run its standard gauge line between Truro and Penzance. Also after years of 'calling the shots' on many issues pertaining to the Plymouth to Truro and Falmouth main line they were later to take over the Cornwall Railway. Thus the GWR owned outright the entire Plymouth to Penzance main line and all branch lines making a junction therewith.

Newquay station in its post-1905 configuration, with a small GWR 2-4-0T ready to leave for Par. Three platform faces are available for the increased rail traffic, substantial awnings and all normal passenger facilities have been provided. Business in the goods yard is brisk and the town is ready for the forthcoming tourist boom in the days when the motor car was a rarity. The platforms would again be extended between 1928 and 1938. *Author's Collection*

Judging by the dress of the passengers and the numbers alighting at Newquay from what is clearly a double-headed special train, the crowd in this 1903 photograph may have been attending a religious gathering, a temperance convention or even a Bank Holiday parade. In front of the two GWR 0-6-0 saddle tanks is the soon-to-be-replaced locomotive turntable. In the background are the station and the gasworks, while to the bottom left is an advertisement for the 1903 GWR Tourist Guide. *Woolf/Greenham Collection*

Having already influenced the CMR's original motive power by returning half of the fleet to the builders, rebuilding the remainder and then transferring away the majority of the Sharp, Stewart locomotives the GWR imported its own locomotives. In addition to the '850' class 0-6-0T many other classes were also transferred to Cornwall and used on CMR lines, including the little 2-4-0 'Metro' tank locomotives. From the 1880s GWR passenger coaches replaced the original CMR examples and after the conversion of gauge of the main line in 1892 other GWR stock was decanted, including some 6-wheelers and some splendid clerestory-roofed bogie coaches. In later years more modern designs of steam locomotive were used ranging from humble pannier and prairie tank locomotives to more illustrious named 4-6-0 tender locomotives. The GWR even tried steam railmotor coaches for a short while in late Edwardian times, particularly on the Chacewater to Newquay services.

The GWR had enormous influence and both before and after the advent of the motor car and motor bus they publicised and improved the railway services thus encouraging usage. The GWR were instrumental in embarking on a series of station name changes, with some stations having as many three different names but not at the same time! In November 1878 Halloon became St Columb Road, within a couple of months Par (CMR) became St Blazey, Holywell became Victoria and in November 1904 Roche, and in May 1905 Bridges was renamed Luxulyan. As already mentioned the envisaged station at Bodmin Road Junction, later St Dennis Junction, was never built. Finally Treloggan Junction, just to the east of town was renamed Newquay Junction and finally Tolcarn Junction. A small halt was built and opened by the GWR at Quintrel Downs in 1911 and the only consistency was that since opening to passengers in 1876 the name of Newquay and Bugle stations never changed!

Although during the 1877 to 1896 period the GWR were, technically, merely the operators of the CMR there is no doubt that they had enormous influence and most of the major changes implemented by the CMR would have had a 'nod' from the GWR. Following the opening by the CMR of the Goonbarrow and Wheal Rose branches in 1893 and the Lostwithiel to Fowey line in 1895, the first major project undertaken by the GWR was in 1903/1905 when a branch line from Chacewater to Newquay via Perranporth opened throughout. This effectively gave a through service from Truro and Penzance to Newquay, although a change of train at Chacewater was often necessary. The story of the building and opening of this line is described in Chapter Eighteen.

In anticipation of the opening of the new line a significant capital investment was made in the Newquay station area. The terminus was enlarged and modernised, starting with a W.H. Smith & Sons news agency in 1896. The pre-1905 changes included the abolition of the original end-of-platform turntable, the construction of a new and repositioned engine shed, and the provision of a brand new signal box to control new lines and providing additional platform accommodation. All of this work was not only to accommodate the new branch service and an increase in freight traffic but with an eye on the future. The envisaged 'future' came to fruition in May 1906 when the first through trains from London, Paddington to Newquay commenced. The journey time was 7 hours and 55 minutes, compared with current times using High Speed Train units of about 5 hours.

These through workings were the main catalyst for a burgeoning holiday industry that was to grow significantly in the following three decades, subject to

Although this 1922 view of the Newquay terminus is technically deficient it does show the three platforms in use at that time. There are some goods wagons in the yard and some stock at platform 3 but the main features are the lovely lamps and the pagoda hut.   *Author's Collection*

Almost coinciding with the opening throughout of the Chacewater to Newquay branch in 1905 was the introduction of steam railmotors by the GWR. These vehicles were introduced on branch lines in 'quiet' areas and they performed very well indeed, until a trailer coach was added. The early examples, such as No. 30, built in January 1905 and seen here leaving Newquay in 1913, were painted in crimson lake livery. Note the magnificent gas lamp.

Woolf/Greenham Collection

Although previously published this is one of the finest views available of an Edwardian Par to Newquay train entering Bugle and to omit it from this compilation would have been inexcusable. A Dean 2-4-0T arrives at what was then the single platform with two magnificent clerestory six-wheelers, a bogie coach and a guard's van. On the right is a crane used for loading casks (barrels) of china clay into goods wagons, while in the background the up goods yard is well populated. The signal box is of 1874 CMR origin and was the last of its type to survive, being replaced in 1916. *Author's Collection*

This fine 1907 study of the second, 1874, Trenance viaduct finds one of Churchward's very successful '4500' class 2-6-2 prairie tanks heading a superb rake of stock towards Par. Included in the formation are two bogie clerestory coaches and three six-wheelers, two being four-compartment and one a five-compartment example. Many years later Newquay Zoo would occupy the field on the left and a massive caravan park the field on the right. *Woolf/Greenham Collection*

There were only two significant centres of population on the Chacewater to Newquay branch line, St Agnes and Perranporth. In this 1914 view of St Agnes, with the original station and track layout, the station master Mr Julian (*centre*) and the porter Percival Trembath (*right*) pose for the cameraman with staff and passengers. The station was nearly one mile from the village, to the disappointment of the local community. The track layout and platform configuration was radically changed in 1938. *Cornish Studies Library*

The GWR were not immune from accidents and operating problems and in this Edwardian view at the junction of Par 0-6-0ST No. 1825 has overrun signals to collide with a goods train on the up main line. The locomotive has been jacked-up onto blocks but recovery of the upturned wagons will require rather more effort. The camera has also captured 16 railway personnel in attendance. *M. Dart Collection*

A GWR '4500' class prairie has just arrived at Newquay station during the 1920s. Of the three-compartment coaches two have clerestory roofs, with a guard's van and a four-wheeled wagon at the rear of the train. A poster advertises Navy Week at Plymouth and in the background is the 1886 gasworks.   *Author's Collection*

With the heyday of small wooden sailing ships long past, commercial traffic at Newquay Harbour sharply declined. The last loads were exported/imported in 1921/1922 and the GWR formally closed the tramway in 1926, with the land being transferred to local authority ownership. In this May 1922 photograph the harbour lines have seen their last wagon and the incline tunnel stands silent.   *Woolf/Greenham Collection*

This view from about 1930 shows just how near to the sea Newquay station is located. In addition to spare stock there are over 20 goods wagons in the adjacent yard while bottom left the Newquay Harbour tramway alignment can be seen, although the road crossing point is obscured by houses. Newquay is now just a single line stub with the yard, goods shed, multiple platforms, station building and long awnings all obliterated. *Woolf/Greenham Collection*

a World War I 'blip'. It was not long before other seasonal trains worked through to Newquay in the height of Summer, particularly on Saturdays, from an array of cities in the Midlands, the North of England and even Scotland. Peak holiday period traffic became so intense that the GWR was obliged to double long sections of the erstwhile single track. The section from Tregoss Moor to St Dennis Junction was doubled as early as 1921 and Goonbarrow Junction to Bugle followed in 1930. The short section from Tolcarn Junction to Newquay was doubled in two stages, 1940 and 1946 following the construction of the new all-masonry Trenance viaduct, which replaced the 1873/1874 CMR masonry and iron example. Smaller changes to track configuration and extending certain passing loops had taken place many years before, including Luxulyan 1910, 1916 and 1936, Bugle station area 1930/1931, St Columb Road in 1931 and the re-instatement of the east to south chord at Tolcarn Junction in the same year (*see Chapter Seventeen*). Other modifications are described in the 'journey along the line' text.

Other changes to the main Newquay branch and its sidings and branches during the 1896 and 1947 period were numerous with changes occurring in most years. Sidings were installed, lifted or modified as the huge numbers of rail-served industrial sites opened, closed or enlarged. Major events included the severing of the line from Burngullow to St Dennis Junction from 1909 until 1922 at Carpella due to the Carpella Mining Company exercising its rights to extract minerals from the part of its land that carried the Newquay & Cornwall Junction line. Also the GWR extended the Retew branch from Melangoose Mill along the River Fal and down to Meledor Mill in 1912, to serve an increasing number of clay works.

Changes in the railways of the County of Cornwall during the reign of the GWR were considerable, including the doubling of the main line from Saltash to Penzance, in various stages, the opening (and closing) of various branch lines, changes to stations and signalling, new locomotives and rolling stock and changes to services. Other more detailed changes were numerous but outside the geographical boundaries of this volume. The GWR were always keen, in public relations terms, to present an efficient and businesslike image and they kept a watchful eye on commercial viability. When it suited them they did not shy away from closing certain lines and particular installations. For example in September 1931 the GWR closed Burngullow station on the Cornish main line. They also withdrew passenger services between Fowey and St Blazey on 8th July, 1925, although a non-timetabled workmen's train ran for several years afterwards. They closed and then re-instated the freight line between Shepherds and Treamble, the track being lifted for the war effort in 1917 and then after relaying reopened the route on 16th February, 1926. The last traffic on the line was in 1949 and formal closure took place in 1952, the track being finally lifted in 1956, eight years after the GWR ceased to exist.

Traffic volumes handled at Newquay Harbour had been dwindling since the latter days of the CMR and had reached a trickle as the small wooden ships of yesteryear gradually disappeared from the commercial scene. Large modern ships could not use the tiny tidal harbour and the horse-drawn operation was by then an anachronism and an operational inconvenience, as was the use of an incline to reach the point of shipment. One of Cornwall's recessions was imminent and unemployment was on the increase. Many local china clay producers had large stocks and many small companies had closed. The last outbound commercial vessel from Newquay Harbour that involved usage of the original tramway was in 1921 and reports suggest the last inbound load was a year later when in 1922 the good ship *Hobah* landed some agricultural fertilizer. The Harbour line became disused and was formally closed by the GWR in 1926. It is hardly surprising that the tramway to Newquay Harbour closed because for many years most of the china clay had deliberately been transported to the southern ports.

Between 1896 and the start of World War I the value of clay exports doubled and Fowey had become established as the primary port for handling china clay and china stone, followed in terms of volume throughput by Par Harbour. There was a post-World War I boom in the china clay industry but this trend was soon reversed. There was considerable consolidation in the china clay industry at this time and in April 1919 the English China Clays company was incorporated. The GWR embarked on a modernisation scheme at Fowey with the objective of hugely increasing handling capacities and replacing many old manual processes with up to date machinery. New jetties were also built and No. 8 jetty could handle ships with a capacity of some 9,000 tons, a dramatic contrast with the 30 to 250 ton tiddlers that once called at the small Cornish ports. This jetty was over 2,400 ft long and the machinery was powered by electricity generated in a small power station at the docks site.

Between the two World Wars china clay production was fairly steady and in most years exceeded 800,000 tons, the exceptions being the years of the great depression. During World War II china clay production was adversely impacted and although the railways in Cornwall were still carrying an annual china clay tonnage in excess of 130,000 much of the output was exported from Bristol and Avonmouth as a wartime expedient, these being safer ports than those on the submarine-infested English Channel. However, by the time the Nationalisation of the railways took place in 1948 the GWR was able to hand over to the newly formed British Railways a source of rail traffic that was in very good shape and 'a nice little earner'!

In order to save on the use of raw materials, such as coal, china clay production during the war years was concentrated on just 23 pits, with over 70 others being closed or mothballed. This situation was made easier by the consolidation that had taken place. In fact between 1919 and 1985 English China Clays (later English China Clays International, and from 1999 Imerys) acquired no less than 100 smaller privately-owned china clay companies! It should be mentioned that not all china clay and china stone was conveyed by rail. Quite large volumes have always been and continue to be transported by road and over the years there have been significant developments in pipeline technology, whereby large volumes of clay in liquid slurry form are piped over considerable distances from the clay pits primarily to the massive clay drying plant at Par Harbour. To use a modern expression, clay continues to be dried there '24/7' and although there have been signs recently that the international commodity market is favouring china clay produced in far off places, such as Brazil, where unit costs are cheaper, Par remains a major hub of the industry in Cornwall.

Returning to the many minor modifications made to track layout at the various industrial works, between 1877 and 1948 these changes were never-ending and the cost of most of the alterations was met by the individual companies that owned the sidings rather than the GWR. Every change involved a legal agreement containing precise details and a full statement of costs. Every contract contained scores of regulations and stipulations about the movement of railway wagons, maintenance of the permanent way, fencing provisions, access to running lines by non-railway employees etc.

Although following a successful inspection by the Board of Trade's Railway Inspectorate prior to opening, the CMR lines were deemed to be perfectly safe for goods and passenger operation, over the years the GWR greatly improved standards. These changes saw the introduction of a comprehensive Rule Book, improved public notices and signs, brighter station and yard lighting but above all an increase in the quality of the track and permanent way. The latter included all aspects of signalling and between 1877 and 1916 the GWR closed and replaced every one of the original CMR signal boxes.

Returning to GWR motive power (much of which was transferred to the Western Region of BR after Nationalisation in 1948), until it was closed during the early 1930s there was an active engine shed at Newquay. However, the majority of the locomotives used on the Newquay branch lines were based at St Blazey motive power depot. The main exceptions were locomotives that worked the Chacewater to Newquay branch, which were often worked by Truro shed, and the sole CMR locomotive that worked the Goonbarrow branch for many years. As already mentioned, after the CMR tank locomotives departed the GWR '850' class saddle tanks arrived and over the years there followed a bewildering array of locomotives from the design offices of Dean, Churchward, Collett and Hawksworth. St Blazey's allocation comprised mostly small tank locomotives, necessary to cope with restricted access, weight restrictions and severe curvature on the sidings and freight lines over which they operated. A sample of these included '3500' class 2-4-0 'Metro' tanks, 0-6-0 pannier tanks of the '2021', '2181', '5700' and '1600' classes and Prairie 2-6-2 tanks of the '4500', '4575' and '5100' classes. Tender locomotives appeared for ex-St Blazey freights that worked longer distances on the main line and express passenger locomotives regularly appeared at Newquay at the head of through trains in the holiday season. These included 'Manors', 'Granges', 'Halls', 'Castles' and the handsome '4300' and '6300' class 2-6-0s. In later years 'County' 4-6-0s also appeared regularly. For use between St Dennis and Fowey the depot at St Blazey often had an allocation of heavy and powerful '4200' class 2-8-0 tanks and '7200' class 2-8-2 tanks, which dated back to GWR days but in Cornwall were more synonymous with the BR era. St Blazey was also home to a handful of '1400' class 0-4-2 tanks but these were mainly used on the Lostwithiel to Fowey branch.

Particularly in the summer months services over the Par to Newquay line were quite intensive. From the two or three return workings over the line in CMR days the frequency gradually improved. In April 1910 there were five down and four up trains and by January 1927 there were seven down and six up trains. By the high summer of 1938 no fewer than 12 trains traversed the branch from Monday to Friday with a maximum of 14 trains on summer Saturdays.

Straying outside of the GWR era, by comparison the summer Saturday 1958 timetable shows a staggering 21 peak period departures from Par to Newquay, whereas there were just four round trip branch workings in the autumn of 2007! Over the years summer through trains from Newquay have run to a huge variety of destinations, for example in 1989 InterCity 125 units worked through

This unusual scene depicts Newquay goods yard about 1930. In the yard are four-wheeled wagons of GWR, LNER and LMS origin, while in the background is an impressive collection of main line stock. The goods shed and the yard crane are clearly visible as well as a horse-drawn delivery wagon.   *HMRS*

This delightful picture shows a rarely photographed GWR 2-4-0 'Metro' tank locomotive at Newquay, which has just arrived from Truro via Chacewater with two vintage coaches in tow. In this *circa* 1933 view coaching set 'Newquay Branch No. 2' is at the adjacent platform. The locomotive, No. 1500, was built in September 1892 and it was withdrawn from St Blazey during 1937.   *Author's Collection*

After the closure of the tramway to the harbour the rails were lifted in 1928 but little development occurred. In the late 1930s there was little fishing activity and the lifeboat service was withdrawn (from the headland) in 1934. A small fun fair was established beside the harbour and a helter-skelter appeared. However, in 1938 the local authority withdrew permissions for such a contraption to continue in operation and the fun fair closed. In this rare 'snapshot' the structure looks to be something of an anachronism.

Newquay Old Cornwall Society

to Manchester, Glasgow, Leeds and London, while in 2007 Manchester, Glasgow and London were served. On the Chacewater to Newquay branch line services doubled between 1910, when there were six round trip workings plus an extra one on Saturdays, and the summer of 1938. In later years there was even a Saturdays Only through train between Perranporth and London, Paddington and vice versa.

Traditionally many of the summer dated 'express' trains have not been booked to stop at the intermediate stations between Par and Newquay but with single track, gradients and speed restrictions the fastest non-stop journey time between the stations has historically been about 45 minutes for the 20¾ mile journey, an average speed of about 27 mph! Between 1888 and 2007 stopping train journey times have been reduced from 56 minutes to 50 minutes, the latter representing an average speed of a shade under 25 mph.

During World War II holiday traffic was suspended and even after hostilities had finished there were still numerous restrictions on travel. There had understandably been minimum maintenance undertaken to locomotives, track and infrastructure during the war and the entire system was decidedly run down. Newquay traffic had peaked just before the war and it would be the early 1950s before there was any return to normal and previous traffic volumes. The end of the 71-year-long GWR operating era on the Newquay branch ended when the railways were nationalised in 1948. In retrospect it only seems a shame that the era did not end on an operational 'high' after the GWR's remarkable role in the development of Newquay.

Proving that not everything Great Western died on 1st January, 1948 when the railways were nationalised, is this 28th August, 1948 scene at Chacewater. Prairie No. 5500 has the initials 'GWR' emblazoned its side tanks as it heads a Truro to Newquay branch train. It looks as though a relief footplate crew is boarding the leading compartment, perhaps to work the train back to Truro.   *M. Dart Collection*

Another splendid scene from the BR 1950s era sees 0-6-0PT No. 9655 leaving St Blazey and starting its way along the single line to Newquay with a branch train from Par. The train is crossing the River Par and is approaching Middleway crossing with its three blood and custard liveried coaches and a four-wheeled van. Wagons in the down sidings can be seen on the right.
R.C. Riley/Courtesy Transport Treasury

Chapter Eight

British Railways to Privatisation

The transport systems of the UK were in rather a poor state of repair by the end of World War II. The Labour government's solution was to nationalise just about every major transport enterprise, from railways to canals and from buses to airlines. The legislation was contained in the 1947 Transport Act. The controlling organization was the British Transport Commission (BTC) and its main holdings were the assets of the 'Big Four' railway companies. The total undertaking was quite unwieldy with a staggering 688,000 staff! By the late 1950s the BTC was in serious financial difficulties mainly due to the under performance of the loss making railways. Accordingly the BTC organization was broken-up and finally abolished by Harold MacMillan's Conservative government, under the 1962 Transport Act. Dr Beeching was the last BTC Chairman. From that time the railways were to be controlled by the British Railways Board, of which Dr Beeching became the first Chairman.

Once the post-war dust had settled it was clear that the national railway system needed modernisation and a plan was drawn up. The Modernisation Plan was extensive and covered motive power, rolling stock, freight wagons, the permanent way, signalling and other infrastructure. From the railway enthusiasts' standpoint the report was infamous for extending electrification and in other areas replacing steam by diesel traction. Cornwall and the south-west was to be one of the first areas of British Railways (BR) to be completely dieselised. This process commenced with the arrival of the first main line diesels in 1958 and by 1962 the exercise had been substantially completed.

Another exercise conducted in the early 1960s was Dr Beeching's review of loss making railway lines and to report and make proposals for economies. There will never be a meeting of minds between a tax paying motorist and a non-car owning railfan but times were changing, motor car ownership was growing rapidly and some BR lines and services were hopelessly unremunerative. Certainly Cornwall would have suffered greatly if all loss making lines had been closed. Indeed one map of the notional post-Beeching network showed no railway lines at all west of Plymouth. The Newquay branch was certainly loss making but together with Gunnislake, Looe, Falmouth and St Ives it survived through subsidy, based to some extent on its summer usage. Bude, Launceston, Callington, Bodmin General, Bodmin North to Padstow, the North Cornwall line, Fowey, Chacewater to Newquay, the Helston branch and a number of freight lines were not so lucky and were subsequently closed and lifted.

Initially BR continued where the GWR had left off, coping with mostly pre-World War II locomotives, coaches and infrastructure. Some new Hawksworth steam locomotives were produced and found their way into Cornwall and on the main line 'Britannia' Pacifics, designed and built by BR, put in an appearance but on the Newquay branch it was the usual crop of ex-GWR named 4-6-0s, 2-6-0s, 0-6-0 pannier tanks, 2-6-2 Prairie tanks and on some clay trains 2-8-0 and 2-8-2 heavy tanks that continued to power the trains. As detailed in Chapter Eleven, most classes of main line diesel locomotive that appeared on the Western Region (WR) between 1959 and 1997

The demands of the Newquay branch through the Luxulyan valley and the epitome of BR steam on summer Saturdays are both depicted in this classic shot. The heavy 12-coach 9.30 am Paddington to Newquay through train on 9th July, 1955, is headed by 'Hall' class No. 5972 *Olton Hall* and '4300' class mogul 2-6-0 No. 6397 and banked by 2-6-2 prairie tank No. 5519. The maximum load for the two tender engines up the 1 in 37 was 370 tons whereas the train would have exceeded 400 tons, hence the banker.   *R.C. Riley/Courtesy Transport Treasury*

Although of GWR design 0-6-0 pannier tank No. 7446 was built in 1950, during the BR era. In BR black livery with 'lion and wheel' emblem, the smart looking locomotive is seen shunting at St Blazey yard with a typical shunters match wagon in tow. The photograph was probably taken from St Blazey signal box, 3rd September, 1954.   *R.C. Riley/Courtesy Transport Treasury*

Table 99 PAR, BUGLE and NEWQUAY

MONDAYS TO FRIDAYS

Miles		am	am		am		am		am		pm		pm		pm		pm		pm		pm	pm D	
	Par dep	**6 10**	**6 45**	..	**7 20**	..	**9 30**	..	**1034**	..	**1220**	..	**2 40**	..	**3 20**	..	**4 25**	..	**6 25**	..	**7 45**	**9 20**	..
4¼	Luxulyan	....	6 59	...	7 34	...	9 44	...	1049	...	1238	...	2 56	...	3 34	...	4 39	...	6 42	...	7 59	9 34	...
6½	Bugle	6 29	7 4	..	7 40	..	9 50	..	1055	..	1247	..	3 3	..	3 40	..	4 45	..	6 48	..	8 5	9 39	..
8¾	Roche	6 35	7 10	...	7 46	...	9 57	...	11 1	...	1254	...	3 10	...	3 46	...	4 50	...	6 54	...	8 11	9 43	...
14¼	St. Columb Road	6 50	7 24	..	8 0	..	1012	..	1116	..	1 8	..	3 25	..	4 2	..	5 6	..	7 10	..	8 26	9 58	..
18½	Quintrel Downs	....	7 33	...	8 9	...	1022	...	1125	...	1 16	...	3 35	...	4 12	...	5 15	...	7 19	...	....	....	...
20¾	**Newquay** arr	**7 5**	**7 41**	..	**8 16**	..	**1030**	..	**1131**	..	**1 25**	..	**3 45**	..	**4 20**	..	**5 25**	..	**7 30**	..	**8 40**	**1012**	..

SATURDAYS

	am	am	am	am	am	am H	am	am	am		pm	pm	pm	pm	pm A	pm	pm	pm	pm	pm	pm	pm	
Par dep	**4 50**	**5 10**	**6 10**	**6 50**	**7 45**	**8 10**	**9 20**	**10 5**	**1045**	..	**1225**	**1 35**	**2 5**	**2 40**	**3 10**	**3 25**	**5 30**	**6 12**	**6 50**	**7 30**	**8 15**	**9 20**	..
Luxulyan	....	....	....	7 6	8 0	....	9 34	....	11 0	...	1239	1 53	....	2 56	....	....	5 45	6 27	....	7 44	8 31	9 34	...
Bugle	..	..	6 29	7 13	8 6	..	9 42	..	11 6	..	1246	2 0	..	3 3	..	..	5 52	6 35	..	7 50	8 38	9 39	..
Roche	....	....	6 35	7 19	8 13	....	9 50	....	1110	...	1253	2 6	....	3 10	....	....	5 58	6 42	....	7 56	8 44	9 43	...
St. Columb Road	5 30	5 50	6 50	7 33	8 32	9 10	1010	1042	1130	..	1 12	2 23	2 44	3 25	3 50	..	6 18	6 58	7 35	8 16	8 59	9 58	..
Quintrel Downs	....	....	....	7 42	8 42	....	1020	....	....	...	1 21	2 33	....	3 35	....	....	....	7 7	....	....	....	....	...
Newquay arr	**5 50**	**6 15**	**7 5**	**7 50**	**8 50**	**9 25**	**1031**	**11 0**	**1146**	..	**1 30**	**2 40**	**3 0**	**3 45**	**4 5**	**4 30**	**6 35**	**7 15**	**7 50**	**8 32**	**9 13**	**1012**	..

MONDAYS TO FRIDAYS

Miles		am		am		am		am		pm		pm		pm		pm	pm B	pm		pm	pm B	pm	pm G
	Newquay dep	**8 12**	..	**9 45**	..	**1045**	..	**1130**	..	**1250**	..	**1 45**	..	**4 45**	..	**6 0**	**7d20**	**8 5**	.	**9 8**	**9d45**	**1015**	**10d50**
2¼	Quintrel Downs	8 20	...	....	...	1051	...	....	...	1257	...	....	...	4 52	...	6 7	....	8 11	...	9 16	....	1022	...
6½	St. Columb Road	8 30	..	10 0	..	11 2	..	1145	..	1 8	..	2 1	..	5 4	..	6 18	..	8 24	.	9 27	..	1033	..
12	Roche	8 44	...	K	...	1116	...	1159	...	1 21	...	2 16	...	5 18	...	6 31	...	8 38	...	9 42	...	1047	...
14½	Bugle	8 50	..	1020	..	1123	..	12 5	..	1 27	..	2 22	..	5 24	..	6 37	..	8 43	.	9 50	..	1052	..
16½	Luxulyan	8 55	...	....	...	1129	...	1211	...	1 33	...	2 28	...	5 30	...	6 42	...	8 49	...	9 56	...	1058	...
20¾	**Par** arr	**9 9**	..	**1040**	..	**1143**	..	**1228**	..	**1 46**	..	**2 42**	..	**5 43**	..	**6 56**	**8 12**	**9 3**	.	**10 9**	**1042**	**1111**	**11 40**

SATURDAYS

	am	am		am	am Z		am	am		am		pm	pm		pm	pm		pm	pm		pm	pm	
Newquay dep	**7d50**	**8d 5**	..	**8d50**	**10 0**	..	**11d0**	**11d15**	.	**1152**	..	**1230**	**12d40**	.	**1 45**	**5 0**	..	**6 0**	**8 0**	.	**9 8**	**1015**	..
Quintrel Downs	....	....	...	8d59	....	...	....	....	...	1159	...	....	12d48	...	....	5 7	...	6 7	8 7	...	9 16	1022	...
St Columb Road	..	8d20	..	9d10	10θ15	..	..	11d28	.	1210	..	..	1d 0	.	2 1	5 19	..	6 18	8 18	.	9 27	1033	..
Roche	....	8d35	...	9d24	....	...	....	11d42	...	1224	...	....	1d14	...	2 16	5 34	...	6 31	8 31	...	9 42	1047	...
Bugle	..	8d42	..	9d30	..	..	..	11d48	.	1230	..	..	1d20	.	2 22	5 40	..	6 37	8 37	.	9 50	1052	..
Luxulyan	....	8d48	...	9d38	....	...	....	11d54	...	1235	...	....	1d26	...	2 28	5 46	...	6 42	8 42	...	9 56	1058	...
Par arr	**8 42**	**9 5**	..	**9 55**	..	..	**1147**	**12 9**	.	**1252**	..	**1 15**	**1 42**	.	**2 42**	**6 0**	..	**6 56**	**8 55**	.	**10 9**	**1111**	..

SUNDAYS

	am	am	am	am		pm	pm	
Par dep	**8 35**	**9 30**	**1040**	**1115**	..	**5 8**	**7 5**	..
Luxulyan	8 48	9 44	....	1129	....	5 22	7 19	...
Bugle	8 55	9 50	..	1134	..	5 28	7 25	..
Roche	9 1	9 56	....	1140	....	5 34	7 31	...
St. Columb Road	9 16	1012	1122	1157	..	5 48	7 46	..
Quintrel Downs	....	1021	....	....	....	5 58	....	...
Newquay arr	**9 30**	**1030**	**1140**	**1210**	..	**6 8**	**8 0**	..

SUNDAYS

	am	am		pm	pm	pm	pm	pm	
Newquay dep	**9 55**	**1110**	..	**1 50**	**5 17**	**7 5**	**7 20**	**9 5**	..
Quintrel Downs	....	....	....	....	5 24	....	....	9 13	...
St. Columb Road	1010	1125	..	2 4	5 35	..	7 35	9 23	..
Roche	N	1140	...	2 19	5 49	...	7 49	9 36	...
Bugle	1029	1146	..	2 25	5 55	..	7 55	9 42	..
Luxulyan	....	1153	...	2 31	6 1	...	8 1	9 48	...
Par arr	**1050**	**1210**	..	**2 44**	**6 15**	**7 53**	**8 15**	**10 4**	..

A Will not run after 30th August
B Runs Fridays 1st, 8th, 15th and 22nd August only.
D Fridays only; also runs on Monday 4th August
d Passengers travelling by this train to certain stations beyond Par are required to hold Regulation Tickets (see page 30)
G Runs Fridays, 1st, 8th, 15th, 22nd and 29th August only.
H Runs 28th June to 23rd August inclusive
K Calls at 10 12 am to pick up passengers for London only on notice being given at the Station by 9 30 am
N Calls at 10 20 am to pick up passengers for London only on notice being given at the Station by 9 30 am
θ Calls to pick up passengers only
Z Restaurant Car Train to London (Paddington) arr 4 55 pm (Table 81)

Table 100 TRURO, CHACEWATER, PERRANPORTH and NEWQUAY
(Second class only except where otherwise shewn)

Miles		Week Days am	am S	am E	am	am E	am S	am T	pm	pm	pm P	pm	pm E	pm S	pm T	pm S	Sundays am	am	am T	am	pm	pm	pm	pm T	pm T
	Truro dep	**6 5**	**7 10**	**717**	**8H45**	**10 8**	**1010**	**1140**	**1H15**	**2J48**	**3 45**	**4L15**	**5H43**	**6 15**	**7 42**	**910**	**845**	**9 25**	**1125**	**1155**	**151**	.	**440**	**542**	**725**
5	**Chacewater**	**616**	**7 25**	**729**	**9 15**	**1020**	**1023**	**1154**	**1 35**	**2 58**	**3 55**	**4 39**	**5 58**	**6 25**	**8 0**	**922**	...	**9 37**	**1140**	**12 6**	**2 2**	...	**451**	**553**	**736**
6¾	Mount Hawke Halt	621	7 30	734	9 20	..	..	1159	1 40	3 3	..	4 44	6 3	6 30	8 5	927	.	9 42	1145	1211	2 8	.	456	558	741
8½	St. Agnes	626	7 35	739	9 25	1028	1030	12 4	1 45	3 8	4 5	4 49	6 8	6 40	8 10	932	...	9 47	1150	1216	214	...	5 1	6 4	746
9	Goonbell Halt	629	7 38	742	9 28	..	..	12 7	1 48	3 11	..	4 52	6 11	6 44	8 13	935	.	9 50	1153	1219	217	.	5 4	6 7	749
10¾	Mithian Halt	634	7 43	747	9 33	....	....	1212	1 53	3 16	....	4 57	6 16	6 49	8 18	940	...	9 55	1158	1224	222	...	5 9	612	754
13	Perranporth Beach Halt	639	7 48	752	9 38	1038	1040	1218	1 59	3 21	..	5 2	6 21	6 55	8 22	945	.	10 0	12 3	1229	227	.	513	617	759
13½	**Perranporth**	**641**	**8F 2**	**882**	**9 41**	**1040**	**1044**	**1221**	**2 4**	**3 23**	**4 20**	**5 5**	**6 24**	**6 57**	**8 24**	**948**	**912**	**10 2**	**12 5**	**1230**	**230**	**435**	**515**	**620**	**8 1**
15¾	Goonhavern Halt	649	8 10	810	9 49	..	..	1230	2 12	3 31	..	5 14	6 33	7 5	8 32	.	.	1010	1212	..	237	442	523	628	8 9
17¾	Shepherds	656	8 17	817	9 56	1052	....	1236	2 19	3 39	....	5 20	6 40	7 11	8 39	...	...	1018	1218	....	244	449	530	637	816
19	Mitchell and Newlyn Halt	659	8 20	820	10 0	..	..	1240	2 22	3 43	..	5 24	6 43	7 15	8 43	.	.	1022	1222	..	248	453	534	641	821
21	Trewerry and Trerice Halt	7 4	8 25	825	10 5	....	....	1245	2 27	3 48	....	5 29	6 48	7 20	8 48	...	...	1027	1227	....	253	458	539	646	826
23¾	**Newquay** arr	**712**	**8 32**	**832**	**1015**	**11 6**	..	**1255**	**2 35**	**3 55**	..	**5 36**	**6 56**	**7 29**	**8 55**	.	**940**	**1035**	**1235**	..	**3 0**	**5 5**	**547**	**655**	**835**

Miles		Week Days am S	am E	am K	am	am S	am ET	am	pm	pm S	pm E	pm	pm	pm	pm	Sundays am	am T	pm	pm	pm	pm T	pm T	pm
	Newquay dep	**7 20**	**7 24**	..	**9 12**	..	**11 0**	**1150**	**1 35**	**2 55**	**3 20**	**4 35**	**5 52**	**7 55**	**9 15**	**10 0**	**1050**	..	**1 30**	**4 0**	**620**	**8 0**	**8 50**
2¾	Trewerry and Trerice Halt	7 27	7 31	....	9 19	....	....	1157	1 42	3 2	3 27	4 43	5 59	8 2	9 21	10 6	....	....	1 37	4 6	626	8 6	8 56
4¾	Mitchell and Newlyn Halt	7 33	7 37	..	9 24	..	..	12 3	1 48	3 8	3 33	4 49	6 5	8 7	9 27	10 12	..	..	1 43	412	633	812	9 2
6	Shepherds	7 37	7 41	....	9 28	....	1114	12 7	1 53	3 12	3 38	4 53	6 9	8 11	9 32	10 17	11 3	....	1 47	417	637	817	9 7
8	Goonhavern Halt	7 43	7 47	..	9 33	..	1120	1212	1 58	3 17	3 43	4 59	6 14	8 16	9 37	10 22	..	..	1 52	422	642	822	9 12
10¼	**Perranporth**	**7 50**	**7 54**	**8 15**	**9 39**	**11 0**	**1125**	**1220**	**2 4**	**3 24**	**3 49**	**5 5**	**6 23**	**8 25**	**9 43**	**10 28**	**1116**	**1 10**	**1 58**	**428**	**649**	**828**	**9 18**
10¾	Perranporth Beach Halt	7 51	7 55	..	9 41	11 2	1127	1222	2 5	3 25	3 51	5 7	6 25	8 26	9 47	10 30	..	1 11	2 0	.	651	830	9 20
13	Mithian Halt	7 58	8 2	....	9 48	....	....	1229	2 12	3 32	3 58	5 14	6 32	8 33	....	10 37	....	1 18	2 7	...	658	837	9 27
14¾	Goonbell Halt	8 4	8 8	..	9 54	..	..	1235	2 18	3 38	4 4	5 20	6 38	8 39	..	10 43	..	1 24	2 13	.	7 4	843	9 33
15¼	St. Agnes	8 7	8 11	8 28	9 57	1114	1139	1238	2 21	3 42	4 7	5 23	6 42	8 42	9 58	10 46	1130	1 27	2 16	...	7 7	846	9 36
17	Mount Hawke Halt	8 11	8 15	..	10 1	..	..	1242	2 25	3 46	4 11	5 27	6 46	8 46	..	10 50	..	1 31	2 20	.	711	850	9 40
18¾	**Chacewater** arr	**8 17**	**8 21**	....	**10 7**	**1121**	**1148**	**1248**	**2 31**	**3 52**	**4 17**	**5 33**	**6 52**	**8 53**	**10 9**	**10 56**	**1139**	**1 37**	**2 26**	...	**717**	**856**	**9 46**
23¾	**Truro** „	**8H35**	**8H34**	**8 48**	**10 20**	**1133**	**12 2**	**1H13**	**2Z41**	**4 5**	**4H50**	**5D55**	**7 2**	**9 3**	**1020**	**11 6**	**1150**	**1 48**	**2 36**	.	**730**	**9 6**	**10 0**

B Arr 7 55 am
D Change at Chacewater. On Saturdays arr 5 45 pm without changing
E Except Saturdays
F Arr 7 50 am
H Change at Chacewater
J Change at Chacewater on Saturdays
K Saturdays only. First and Second class. Through Train to London (Pad.) arr 3 55 pm (Table 81)
L Change at Chacewater, dep 4 25 pm on Saturdays without changing
P Saturdays only and not after 30th Aug. First and Second class. Through Carriages from London (Pad.) dep 8 25 am (Table 81)
S Saturdays only
T Through Train from or to Falmouth (Table 101)
Z Change at Chacewater on Saturdays and arr Truro 3 5 pm

Newquay branch timetables from summer 1958.

As a result of the 1955 BR Modernisation Plan the west country was one of the first areas to be designated 'all diesel', an objective substantially achieved by 1962. The twin-engined 2,200 hp B-B 'Warship' class diesel-hydraulics arrived in Cornwall in 1958 and they could soon be found working on the lines featured in this volume. Shortly after delivery No. D816 *Eclipse* is seen beside the St Blazey roundhouse with train 9B25, a load of china clay destined for Fowey Docks.
R.C. Riley/Courtesy Transport Treasury

Another of the early diesel arrivals in Cornwall were the short-lived 1,100 hp (later class '22') diesel-hydraulics. In this exceptional study triple-headed 'D63XX' class, Nos. D6325, D6322, D6349, head the maroon stock forming the 10.05 am Newquay to Paddington. In the background is one of the North British Locomotive Company built 'D8XX' class 'Warship' diesel-hydraulics No. D850 *Swift* that will head the 11.45 am Newquay to York. Father and son (who will now be in his fifties) admire the non-steam motive power! *T. Mahoney*

also worked on the Newquay branch, with the more powerful locomotives either working china clay trains to Goonbarrow Junction or class '1' passenger trains to Newquay on summer weekends. In this respect the main Newquay branch posed no route availability problems, although this was not the case with most of the branches and sidings along the way. Class '22s', '25s' and later class '37s' worked most of the branch freights, although at Ponts Mill and Par Harbour class '08' shunters ruled.

Once steam had breathed its last gasp in 1962 most local branch passenger services for the following 30 years were in the hands of various classes of diesel-mechanical multiple units, although in the early 1960s 'D63XX' class locomotives and coaching stock appeared for a short time. Class '121' and '122' single car 'Bubble' units were regular performers. During the 1986/1987 period there was a departure from the norm when two-coach four-wheeled class '142' 'Skipper' units appeared. They were remarkably unsuccessful with no sanding equipment available, doors that operated erratically and a long wheelbase non-bogie arrangement that caused squealing and flange wear on the curves. Once steam ended on the Chacewater to Newquay branch it was also a combination of dmus and 'D63XX' locomotives and stock that worked the branch, although this era was short-lived with the line closing in 1963. In the early 1990s a new generations of diesel units appeared on the branch, mostly class '150/2s' and '153s'.

During the BR era many sidings and lines closed including St Blazey to Fowey, Ponts Mill siding, the Goonbarrow, Wheal Rose and Carbis Wharf branches, the line from Parkandillack to St Dennis Junction, the Retew branch and the Chacewater to Newquay line. In addition dozens of minor sidings off these branches also closed.

During the BR years there was much rationalisation including the singling of much of the Newquay branch, the abolition of passing loops, signal boxes and the

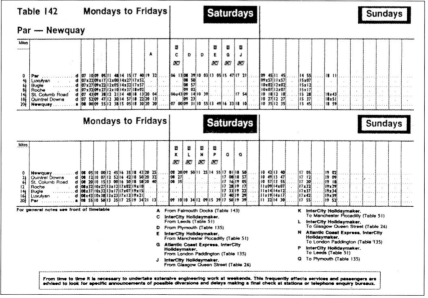

Newquay branch timetables from summer 1989.

One full length platform has been retained at Newquay to accommodate 'IC125' units in the summer months. No. 43147 will soon be leaving for Paddington in August 1992. *Author*

signals they controlled and the de-manning of stations. Above all else it was the withdrawal of general goods services (as distinct from china clay) from all lines and stations included in the scope of this book that had a profound affect on the potential usefulness of the Newquay branch. Eventually only china clay products were hauled by rail, except for a little coal and seaweed traffic at the southern end of the Drinnick Mill branch and some pipes and scrap metal at St Blazey.

Between 1983 and 1986 an experiment was conducted whereby 'Cornish Railways' was established to run most Cornish rail services as a franchise, with delegated responsibilities for many operational and financial matters. The experiment was not perpetuated but it turned out to be the precursor of the sectorisation and then the privatisation of our railways. The Railfreight sector of BR became established in Cornwall in 1986. Phase 2 saw the business divided into sectors, such as distribution, construction, petroleum, metals and coal, followed by the establishment of three 'shadow' freight operating companies, including Transrail in 1994. Finally privatisation arrived, with English Welsh & Scottish Railways winning the freight franchise in 1996. Passenger services in Cornwall also went through various stages, operators including InterCity, Regional Railways, Wales and West, Wessex Trains, Virgin Trains, First Great Western etc. With these various sectors and train operating companies (TOCs) came a raft of new liveries, which made a welcome change from years of all blue or blue and grey. However, by 1996/7 the good old days of BR had ended and, bearing in mind the many political and financial constraints placed upon the organization, it did a pretty good job.

Table 6 — Newquay to Par — Monday to Friday until 16 September

Train Operator		WE	T10	WE	T10	WE	T10	WE	WE	WE	WE	WE
Newquay	d	0757	0925	1017	–	1217	–	1417	1607	1825	2012	2210
Quintrell Downs	d	0803	–	1023	–	1223	–	1423	1613	1831	2018	2216
St Columb Road	d	08x09	–	10x30	–	12x30	–	14x31	16x21	18x39	20x25	–
Roche	d	08x21	–	10x42	1045	12x42	1245	14x43	16x33	18x51	20x37	–
Eden Project	a	–	1015	–	1105	–	1305	–	–	–	–	–
Bugle	d	08x25	–	10x46	–	12x46	–	14x47	16x37	18x55	20x41	–
Luxulyan	d	08x30	–	10x51	–	12x52	–	14x53	16x43	19x01	20x47	–
▓Par	a	0845	–	1105	–	1305	–	1505	1655	1916	2100	2255
Penzance	a	1023	–	1228	–	1433	–	–	1902	2100	–	0007
Plymouth	a	0950	–	1201	–	1516	–	1602	1757	2037	2153	2355
London Paddington	a	–	–	1505	–	–	–	1905	2120	–	0511

Table 6 — Newquay to Par

Train Operator		T10 K	WE	WE	T10 K	WE	WE
Newquay	d	0925	1017	1217	1305	1417	2012
Quintrell Downs	d	–	1023	1223	–	1423	2018
St Columb Road	d	–	10x30	12x30	–	14x31	20x25
Roche	d	1001	10x42	12x42	1341	14x43	20x37
Eden Project	a	1015	–	–	1355	–	–
Bugle	d	–	10x46	12x46	–	14x47	20x41
Luxulyan	d	–	10x51	12x52	–	14x53	20x47
▓Par	a	–	1105	1305	–	1505	2100
Penzance	a	–	1228	1433	–	–	–
Plymouth	a	–	1201	1516	–	1619	2153
London Paddington	a	–	1505	1905pq	–	1905	–

Newquay branch timetables from 2005, showing the difference between the summer (*left*) and winter Monday-Friday (*right*).

Chapter Nine

Fowey-St Blazey and Par Harbour

Fowey to St Blazey

Fowey and its natural deep-water harbour sprang to prominence in the early 14th century. In the early days it was an important centre for naval activities and in 1342 it was reported that Fowey had dispatched 29 ships and crews, numbering 720 men, to take part in naval operations in Scotland and France. In medieval times Lostwithiel, the upriver ancient Capital of Cornwall, had begun to lose the tin trade as mining activities began to silt up the River Fowey at that point. In times past the quays at Lostwithiel had been operational and as if to prove the point old lime kilns can still be seen on the quayside. Fowey was the beneficiary of Lostwithiel's problem. It was not until the mid-1850s, however, before Fowey really came into its own right as an important port, firstly for loads of timber, but following the opening of the Lostwithiel and Fowey Railway (L&FR) in 1869, and the Cornwall Minerals Railway in 1874, for large volumes of china clay, china stone and other mineral traffic.

The L&FR ran from Lostwithiel to a point known as Carne Point, about half a mile north of the ancient town of Fowey. The broad gauge line hugged the western bank of the river and consequently there were no problems with gradients. The line was worked by the Cornwall Railway - the company which also owned the Cornish main line east of Truro. The L&FR had ambitious plans for Fowey. They wanted to set up a Fowey Harbour Board on which the railway would be heavily represented. They wanted to build a line of quays from one end of the Carne Point river frontage to the other and to levy rates.

There were many objections to the plan as locals saw advantages only for the railway company. Lostwithiel in particular saw the prospect of their ancient rights being eroded. Above all else the huge cost of these developments, amounting to some £60,000, far exceeded the asset value of the company and accordingly there would be little security for those advancing money. Eventually, however, just three jetties were built that were sufficient for the railway company to commence trade and for them to convey nearly 29,000 tons of freight, primarily china clay, during the year 1872. The next two years saw the L&FR consolidate its position, but in the meantime the CMR was driving through its direct line from St Blazey to Fowey which offered direct access to the heart of china clay country as well as a direct line to Newquay.

The opening of the CMR spelt disaster for the L&FR. The possibilities of a route from the Par area had been on the cards for many years. Indeed, back in 1825 Joseph Thomas Treffry had proposed such a line to capitalise on the improvements he had set in motion at Fowey in 1811, when the building of a completely new quay at the harbour commenced. Treffry had tried to capture some of Charlestown's trade by publicly stating that Fowey was better than any other harbour in the West of England for wet and dry docks, on a scale suitable for merchantmen. Treffry knew that without a railway Fowey could not expand to the envisaged degree and there was a setback in 1825 when the Rashleigh

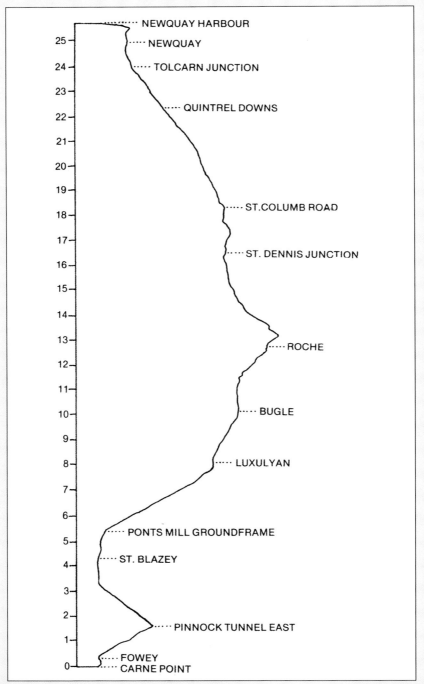

Gradient profile of the Cornwall Minerals Railway main line from Carne Point, Fowey to Newquay Harbour.

family would not let him build a railway over their land. To detour around their land would have been too expensive. Treffry uttered, 'I though my idea of a railway was a sound one, but I have been prevented from carrying it out through the influence of a neighbouring country gentleman'. It was thus nearly 50 years later that the CMR overcame these difficulties with the opening of its line on 1st June, 1874, with a passenger service from 1876.

Almost immediately the L&FR tonnage dropped to only one-third of its 29,000 ton peak of 1873 and by 1879 it grossed less than 8,000 tons. The CMR had not entered the transportation fray without investing in its own infrastructure at Fowey. The CMR built three large jetties south of Carne Point, each ranging from 90 to 114 ft in length. Each jetty was served by double tracks which partially merged and were served by a single wagon turntable on the mainland sidings. Both horses and capstans were used in the movement of wagons on the jetties. During the mid-1870s there developed a battle between the L&FR and the CMR with each trying to undercut its competitor's rates. Whatever the rate the Cornwall Railway and the L&FR came up with the CMR did better. Due to a combination of a disastrous reduction to 2s. 2d. per ton carriage for china clay from Burngullow to Fowey, which the L&FR could ill afford, followed by the Lostwithiel and Fowey line becoming unsafe, it closed from 31st December, 1879. By then the L&FR simply did not have the money available to repair its line. The CMR had deliberately not linked with the L&FR - there being a gap between the two routes of about half a mile. The recession in the china clay industry in 1877/1878 had not helped the L&FR in its fight. Ironically, after the closure of the L&FR, business boomed. Between the years 1885 and 1890 Fowey shipped the largest tonnage of china clay of any port in Cornwall due to vessels using the port having significantly increased in size, Fowey's ability to handle deep-draught ships, combined with a vigorous overseas export trade. During this period the average annual tonnage league made interesting reading: Fowey 110,000, Par 85,000, Charlestown 55,000, Pentewan 20,000 and Newquay 4,000. Insignificant amounts were shipped from other Cornish ports.

With the involvement of the GWR the CMR reconstructed the Lostwithiel to Fowey line as a standard gauge branch in 1895, which carried both freight and passenger traffic. By this time all GWR broad gauge lines had been converted to standard gauge. With the opening of the 'new' line in September 1895 came the joining of the former L&FR line with the CMR line, the entire route being in the hands of the GWR from July 1896 when they absorbed the CMR. The GWR invested a fortune in the Carne Point area, adding to the CMR jetties so that by the Edwardian era, seven jetties were in operation. Tonnages doubled and redoubled reaching a peak of nearly 600,000 tons before World War I. Due to the loss of European markets the volumes had dropped to 400,000 by 1918.

The GWR expanded the original 1874 CMR Fowey station site by building two through platforms, a centre road and a bay platform at the west (St Blazey) end of the station. There was a signal box on the down platform at the Lostwithiel end of the station. An imposing footbridge connected the platforms but in later years the centre through road became a dead end siding when, in 1936, buffer stops were erected at the west end. This siding was lifted in 1951 and the little used up platform and the footbridge were demolished. There was originally a goods shed at the Lostwithiel end of the station but the general goods shed and yard were at

Reproduced from an old postcard, this view shows a wonderful era at Fowey Docks, when steam was replacing sail. The CMR and later the GWR greatly increased the handling capacity of the deep water port of Fowey and many additional jetties were built. Each was rail-served with wagons being turned through 90 degrees on turntables and powered along the jetties by horse. Note the casks of china clay in the foreground wagons, the shunting horse, the steam ship, the distant sailing ships and, in the background, the town of Fowey. *Author's Collection*

After the end of steam Blackstone-engined (later class '10') diesel-electric shunters and later English Electric class '08s' took over operations at Carne Point, Fowey. The 'clay hood' wagons were withdrawn in February 1988 and they were replaced by air braked, roller bearing, CDA wagons as seen here in April 1990. Railfreight-liveried No. 08954 is seen at work on the quayside, with the River Fowey behind. *Author*

It is now well over 40 years since one could experience the delightful experience of catching a typical GWR/BR branch train from Lostwithiel for a run along the banks of the River Fowey down to the ancient town of Fowey. Photographed on 21st June, 1956, 0-4-2T No. 1408 is seen at the now long-demolished station before propelling its auto-coach back to Lostwithiel. Passenger services were withdrawn in January 1965.   *Hugh Davies*

The CMR Fowey to St Blazey line opened in 1874 and the route included the longest railway tunnel in Cornwall, the 1,173 yds-long Pinnock tunnel. On 9th May, 1963 'D63XX' class diesel-hydraulic No. D6342 emerges from the tunnel into sunlight with a St Blazey-bound train of empties. The locomotive is in green livery with small yellow warning panel and it would have a life of only six years. The entire line was converted to a road for exclusive use by ECC lorries in 1968.   *Carey Bachelor*

From 1874 until 2008 the hub of china clay and Cornish freight workings in mid-Cornwall was St Blazey. With the old closed St Blazey station ('Par' in CMR days) immediately behind the locomotive 0-6-0PT No. 7446 toys with a couple of wagons and a brake van on 3rd September, 1954. In 2008 these sidings still existed and were used mainly for loading wagons with scrap metal. *R.C. Riley/Courtesy Transport Treasury*

This nostalgic flash-back to 7th August, 1956 finds one of the aesthetically pleasing '4500' class 2-6-2Ts approaching Par Bridge crossing with Fowey to St Blazey clay empties. Points to note in this beautifully lit scene are the line to Par Harbour on the right, the classic lower quadrant semaphore signals controlled by the nearby signal box, the Plymouth to Penzance main line on the low profile arches behind and the large BR 'lion and wheel' transfer on the locomotive's side tanks. *Les Elsey*

the St Blazey end, until closed in July 1965, the same year as passenger services ceased. The entire site and all buildings were razed in 1968 when the line to St Blazey was closed and converted into a road.

The following decades produced plenty of technological innovation. The GWR installed mechanical devices to facilitate high-speed loading, they built a power station adjacent to the harbour and, in 1923, an eighth jetty was built. The second Carne Point signal box was closed in 1925 and another more modern signal box was opened on the river side of the sidings at the north end of the complex. For decades the scene did not change greatly, although when the passenger service between Fowey and St Blazey closed in 1925 the only access for rail travellers was via Lostwithiel. Before closure in 1925 there was but one train per day each way between St Blazey and Fowey. During the World War II there was again a significant decline in traffic. In 1950 jetties Nos. 5 and 6 closed and in 1954 Carne Point signal box was abolished. In 1962 the use of No. 7 jetty was reduced. In the same year 900 vessels were loaded at Fowey. It was during the mid-1960s that negotiations between BR and the English China Clay Company (ECC) commenced about the long term future of Fowey. ECC had for some time perceived a need for good road access to Fowey Docks. The local roads were narrow and did not lend themselves to heavy use by 38-tonne lorries conveying china clay. On the other hand, BR was keen to enter into a long term arrangement with ECC for a guaranteed minimum annual tonnage of china clay for transportation by rail. BR's steeply graded line from St Blazey ran past ECC's massive drying plant at Par Harbour and BR had access directly to Par Harbour and via Lostwithiel to Fowey. Accordingly, part of the overall 'deal' was for BR to close its Fowey to St Blazey line and for this section to be converted into a private road for the exclusive use of ECC.

ECC leased the deep-water loading jetties from BR and the major Fowey Docks Development scheme ensued. There would be four modern operational jetties; three equipped for road and rail usage and a fourth for china clay slurry only. There would be a 22,000 ton bulk store and rapid loading equipment with a maximum capacity of 1,000 tons per hour. The old CMR railway line closed in October 1968 and work on the conversion to road began immediately. The 3.2 mile stretch had to be widened to provide a two-lane road. The 1,173 yd tunnel presented special problems, traffic lights had to be installed because the narrow tunnel could take only a single-lane road. Finally, during 1987/1988, in anticipation of the end of the old vacuum-braked clay hood wagons, the old traverser and tipping equipment had to be modified and partly replaced to accommodate the new air-braked CDA wagons, which have a payload of nearly three times that of the old wooden-bodied wagons.

At Fowey it was normally the CMR/GWR/BR locomotive which headed a train to the docks which then performed the shunting duties. Horses were used on the jetties but at the sidings it was nearly always a tank locomotive that moved the goods wagons filled with their 'white gold'. This was not always the case when the heavier 2-8-0T and 2-8-2T types worked over to the docks from St Blazey. Their wagons would be shunted on certain of the sidings with whatever motive power was in the area. However, after the 1968 development plan ECC purchased some redundant ex-BR class '10' Blackstone-engined diesel-electric shunters (Nos. D3452, D3476 and D3497). Once BR's diesels brought their load into the Carne Point sidings it would

Accelerating away from the abandoned platforms of the closed St Blazey station on 5th July, 1955 with the evening 7.45 pm Par to Newquay branch train comprising three red non-corridor suburban coaches is prairie tank No. 5526. The locomotive has an 83E St Blazey shedcode disc on the smokebox.   *R.C. Riley/Courtesy Transport Treasury*

St Blazey normally had an allocation of about 36 steam locomotives and included therein were a couple of heavy 2-8-0 or 2-8-2 tank locomotives for hauling heavy loads from St Blazey to Fowey and occasionally to and from St Dennis Junction. These chunky tanks could haul 40 per cent more than a 2-6-2 prairie. Here '4200' class No. 4273 pauses to pin down the wagon brakes while running from Fowey to St Blazey in 1955.   *R.C. Riley/Courtesy Transport Treasury*

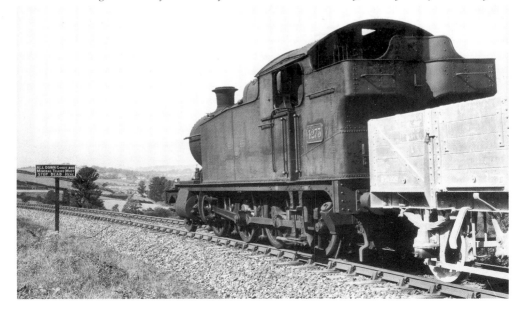

Long after the direct line from St Blazey to Fowey closed occasional traffic to Par Harbour continued. To the present day approximately daily workings trip down from St Blazey to deliver empty wagons for loading. For several decades such trains were powered by class '08' shunters, such as that seen here in February 1993. The train is passing the St Blazey turntable.   *Author*

A through train from Newquay is seen slowly passing the disused platforms of the old St Blazey station in September 1987 before being stopped by the semaphore signal. Powering the train is blue-liveried class '47' No. 47596 *Aldeburgh Festival* that was allocated to Stratford depot and, perhaps not surprisingly, carried a 'Stratford' silver roof.   *Author*

This general view shows to advantage Treffry's 1830s creation of Par Harbour, which was to become the second busiest UK port for the exportation of china clay products, transported mainly by coasters. Seen in the early 1950s, all quays were rail served by an extensive complex of standard gauge lines. The 1,200 ft-long breakwater can be seen on the right, with Par Sands on the left and Polkerris in the distance.

Author's Collection

be the ECC shunter that propelled the wagons onto the tipping/traversing equipment. These elderly shunters were replaced in 1987 by class '08s'.

From St Blazey to Fowey steam locomotives would always work bunker first. The smoke and steam from a steam locomotive as it blasted up the 1 in 36 and through the narrow granite-lined Pinnock tunnel would have asphyxiated a crew if operating in chimney-first mode. When returning from Fowey to St Blazey the locomotive would, of course, be chimney first and there was still the one-mile climb to Pinnock signal box, but beyond the box and through the tunnel the journey was downhill and in any event, on the return journey the wagons were empty which would have called for only modest regulator opening.

The small 6-lever Pinnock signal box was opened on 8th January, 1908 and after a short period of temporary closure it was closed completely in 1958. It is said that the box was re-erected at Par as a BR painters' shop. Trains used to stop at the east entrance to the tunnel on the down run to have their brakes pinned down. There was a further stop board at the west end of the tunnel. The tunnel was difficult to build, the rock being comprised entirely of granite. More importantly, the tunnel was the longest railway tunnel in the County of Cornwall at 1,173 yards. The single-line branch meandered down from the tunnel towards Par Sands through rolling farmland. At Par Sands trains again stopped to have their brakes picked up. In the reverse direction brakes were picked up at Fowey station.

Once across Par Sands, which still plays host to holiday-makers and caravanners, the branch converged towards the Par Harbour branch having curved northwards to pass under the main line. The approach to Par Bridge Crossing was controlled by the signals of Par Bridge Crossing signal box, which closed with the line to Fowey from 6th October, 1968. The gated crossing survives and is used by approximately daily clay trains from St Blazey to Par Harbour, with the on-train shunter operating the gates manually. In its final years the St Blazey to Fowey line was operated by diesel-hydraulic 'D63XX', 'D6XX' and 'D8XX' class locomotives. From 1968 all china clay trains destined for Fowey ran via Lostwithiel, necessitating a reversal there for eastbound trains to reach their Carne Point destination.

Par Harbour

Once Treffry's plans to build a railway from the Par area to Fowey had been thwarted by local landowners, especially the Rashleigh family, his attentions turned to Par and the possibilities of building a harbour there. As detailed in Chapter Four, by 1828 plans had been drawn up for a completely artificial harbour occupying some 35 acres. The harbour would be tidal which would place some restrictions on access and the size of vessel using the port. Following the construction of a 1,200 ft long breakwater, sufficient progress had been made by 1833 for the port to receive its first commercial vessel. Shipments mainly comprised copper ore, granite and china clay, while incoming loads included coal, timber, lime and sand; in fact any commodity which could not easily be transported overland - the main line railway from Plymouth and beyond not reaching Par until 1859.

Over the decades the Port of Par has had a remarkable and varied array of motive power. Seemingly secured by a large anchor, this 1927-built Sentinel locomotive No. S6520/27 was named *Toby* but by the time it was photographed in January 1960 it had run its last mile.   *M. Dart Collection*

The most famous of all the Par Harbour motive power were the two cut-down cab Bagnall 0-4-0 saddle tanks, No. 2572 of 1937 and No. 3058 of 1953. They were called *Judy* and *Alfred* respectively and fortunately, although displaced at Par several decades ago, both have been preserved at the Bodmin & Wenford Railway. The pair are seen at work with china clay wagons on 1st September, 1954 with the SS *Simultaneity* in the background.   *R.C. Riley/Courtesy Transport Treasury*

As the business in copper ore and granite diminished, and following the opening of the canal from Ponts Mill to Par, and later the Treffry Tramway from Mollinis, near Bugle, china clay became all important. By 1855 15,000 tons of china clay was shipped from Par, a figure which exactly doubled by 1860. By 1865, 44,000 tons of china clay were shipped and during 1870 the total had reached 52,000 tons. Although there was over-production leading to a depression in the china clay industry in 1876/77, by the late 1880s the volume shipped from Par Harbour tonnage had risen to 85,000 tons per annum. Other industries in the Par Harbour area at this time included a large smelter and a local brickworks. Completion of the CMR lines brought more prosperity to the Port of Par, although for a year or two it seemed that there would be competition between Fowey and Par. The involvement of the GWR at both ports ensured an unique identity for each port: Fowey dealing with large ocean-going vessels and heavy long-haul loads, with Par taking coasters of a smaller size for domestic UK and cross-channel shipments.

Not all of the china clay shipped from Par came from a great distance. Just to the north of the harbour area there were a number of driers in the Par Moor complex, which included Hensbarrow, Hallaze, Pentruff, Great Treverbyn, Ruddle Common and Carvear. Not all were rail-served and all have now closed. However, the greatest impact on Par Harbour was undoubtedly the advances in pipeline technology. Gradually over the early decades of the 20th century china clay in slurry form was increasingly transported over several miles by mainly underground pipeline. As a result of this, ECC built a vast centralised clay drying plant adjacent to Par Harbour and even today steam can be seen rising from the four tall modern stacks 24 hours a day, seven days a week. Clay is piped for several miles from a variety of clay works. Only a modicum of clay now leaves Par Harbour by rail, along the only surviving access line from St Blazey.

The throughput of Par Harbour continued to steadily increase and by 1933 the annual total for china clay reached 100,000 tons per annum. In its first 100 years of operation Par had seen the transition from wooden 50-ton schooners to 2,000-ton coasters. It was after World War II that the large ECC Company took out a 999-year lease on the port and the company produced long-term plans for modernisation. Initially changes were minor but in 1961 large sums of money were spent modernising and enlarging the port. A total of 10 berths were provided with the largest some 280 ft in length. All of the quays were concrete and modern loading equipment was provided. In 1964 ECC purchased the port outright. In 1965 a total of 1,500 vessels were loaded at Par Harbour. Since the conversion of the St Blazey to Fowey line from railway to private road, much of the dried china clay produced by the harbour plant is taken by lorry to Fowey where it is loaded onto the larger ships or placed in store. However, Par still enjoys a lucrative trade with large tonnages leaving from the still-tidal harbour.

There were once two points of access to the not inconsiderable railway network within the confines of the harbour. There has always been the existing and surviving access direct from St Blazey but until 1965 there was also access from the main line to the west end of the harbour area. There was also one other line which left the harbour complex on a spur which ran under a very low bridge beneath the main line and across the coastal road which served the aforementioned clay driers. It was for this reason that Par Harbour required its own shunting locomotives, all with cut-down cabs.

Over the years these locomotives attracted some degree of notoriety. The most famous were a pair of Bagnall 0-4-0 saddle tanks: No. 2572 *Judy* of 1937 and No. 3058 *Alfred* of 1953. Earlier locomotives included an old 1879-built 0-4-0ST called *Punch* (Manning, Wardle No. 713, rebuilt with a vertical boiler in 1936) and a 1927-built Sentinel (No. 6520) called *Toby*. Other shunters appeared from time to time and in recent years one of the most important was a specially adapted road-going Ford tractor. Happily both *Alfred* and *Judy* have been preserved as reminders of Par Harbour's past. Since the early 1970s there have been no dedicated shunting locomotives in the harbour area and the only sign of railway motive power is when a locomotive works down from St Blazey to leave or remove wagons on the surviving siding. In times past it was a class '08' shunter that worked to the harbour but in recent times 125 tonne English Welsh & Scottish Railways' (EWS) General Motors class '66s' perform the trip.

In terms of railways the Par Harbour area is but a shadow of its former self. The little clay wagons no longer run along the quayside and the former locomotive shed is no longer used. However, despite rationalisation, the harbour area is at least rail connected - by the aforementioned siding that runs from the south end of St Blazey depot across Par Bridge Crossing to the massive Cambrian China Clay store. Workings are as and when required but three or four times per week would be typical. In terms of lorry traffic Par Harbour is still very busy with commercial vehicles frequently arriving at and leaving the complex. However, most lorry traffic is between the drying plant and the docks at Carne Point, Fowey, using the private road.

A remarkable anachronism that commenced in 2007 was the displacement of 350 hp class '08' shunters on the short St Blazey to Par Harbour run by 3,200hp 125 tonne high-tech North American-built class '66' locomotives. Another anachronism in Cornwall is a set of manually operated crossing gates, worked by the train crew. No. 66129 was recorded on 3rd October, 2007 hauling four wagons across Par Bridge crossing on its return trip to St Blazey.   *Author*

Chapter Ten

Par Main Line Station

'Par – change for Newquay' was for many years the message offered by the main line station running-in boards. Indeed between the years of 1879, when the CMR built a connecting loop from its own Par (later St Blazey) station to the Cornwall Railway's main line Par station, and 1892 when the GWR abandoned its broad gauge, a change at Par for Newquay was unavoidable. Prior to 1879 the Newquay locomotives and stock were provided by the CMR, as already described. But from that date there was a gradual increase in influence by the GWR. After 1892, when all of the railway lines were of the same standard gauge, greater interchangeability of locomotives and stock took place. With the growing importance of Newquay as a resort the GWR was operating through coaches from Paddington to Newquay from 1906. Within a few years trains from many parts of the UK worked through to Newquay in the summer months, with summer Saturdays in particular being extremely busy.

Between the years of 1876 and the last day of 1878 there was no railway link between the CMR and the CR, only horse-drawn coaches. However, once open, passenger trains using the connecting spur adopted unusual patterns in connecting with workings both to and from Fowey and to and from Newquay; the former requiring a reversal at St Blazey (CMR). In the main, trains leaving Par were split at St Blazey with half travelling south for the 12 minute journey to Fowey and the other half heading north for the 55 minute trip to Newquay. Trains would be joined at St Blazey in the opposite direction. A handful of trains ran from Par to Fowey only and similarly (but especially in the Edwardian era) trains also ran only from Par to Newquay. In fact, in the 1910 *Bradshaw*, the Par to Fowey and Par to Newquay timetables are shown separately, although it is obvious that some departures and arrivals were still 'joint' trains. The passenger traffic on the Par-St Blazey-Fowey line did not increase once the Lostwithiel to Fowey passenger service commenced in 1895 and by 1925 the receipts did not begin to pay for the cost of providing the service, which was withdrawn from July of that year. Workmen's trains continued to run, however, until 1934. St Blazey station closed from 21st September, 1925, although it continued to be used by workmen until 31st December, 1934.

In later years it was not always necessary to change at Par for Newquay, even on a local train. Some trains started from Plymouth and ran through to Newquay. In the 1968/69 working timetable, all Newquay branch services started and finished their journeys to Newquay at Bodmin Road station on the Cornish main line. At the beginning of the 1988 summer timetable there were two through local trains from Newquay to Plymouth and one in the opposite direction. Over the decades there have been other starting points, such as Falmouth, Exeter and even Gunnislake. However, by way of example in 1989 the timetables still contained the unequivocal message, 'Par - change for Newquay', for each of the half-dozen branch trains per day, except the 7.32 pm from Par to Newquay which started its journey at Falmouth Docks!

More problems in the Par area but this time in the late 1950s. On the 1879-built spur between St Blazey and Par main line station 'Hall' class 4-6-0 No. 7929 *Wyke Hall* became derailed on the up road. Re-railing was achieved by the use of jacks and wooden blocks.   *Author's Collection*

An easy task for 'Hall' class 4-6-0 No. 5915 *Trentham Hall*, seen departing from Par station for Newquay with just three coaches in tow during the 1950s. Until 1892, when the broad gauge was abandoned, a change of gauge and therefore of train was necessary for passengers travelling beyond Par, towards Newquay.   *M. Dart Collection*

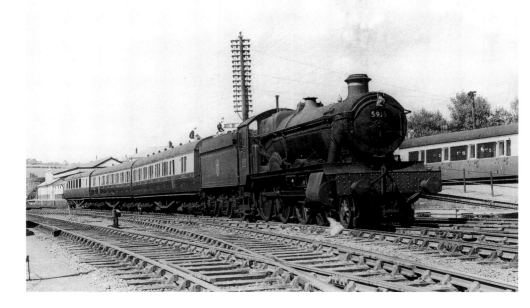

Par station was opened by the Cornwall Railway on 4th May, 1859, although the 'Associated Companies', the Bristol & Exeter, South Devon and Great Western Railway, had a controlling financial interest in the entire CR operation. The station comprised a main stone-built station building and platform on the down side and less permanent wooden structures located on an island platform on the up side. The standard gauge loop line to St Blazey and Newquay was opened from 1879 and Par's junction status came into its own when the broad gauge main line was abolished in 1892. Sidings were provided on the up side of the station where there was a large goods shed which doubled as a transhipment shed prior to 1892.

The station provided a main line passing loop between 1859 and 15th October, 1893 when the line to St Austell was doubled, and 19th December, 1894 when the line to Milltown viaduct, just above Lostwithiel, was also doubled. A signal box was, and still is, located at the south end of the up platform, now the oldest box in Cornwall. A new 57-lever frame was installed in 1913. The platforms were lengthened in 1913 and the branch platform (up side of the island) was lengthened in 1924. There were later carriage sidings on both the up and down sides of the station and the down siding, just outside the station, was converted into a down loop on 5th April, 1943. There were a number of detailed changes to the overall track layout and sidings over the years including provision for a short-lived Freightliner terminal in 1968.

However, in 1974 there were drastic alterations at Par. Various sidings and complicated slip points were removed and the entire layout was rationalised and simplified. The wooden goods shed was removed as were most of the up side station buildings, leaving just a short awning and a mainly glass-sided waiting room. The roof of the station footbridge connecting the platforms was removed. In the 1980s, following the closure of both St Austell and Burngullow signal boxes, an electronic signalling control panel was installed in Par signal box, although levers continued to control signals and points at Par. The box then interfaced with Lostwithiel, Truro and St Blazey signal boxes. A signalling and telecommunications depot was established on the north side of the station area.

Par and Lostwithiel stations are the busiest in Cornwall. In addition to main and branch line passenger trains, china clay traffic from Rocks on the Newquay branch and Parkandillack on the Drinnick Mill branch (to Carne Point, Fowey) and main line air-braked freights pass the station. Those making for St Blazey from the west must reverse at Par, with the locomotive running round. The daily sleeping car trains to and from London call at the station, albeit at an unsocial hour. Other sundry workings can include engineer's ballast and spoil trains and empty coaching stock workings. There are also block trains, such as the recently discontinued Burngullow to Irvine china clay slurry tanks and occasional china clay waste and scrap metal trains. Also in the winter months a Railhead Treatment Train run by the Colas Rail company is berthed in Chapel sidings south of the station.

For the time being it is not only the sighting of these trains which is of interest but also the operation of semaphore signals, which control all movements in the area. On summer Saturdays, when High Speed Trains and Voyager units run

This late afternoon view of Par station on 22nd April, 1987 shows the up and down main lines on the left and No. 37207 *William Cookworthy* on the right heading 40 empty clay hood wagons from Carne Point, Fowey to the ECC Rocks works at Goonbarrow Junction on the Newquay branch. The stacks of Par Harbour clay drying plant can be seen in the distance.

Author

The lines on the up or west side of Par station are not only used by Newquay branch trains but also by all freight traffic to and from St Blazey yard. On this April day in 1990 the Newquay branch single power car had failed and it was being rescued by class '37' No. 37670 in Railfreight Distribution livery, seen here removing the unit to St Blazey depot. *Author*

The 3rd October, 1987 was a very significant day on the Newquay branch line when the last ever *scheduled* locomotive-hauled train worked out of the seaside town. The train was the 17.17 Newquay to Plymouth headed by original Network SouthEast-liveried class '50', No. 50026 *Indomitable*. In appalling conditions the up starting signal is off for the 2,700 hp machine and its train of air conditioned coaches. *Author*

through to Newquay, it is fascinating to see a traditional GWR junction in full operation with extra trains not only to and from Newquay but to and from Penzance as well. From the enthusiasts' viewpoint it is unfortunate that passenger trains now comprise various multiple unit formations and, except for the sleepers and special trains visiting the Eden Centre, locomotives on passenger trains are a rare sight.

From Par to St Blazey the line is double track but on arriving at St Blazey a train destined for Goonbarrow Junction or Newquay will take the single-line token from the St Blazey signalman. The single line commences just beyond the old St Blazey station and continues through to Goonbarrow Junction.

A recent (October 2007) view of Par station, junction for Newquay. A Penzance to Paddington IC125 unit comprising a rake of Midland Main Line stock is headed by a re-engined First Great Western power car. Also at the island platform is a 2-car class '150/2' diesel unit that will shortly depart for Newquay. Generally the branch line connections at Par are appalling with no connection for Paddington to Newquay passengers until 2 pm.
Author

Chapter Eleven

St Blazey Depot

Being so near to Treffry's Par Harbour, a significant number of early mines, including the vast Fowey Consuls complex, and adjacent to the main Cornwall Railway line, there was perhaps an inevitability that the CMR would site its headquarters at St Blazey. Above all else, the original tramway from Mollinis, via the Carmears Incline in the Luxulyan Valley, also passed the site.

Built on 600 square yards of land to the west of the tramway, but to the north of the main line, the CMR Headquarters was a grand affair. Designed by the great Victorian railway engineer, Sir Morton Peto, the buildings were classic in design and unusual for Cornwall in that they were built of red brick imported from the Plymouth area. The design included not only offices but a substantial works, with a high chimney for the blacksmith's forge, and a locomotive shed. The latter was unusual in that it was designed on a roundhouse and turntable principle with nine 'roads', each capable of taking two CMR tank locomotives, i.e. the entire 1874 fleet. Other buildings included an erecting and repair shop, a boiler house, a fitting shop and a smithy.

Slightly to the north of the main buildings was a wagon shop and a goods shed. Early postcards show a further small engine house alongside the wagon shop. Beyond that was the brick-built Par station, which became St Blazey when the loop to Par main line station was opened in January 1879. In later years the brickwork of the station was rendered. In addition to the many buildings there were a large number of sidings to the west of the wagon shop and more sidings to the east. Over the years there were many modifications to the St Blazey site including a now long-demolished passenger footbridge from the St Blazey road across the sidings to the station.

The GWR demolished the goods shed and replaced it with a loading wharf and crane, while at the south end of the yard a steeply inclined coaling stage was built. Coal wagons were propelled up the incline and unloaded into the bunkers and tenders of the steam locomotives below. At the south end the lines and sidings tapered into just two roads; one leading to Par Harbour and the other to Fowey. In the 1910s, 1920s and 1930s there were further siding extensions including land to the north-west of the station. The two-platform station closed in September 1925 when the passenger service to Fowey was withdrawn (except for workmen's trains which continued until December 1934).

Although the locomotive works ceased to be used for the purpose in the days of the GWR, it was from the 1960s onward that saw the start of significant rationalisation. Although BR could not demolish the listed buildings the original station building did meet its end in the early 1970s. Before that, in 1967, some four years after the end of steam in the area, the lines to the former works and the coaling stage, including the incline, were removed. The line to Fowey was closed and lifted in 1968 and by then little-used sidings were being removed. The sidings down to the large loading wharf adjacent to the old

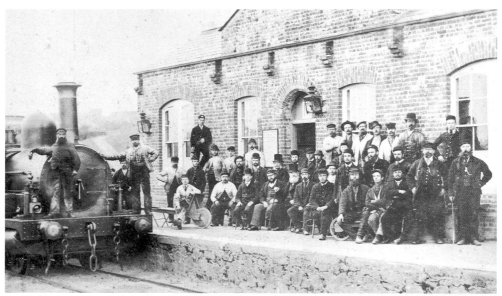

St Blazey station (originally Par CMR) and the nearby depot owe their existence to the CMR. Built in the 1874 period Par station opened to passengers in June 1876 but by 1879, when a spur was built to the Cornwall Railway's main line station, it became St Blazey. Prior to its 1883 modification a CMR 0-6-0T locomotive and 39 staff pose in front of the brick structure.

M. Dart Collection

A large format film camera captures the classic lines of very clean '4500' class prairie tank No. 4584, with prominent British Railways 'lion and wheel' emblem on the side tank, on the St Blazey turntable on 28th September, 1957. To the right a pannier tank is being lifted for works attention.   *Les Elsey*

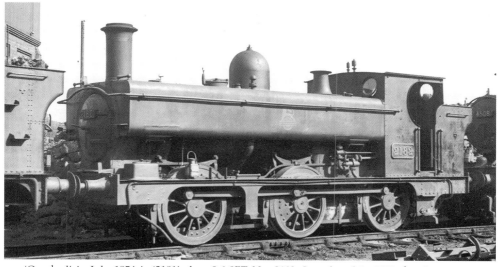

'On shed' in July 1954 is '2181' class 0-6-0PT No. 2182. Introduced in 1939 the class was a development of the 1897 Dean '2021' class but modified to provide increased braking power for heavy gradients. The class became work horses on the many china clay lines and sidings.

M. Dart Collection

This is the sad sight that most steam enthusiasts dreaded. In the foreground is the new order with a pair of 350 hp diesel shunters, with No. D4008 dominant, while in the background is a 204 hp diesel shunter and a line of redundant 0-6-0PT and 2-6-2T steam locomotives. The view shows the coaling stage and ramp to advantage as well as the locomotive works and part of the running shed / roundhouse.

Author's Collection

The old CMR brick roundhouse had nine roads and segments, all accessed via a single turntable. Remarkably the installation was in continuous use between 1874 and 1987, a period of 113 years. Historically tank locomotives would 'peep' out of the shed but in this utterly fascinating mid-1960s view two green liveried dmus are joined by two short-stay four-wheeled railbuses that were mainly used between Boscarne Junction and Bodmin North, with occasional sorties to Wadebridge.

Author's Collection

St Blazey Road were removed in the early 1980s and by that time many of the buildings were showing signs of minimum maintenance by BR. In fact the roof of the roundhouse and supervisor's offices was unsafe. Consequently, in April 1987, the roundhouse was closed, after 113 years of operation.

Many of the sidings to the north-west of the old station were removed at this time and in 1988 work started on a major scheme, which saw completely new offices built north of the roundhouse but to the west of the wagon works. With the withdrawal of the 'clay hood' wagons in February 1988 the wagon works was modernised and equipped to deal with modern air-braked, roller-bearing wagons. The diesel fuelling point was moved from just south of the turntable to the east side of the wagon works building and a large number of sidings were removed. In 1989 the individual roads of the roundhouse were separated by breeze-block walls and each section was leased out as a small industrial unit. New power supplies were provided and the buildings, including the roof, made safe. Diesel locomotives continued to cross the turntable on their way to the wagon works building for minor attention, such as fitting new brake blocks. The GWR signal box and a reasonable selection of lower quadrant semaphore signals have survived into the 21st century. The remnants of the old St Blazey station platforms remain, although the edging and surface have crumbled with the passage of time. High floodlights now provide new lighting standards for the shunting yard in hours of darkness.

St Blazey was always the hub of the operational wheel in terms of freight and china clay train operations. In terms of locomotive allocation, controlling wagons, customer communications and managing local manpower, St Blazey has shrunk from the halcyon days but until the end of 2007 it was still the nerve centre of the freight operations for central Cornwall. The days of the paper-driven control system, which gave way to Telex after World War II, have gone and computer-based systems with modern communications technology is the order of the day. However, traditionally it has been the St Blazey supervisors, the Freight Manager and railmen who have run the local business. All of this has now changed and St Blazey has reduced in importance, with certain EWS train operations being transferred to Fowey.

While there are fewer clay loading points these days, requirements are constantly changing and it is a nightmare trying to supply wagons at a moment's notice, while at the same time ensuring train crews are able to work the trains, that a locomotive is available and that the logical order of operating can meet all requirements. There are scores of potential problems ranging from crippled wagons, delays of ships in the Channel due to gales and meeting the various company targets and objectives.

The St Blazey train crews have worked diverse diagrams over the years. In days gone by workings varied from minor branch clay trains with small pannier tanks or diesel shunters to main line turns which, especially on summer Saturdays, included several class '1' trains as far as Penzance in the down direction and Exeter up country. In the war years St Blazey drivers regularly worked beyond Exeter, on both passenger and freight workings. In more recent times St Blazey men have worked class '1' trains over the Newquay branch and on to Plymouth. All air-braked china clay trains are now 'Driver Only' -

Many would regard this 1988 scene as modern but in fact it has already become a historic shot featuring withdrawn motive power. At the south end of St Blazey yard is a class '47' in original Railfreight livery at the head of a rake of CDA wagons, while on the left are class '50s' in revised Network SouthEast and new Railfreight liveries. The locomotive on the left is the unique class '50/1' No. 50149 *Defiance* which was converted from express passenger to freight use from 1987 until 1989, when it was re-converted.   *Author*

After its abandonment in April 1987 the already structurally unsound building started to become even more dilapidated, as seen here in September 1988. However, the structure and particularly the roof were repaired and the listed building was leased out as a number of small industrial units, breeze block walls having been built between the nine distinct 'sections'. No. 47446 in large logo livery stands beside the listed building.   *Author*

although a shunter is present on the branches and at major sites. Operations at St Blazey were once literally around the clock.

The classes of steam locomotive allocated to St Blazey have already been described. However, once the diesels took over 36 steam locomotives were replaced by only nine diesels, such was the availability of the modern motive power. In the early 1960s class '03' and '08' shunters were allocated to St Blazey but the smaller class '03s' had certain limitations and by 1964 they had been transferred away.* The earliest main line diesels that could be found on the depot in 1959 were the original twin-engined North British 'D6XX' A1A-A1A 2,000 hp 'Warships' and their small diesel-hydraulic cousins from the same stable, the 1,000 hp (later 1,100 hp) class '22' B-B type '2s'. Hot on their heels were the lighter class '42' and '43' 2,200hp B-B 'Warships' and later still, from 1962, the attractive 2,700 hp class '52' 'Westerns', the definitive UK diesel-hydraulic locomotive design. Gradually diesel-electric classes appeared including 2,580 hp class '47' Brush type '4s' the cumbersome looking 16-wheeled Sulzer engined 1Co-Co1 class '45' and '46' 'Peaks', and the small 1,250 hp class '25s', which replaced the class '22s' after a very short lifespan. The 'Peaks' normally arrived on freight services from the north and after a little Cornish activity they normally returned north. In later years Laira depot at Plymouth had an allocation of class '46s'. English Electric 2,700 hp class '50s' found themselves working in deepest Cornwall from 1975 and they were regular visitors to St Blazey. One example was converted for freight use and between the end of 1987 and the start of 1989 class '50/1' No. 50149 *Defiance* could often be found working from St Blazey depot. In 1979 English Electric 1,750 hp class '37' Co-Cos started to replace the class '25s' and the former were to work Cornish china clay trains for over 20 years. Several carried Cornish names, including No. 37671 *Tre Pol and Pen* and 37675 *William Cookworthy* (previously carried by Nos. 37196 and 37207 respectively). From 1995 class '60s' started to appear on the long distance freights, replacing pairs of class '37s' on certain trains but more significant was the arrival towards the end of 1999 of the first General Motors North American-built 125 tonne class '66s'. These hi-tech locomotives would eventually replace all of the class '37s'. Later still class '67s' started working postal trains and they headed their distinctive rolling stock to St Blazey for servicing on a daily basis, until the postal trains were withdrawn in 2004. Various types of diesel multiple unit were also stabled on St Blazey as well as any visiting strangers, such as a class '56' in 1990.

Times have changed at St Blazey. With reductions in the china clay industry combined with the power of the class '66s', the number of clay trains has been significantly reduced. The class '66s' can take 34 loaded CDA hoppers up to Treverrin tunnel, which would have required at least four trains in the days of steam. Nowadays it is common to find only one or two locomotives on local china clay duties in the area. The future of St Blazey depot and site is uncertain and it may not live to celebrate its 150th anniversary, because at the very end of 2007 the EWS company transferred some of its operations to Carne Point, Fowey. Thankfully the original buildings are Grade II listed.

---

* In this paragraph classifications introduced in 1968 are used for ease of identification.

For nearly 30 years the humble diesel-mechanical unit, in various guises, formed the mainstay of local services on the Newquay branch line. On 1st October, 1987 the 'peg' is off for 2-car unit No. P467, seen approaching Middleway crossing with a Par to Newquay working. Note the old bullhead rail and the foreground signal wires.   *Author*

Chapter Twelve

Middleway to Ponts Mill

Just to the north of St Blazey is Middleway Bridge Crossing which carries the St Blazey to Tywardreath road across the Newquay branch railway line and the River Par. It also crosses the alignment of the old Par Canal. The railway line is single track at this point and in the early years a ground frame and crossing keeper's cottage controlled the crossing. In GWR days a small signal box was built on the down or west side of the line. The small cabin was of interesting design because the point levers and signal wires had to span the River Par to reach the rods and pulleys adjacent to the track. Curiously, although traffic on the Newquay branch could never be described as busy, a substantial wooden pedestrian footbridge was built across the railway and river at this point. It was demolished in the 1930s, however, and was never replaced. It was a sad day in January 1981 when Middleway Bridge Crossing signal box closed; the gates were removed and barriers with CCTV controlled from St Blazey signal box were installed.

The river, old canal and the railway run side by side to the north with trains passing along what appears to be a causeway. On the down run a semaphore signal controls the next crossing at St Blazey Bridge, although in the up direction a colour light controls proceedings. Again, there was once a signal box located on the down side, north of the main A390 road, which it protected. After being physically moved 22 yards to the north in 1973 to accommodate barrier work and bridge widening, it finally closed on 30th September that year, and again control passed to St Blazey box with CCTV. There are the remains of some old disused lime kilns on the up side of the line, and a few years ago a laundry with a splendid stone stack stood on the south-west corner of the crossing. Now there is only the audible warning of an approaching train and barriers to interest the student of railways. The line continues beside the river and old canal alignment to reach Ponts Mill.

The entire Ponts Mill area is steeped in history. As stated in the Chapter Four, the sea once reached this point before 400 years of mining activity produced enough silt and spoil to push the shoreline to where it is now, some two miles to the south. Activity in the area was at its height in the mid-1850s when inclines brought down the substantial output from the Fowey Consuls to Ponts Mill for conveyance to the then new Par Harbour. Granite, ores and china clay were being carried down the Carmears Incline in the Luxulyan Valley from the pits around Bugle and the quarries at the top of the valley. Until 1855 all of this had to be transhipped manually from wagon to barge for the journey along a canal to the sea. Add to this local activity, milling and crushing, combined with the water from man-made leats and the River Par tumbling through, the scene must have been remarkable.

Nowadays the scene is considerably less frantic. At milepost 283 the main Newquay branch starts to climb steeply as it crosses the River Par. Just before the bridge is a ground frame which once controlled the siding down to the now

Middleway Bridge Crossing ground frame controlled an adjacent road crossing plus protecting signals in each direction just north of St Blazey. The mechanical point rodding and signal wires crossed the River Par on some old timbers. The attractive little building was demolished in 1981 when CCTV and barriers, controlled from St Blazey signal box, took over. *Author's Collection*

The line between Middleway and St Blazey Bridge crossing has always been popular with railway photographers as the trains run on an embankment between the river and the old canal alignment. '4500' class No. 5505 picks up speed with its four-coach Newquay-bound branch train on 6th August, 1956. The river is running white with china clay deposits, which would be eliminated in later years as ECC became more environmentally aware. *Les Elsey*

The class '121' and '122' single power or 'bubble' cars as they were to become known, normally had more than sufficient capacity to cope with Newquay branch passenger loadings. They always looked attractive on the single line branch. Here No. 55026 approaches St Blazey Bridge and makes for the hills surrounding the Luxulyan Valley with a down train.   *Author*

Class '37s' Nos. 37181 and 37247 with a long clay train of 46 clay hood wagons from ECC Rocks at Goonbarrow Junction at Middleway on 19th April, 1985. The load was bound for Carne Point at Fowey.   *Author*

An impressive looking InterCity 125 unit, headed by power car No. 253034, accelerates away from Middleway with a summer Paddington to Newquay through train in June 1989. Newquay is now the only Cornish branch line to receive visits from such trains in the peak summer period. *Author*

Adjacent to St Blazey Bridge crossing are some old abandoned lime kilns. These are testimony to the fact that the old canal was navigable beyond this point and limestone would have been conveyed in barges to the kiln for burning, the resulting lime being used for agricultural purposes. Single power car No. 55003 passes with the 4.35 pm Newquay to Par on 4th October, 1991.   *Author*

abandoned ECC Ponts Mill installation (*see map on page 174*). The point levers were unlocked by the shunter travelling in the brake van on the local Ponts Mill goods train - normally worked by a St Blazey class '08', which propelled its train from St Blazey. The ground frame could only be operated in conjunction with telephone communication to the signal box. A control box at the ground frame contained token instrument apparatus. Electric tokens were installed at Ponts Mill siding in October 1914, when they were also introduced at St Blazey and Luxulyan signal boxes.

Just beyond the ground frame a siding left the branch on the opposite, down or west side to serve Prideaux Wood china clay dry from 1912. The only obvious remains of this today are the extended girders on the railway bridge over the River Par, which clearly once carried an additional line. The Prideaux Wood works was built in the 1870s but all around the area was at one time heavily mined, mainly for tin. The planting of a substantial conifer forest by the Forestry Commission in 1960 has obscured many of the mining remains and the clay kiln was demolished by ECC immediately following closure in the early 1960s, although the settling tanks and base of the furnace room can still be traced. The origins of Prideaux Wood and South Prideaux Wood Mines are ancient. In 1881 the historian Robert Symons stated that, 'the open excavations in the coppice wood in which the sett is situated are enormous, if not unparalleled, partly done by the ancients - probably the Phoenicians - and partly by the moderns. The lodes are so numerous and the tin stone so thoroughly combined with the containing killas that the whole of it is fit for the stamps (crushers)'.

The Prideaux Wood china clay kiln was also served by a narrow gauge line, which ran from the linhay through a narrow and low bridge beneath the Newquay branch to a loading wharf, which adjoined the standard gauge Ponts Mill siding. Some remains of the line and one of its turnouts on the wharf can still be traced. In all probability the narrow gauge wagons were horse-drawn.

The single siding to Ponts Mill works branched away from the old tramway route on the down side, and divided into two dead-end roads with the track set in concrete. Normally one train per day visited the works, where once PRA and later PBA Tiger wagons were filled with china clay by front-loading tractors. VDA wagons had bagged clay on pallets loaded into them by forklift trucks. For some years the powdered china clay found its way to the Wiggins Teape mill near Fort William in the West Highlands of Scotland, for use in the manufacture of paper. Latterly there were no no run-round facilities, which is the reason for the train normally being propelled from St Blazey. The works closed at Easter 1992 and the last train ran on 21st April, 1992. After closure but before the track was lifted the works area was used for remedial work to CDA china clay wagons.

Returning to the route of the original tramway on the east side of the siding into Ponts Mill works, there was a siding that veered away from the tramway in an easterly direction on the down side that once served the loading point at the foot of the incline from the Fowey Consuls mining complex. The tramway then crossed a minor road beside the old canal basin and within 100 yards or so the track layout became more complex. There were in effect three routes, the most easterly of the lines serving the Ponts Mill china stone works, the central northerly route being the original Treffry Tramway that started its steep climb

A pleasant study of a typical local work-a-day china clay train of the 1950s. Making for St Blazey near St Blazey Bridge crossing is pannier tank No. 1664 on 3rd August, 1956. The box van would contain bagged clay with the UCV four-wheelers being loaded with powdered china clay. Penpillick Hill is in the background.   *Les Elsey*

The interesting and rarely photographed junction between the Newquay branch line, *right*, and the siding down to the Ponts Mill complex (*left*) is featured here. Class '37' No. 37670 will be on full power for the climb through the Luxulyan valley with its load of empty CDA wagons on 21st March, 1994. The siding had seen its last clay train on 21st April, 1992 but it was subsequently used for Royal Train berthing and for crippled wagons before closing completely.
                                                                                    Author

up the Carmears incline on the eastern side of the Luxulyan valley, and the valley floor tramway that ran beneath the elevated Newquay branch that still passes over the site on the impressive Ponts Mill viaduct. The china stone works closed in the mid-1960s and the track was lifted. For some time that area has been waterlogged and heavily overgrown. The route of the incline is clear to see as it climbs away from the valley floor at a gradient of 1 in 9 and the granite setts (sleepers) are an obvious feature. To the left and heading off in a north-westerly direction is the valley floor line that served two stone quarries and, in later years, Trevanny kiln, a china clay drying plant on the alignment of the valley floor tramway is a substantial and solid-looking loading wharf on the down side, located just before Ponts Mill viaduct, where china clay from Trevanny kiln was once loaded onto railway wagons after the valley tramway closed (*see Chapter Thirteen*). There is one minor curio at this site. Just as the Carmears incline starts its ascent there is a bridge at the foot of the incline, which a Cornish Archaeological survey describes thus:

> The bridge at the foot of the Carmears Incline is a very substantial structure whose purpose is to carry the incline over an obstacle of some importance. It has so far been impossible to establish if this was a road or trackway from Ponts Mill up the valley, or whether it was in fact the line of the early Tramway, preserved for some future use.

A visit to the location is highly recommended, preferably in the winter months for while the ground can be muddy the dense foliage of summer obscures many of the ruins.

This view from the Newquay branch train window on 27th June, 1976 shows the Ponts Mill siding in better days. Once the site of much activity, in its final years a daily train was normally tripped from St Blazey yard powered by a class '08' shunter. Sometimes empty wagons would be left for loading while on other occasions the shunter waited at Ponts Mill while the wagons were being loaded.   *Author's Collection*

It must be added that although the railways at Ponts Mill are broadly described, space does not permit detailed reference to the early primitive cottages and tin miners huts, the once-extensive crushing plant with its many stamps, the buildings of the New Consolidated Mines Company, the many mines such as Wheal Rashleigh, Wheal Treffry etc., the fascinating array of machinery which pumped out mines, controlled the many leats and waterways or that powered the inclines and other equipment.

The last and undoubtedly most significant development at Ponts Mill sidings, towards the end of the 1980s, was its connection with royalty! The Prince of Wales owns, through his Duchy of Cornwall interests, vast tracts of land throughout the County of Cornwall. To visit his estates he regularly uses the Royal Train with its distinctive stock, which includes sleeping accommodation. In past years the Royal Train was berthed overnight on the Bodmin General branch, just around the curve from Bodmin Road (now Parkway) station. After the closure of that branch and its sale into private, preservationist hands, the Royal Train used Ponts Mill siding but now that too has closed. On one occasion both the Prince of Wales and Princess Diana spent the night on the remote Ponts Mill siding, and bearing in mind that such workings are 'topped and tailed' with a locomotive at each end, it may well be that the future King of England enjoyed the last locomotive-hauled passenger train on the Ponts Mill line!

It was common in many of the clay works for the track to be set in concrete, as seen here at ECC Ponts Mill. A regular performer at the little works was No. 08955, seen here with a couple of 38 tonne PRA wagons that would end up in at a paper mill in the West Highlands of Scotland! Note the ECC bagged clay on pallets. Every building in this view was razed after closure of the works in the 1990s.   *Author*

Chapter Thirteen

Luxulyan Valley-Goonbarrow Jn
and the Goonbarrow Branch

Luxulyan Valley to Goonbarrow Junction

Although there were clay dries and china stone crushing plants at Ponts Mill, and large volumes of china clay were taken down the valley to the harbours at Par and Fowey, the granite within the Luxulyan Valley was not kaolinised and hence there is no china clay in the actual valley area. That is not to say that there was no mineral wealth, mining or quarrying activity. There was much activity in ancient times but in terms of railway lines it was Treffry's original plans for a tramway in 1835 which first brought rails to the valley.

Little is known about the original scheme but it is clear that due to the difficult terrain, hard rock and incompetent contractors, work was abandoned. However, Treffry was determined to build the tramway to Mollinis, near Bugle, and eventually on to Newquay where he had just purchased the harbour. As detailed in Chapter Four, after detailed planning in 1837 work started on the tramway in earnest towards the end of that year. By 1841 the Carmears Incline up the eastern edge of the valley and the tramway along level ground, to what would become the eastern end of the Treffry viaduct, and on to Colcerrow and Carbeans granite quarries, was ready for service. A combination of horse and waterwheel power saw the first loads being transported down to Ponts Mill, where they were transhipped to barge for the two-mile canal journey to the then complete Par Harbour.

Historical reports refer to the Carmears Incline as double track with 'down' loads being balanced by 'up' loads, others show single track but with a passing section or loop halfway up, while an archaeological report is specific in stating that the incline was single track only. Further research shows that the incline was single track but judging by the width of the tramway in places it is easy to understand how some have made double-track assumptions. In the last week of February 1844 the magnificent Treffry viaduct/aqueduct was opened for traffic, which later resulted in the first through loads to and from Bugle via Luxulyan. One historian commented that the Treffry viaduct did not have the family crest sculptured on a shield on the stonework, another argued that it did. In a way they were both right, because curiously, the south side of the viaduct shows a blank stone shield whereas the northern face has the family crest proudly carved in a shield above the central arches. Water was carried across the structure beneath the huge granite slabs which supported the tramway. The water fed the leat which powered the Carmears Incline waterwheel.

Although there had been granite quarries around the Luxulyan Valley for many years, a form of pink and black coloured variety, known as Luxulyanite, was quarried in the area, and some of this was used in the construction of the Duke of Wellington's tomb in Westminster Abbey in London. In the early 1850s a branch from the tramway to Colcerrow and Carbeans quarries was built. It formed a trailing connection with the branch in the down direction and ran to the north-north-west past Gatty's Bridge to Cairns Quarry, a shallow working

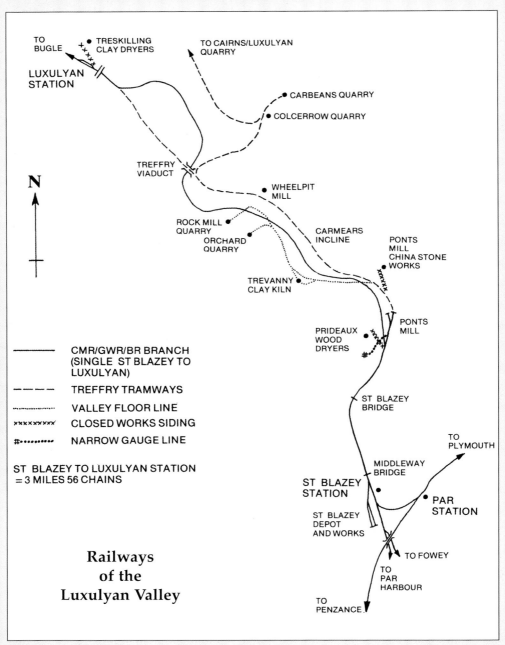

TO
BUGLE

● TRESKILLING
CLAY DRYERS

TO CAIRNS/LUXULYAN
QUARRY

LUXULYAN
STATION

● CARBEANS QUARRY

● COLCERROW QUARRY

N

TREFFRY
VIADUCT

● WHEELPIT
MILL

ROCK MILL ●
QUARRY

ORCHARD ●
QUARRY

CARMEARS
INCLINE

PONTS
MILL
CHINA STONE
● WORKS

TREVANNY ●
CLAY KILN

PONTS
MILL

PRIDEAUX
WOOD
DRYERS ●

—————— CMR/GWR/BR BRANCH
(SINGLE ST BLAZEY TO
LUXULYAN)

– – – – TREFFRY TRAMWAYS

··········· VALLEY FLOOR LINE

xxxxxxxx CLOSED WORKS SIDING

#········· NARROW GAUGE LINE

ST BLAZEY TO LUXULYAN STATION
= 3 MILES 56 CHAINS

ST BLAZEY
BRIDGE

TO
PLYMOUTH

MIDDLEWAY
BRIDGE

ST BLAZEY
STATION

PAR
STATION

ST BLAZEY
DEPOT
AND WORKS

TO FOWEY

TO
PAR
HARBOUR

**Railways
of the
Luxulyan Valley**

TO
PENZANCE

This map shows the railways and tramways through the Luxulyan valley between St Blazey and
Luxulyan stations.

Even with a load of only three coaches and two vans this '4500' class 2-6-2T is working hard in the Luxulyan valley with a Par to Newquay branch train on 2nd October, 1948. The photograph was taken from the Treffry viaduct but such views are no longer possible due to a substantial and unchecked increase in the growth of foliage. *P.Q. Treloar Collection*

With the end of steam rapidly approaching a number of railtours for enthusiasts were arranged, this one by the Plymouth Railway Circle. This busy scene at Luxulyan station on 22nd April, 1961 shows the brake van special on the right with an up clay train held at the island platform. The lines to the left serve the goods yard and Treskilling clay dries, which closed in 1975. 0-6-0PT No. 1626 is taking on water. *Terry Nicholls*

Adding to the variety of Newquay branch motive power is a very smart looking 'Manor' class 4-6-0 No. 7823 *Hook Norton Manor* seen powering a three-coach Newquay-bound local off Rock Mill viaduct in the Luxulyan Valley, on 10th August, 1956. There are destination boards on the carriages, which may suggest a Newquay portion of a down express to Penzance.   *Les Elsey*

Rock Mill viaduct features more prominently in this shot of a 'Hall' class 4-6-0 and a mogul 2-6-0 (probably Nos. 5972 and 6397 as previously featured) double-heading a heavy summer train to Newquay on 9th July, 1955. The leading coach is No. W1775W but its destination board is blank! The sound of the exhausts 'bouncing' off the surrounding hillsides must have been tremendous.
R.C. Riley/Courtesy Transport Treasury

One of the unsung workhorses of the modern traction era was the class '46' version of the 1Co-Co1 'Peak' class of diesel locomotive. The heavy 138 ton 16-wheeled monsters were powered by 2,500 hp 12-cylinder Sulzer engines with Brush electrical equipment. Here steam heating No. 46009 approaches the Treffry viaduct in the Luxulyan valley with the 10.32 am (Fridays Only) Newquay to Manchester Piccadilly of 21st September, 1979. *Author*

In the 1950s Luxulyan station still had the full railway infrastructure of signal box, water tower, GWR station seat, semaphore signals, passing loop, single-storey station building and goods yard, as well as the delightful clerestory-roofed camping coach seen here. All of the above have since been removed leaving just a basic single platform and a crude waiting shelter.

Author's Collection

By October 1991 the scene at Luxulyan was almost desolate with just a single track and a single car unit passing-by four times a day in each direction. The waiting hut had no creature comforts and trains did not stop in the hours of darkness because there were no station lights! In this unusual scene on a truly appalling day there are waiting passengers at the request stop as 'Bubble' No. 55006 prepares to pause at the station in driving rain on its way to Par. Note the line speed limit.

Author

in the hillside behind Luxulyan. This quarry was disused by 1880 but the remains can still be traced.

What was to become one of the most interesting tramways was a horse-drawn extension from Ponts Mill along the valley floor to granite quarries at Orchard Quarry and Rock Mill Quarry. This line was built between 1868 and 1870. When the CMR built its well-engineered line up the valley in the 1872 to 1874 period, to enable locomotive-hauled trains to run from Fowey to Newquay via Bugle, effectively replacing the Treffry Tramway and making the Carmears Incline redundant, stone for the abutments of the viaducts in the valley was conveyed by horse on the valley floor tramway (*see photograph page 92*).

The quarries had been in operation prior to 1840 and evidence of abandoned dwelling houses has been found. The tramway was built by the South Cornwall Granite Company. It diverged up the valley from the foot of Carmears Incline and the rails were anchored to granite block sleepers. The main tramway was to Rock Mill Quarry but just before what was to become Rock Mill viaduct on the Newquay branch a spur branched off to serve Orchard Quarry (*see photograph page 100*). About the turn of the century the Penryn company of John Freeman took over the quarries and on some early maps the name of the quarries are shown simply as 'Freeman's Quarry'.

In the early part of the 20th century the demand for granite declined as cheaper imports from Scandinavia were readily available. While unlike other mining depressions this did not finish quarrying overnight, the two quarries closed just before the World War I and the track from Ponts Mill to both Rock Mill and Orchard quarries was lifted. In the very early 1920s the Central Cornwall China Clay Company built its Central Cornwall Kiln, also known as Trevanny Dry. It was a conventional coal-fired pan-kiln with the linhay facing the valley floor tramway, which was relaid (and slightly diverted), continuing through to the quarries further up the valley. The kiln was unusual in having an all brick stack, which still survives. The kiln has been preserved and it is possible to walk around the site, with protective railings installed on health and safety grounds. The main buildings were built of granite and there is speculation that one of the primary reasons for relaying the tramway to the quarries was to bring down granite for its construction. There is some evidence that granite was sold from the quarry floor but little sign of post-World War I quarrying. The relaid standard gauge line was on wooden sleepers whereas the original valley floor tramway was, in common with the Treffry Tramways, laid on granite blocks, or setts.

The entire line from Rock Mill Quarry to Ponts Mill was lifted in 1938. It was reputed that no granite had come down from the Freeman-owned site since 1928. The track was again relaid almost immediately with upgraded materials but only as far as Trevanny Kiln. From the date of Trevanny Kiln's opening small 4-wheeled Motor Rail 'Simplex' petrol locomotives were used to haul wagons to and from the clay dry. The machines used were No. 1943 of 1919 build and No. 2032 of 1920. One was called *Bessie* and the driver for many years was one Jack Arscott. The locomotives were not powerful and often loaded wagons were brought down from Trevanny under the control of a brakeman, without locomotive. The first of the small locomotives crashed about 1933 and

Right: By September 2006 tall station lights had been provided and a seat had suddenly appeared. With trees taking over on both sides of the track a streamlined Virgin Voyager unit forms a summer Saturday Newquay to Glasgow through train. Within a year this sight would also become history as Virgin Trains lost the cross country operating franchise.

Author

Below: There are few more incongruous sights than a 125 mph express train running along a single track at 25 mph. However that is exactly what happens on the Newquay branch as even in 2007 the 20¼ mile journey from Par to Newquay takes 50 minutes non-stop, at an average speed of 24.9 mph! On 22nd August, 1992 the 08.25 from far-off Edinburgh approaches Luxulyan, powered by Valenta-engined cars Nos. 43090 and 43092, on its way to Newquay.

Author

In addition to through trains from distant locations running to Newquay on summer weekends, from 2007 First Great Western announced that a train would run direct from Paddington to Newquay on Mondays to Fridays between 2nd July and 31st August, in addition to Saturday and Sunday workings. On 8th September, 2007, the very last Saturday of the season, the 'Atlantic Coast Express' looks somewhat out of place as it approaches Bowling Green on its run down to Newquay. *Author*

An extraordinarily difficult task photographically is to record three trains in one frame at Goonbarrow Junction. Waiting in the up loop in April 1991 is the Chipman's Weedkilling train, which was paying its annual visit to the branch powered by Nos. 20901 *Nancy* and 20904 *Janis*, while the down branch train has the road to Newquay as it heads towards the signal box. A class '37' in the sidings at ECC Rocks will follow the weedkiller to St Blazey in about 20 minutes time.
Author

With the sun breaking through the mist No. 37669 heads a rake of CDA wagons, which had been in service for just over a year, past Bowling Green between Luxulyan and Goonbarrow Junction in May 1989. The locomotive is in large logo grey livery, as originally applied to Railfreight sector locomotives.
Author

the other was re-engined with a diesel in 1948. The track to Trevanny was finally lifted in the early 1950s and lorries then took the china clay down to a loading wharf near the foot of the Carmears Incline for transhipment to railway wagons, as previously mentioned. The Central Cornwall/Trevanny installation closed in the mid-1960s while in the ownership of English Clays, Lovering, Pochin & Co. Ltd and Trevanny siding was formally taken out of use on 31st December, 1967. The slate roof on the kiln was removed in the early 1970s.

In the lower reaches of the valley there were a number of stone crushing plants but the last to be rail-connected was Ponts Mill siding which was also taken out of use on 31st December, 1967. From this date there was no commercial reason for the standard gauge line from Ponts Mill ground frame to cross the road beyond Ponts Mill driers.

Originally granite traffic coming off the Colcerrow and Carbeans line, and before 1880 the Cairns Quarry branch, joined the main Treffry Tramway from Mollinis and Luxulyan at a junction just at the south-east end of the Treffry viaduct. From there it ran to the head of Carmears Incline for lowering by cable to the Ponts Mill area. However, once the CMR line (the present Newquay branch) opened in 1874 the incline closed and traffic from the quarries reversed at the junction and was drawn by horses across the viaduct to a gate at a point on the tramway just before it joined the CMR, immediately east of Luxulyan station. From this point CMR, and later GWR, locomotives collected and delivered wagons.

In about 1890 the West of England China Clay Company opened its Wheelpit Mill at the head of Carmears Incline on the site of the incline waterwheel. A new waterwheel of 40 ft diameter was installed in the pit and this drove a pair of grinding pans. China stone was reputedly brought down to the mill by horse-drawn wagons, along the old Treffry Tramway from Luxulyan station and loaded into the mill via wooden chutes. The crushed stone, in slurry form, ran down a 6-inch pipeline laid along the old Carmears Incline to Ponts Mill for drying. The Wheelpit Mill did not work beyond World War I, closing *circa* 1908. Remains of some of the Wheelpit buildings can still be found.

A delightful description of a walk recommended in an 1890 guidebook gives a remarkable insight to this area. Quotes include there being no risk in walking the tramway because 'the trucks conveying the stone are drawn by horses' and on the Colcerrow branch 'we may have to step aside to make way for trucks descending by gravitation'. The branch up to Colcerrow and Carbeans was steep but well graded. There was a smithy at the quarry and a loading bank. Some of the track at the quarry end of the branch was relaid on wooden sleepers rather than the original granite blocks. It seems the 'new' track was ex-broad gauge and purchased from the GWR after 1892 (and, of course, relaid to standard gauge). The track to Wheelpit was lifted in 1915, although few short lengths of rail remain and can still be traced. The granite traffic dwindled, although granite was quarried at Carbeans until the early 1930s when the tramway closed. The 1937 *GWR Magazine* refers to the line being open 'until a few years ago'. It seems traffic dwindled with the last load being taken down in 1933 by one of Matthew Hores' horses from Trethurgy. The Colcerrow track was mostly lifted shortly after closure but other track was removed in the summer of 1940. It was all removed to Par Beach and used in wartime defences

An amusing view that proves it takes 17 Railtrack workers to move just two short sections of track on two trolleys! The gang are about to replace a broken rail behind Goonbarrow Junction signal box in March 1995. A class '37' is lurking between Polybulk wagons on the left and Tiger wagons on the right.   *Author*

The reliable class '37s' were the stalwarts of the Cornish china clay railscene between 1979 and 1999, surviving into the 21st century before being completely replaced by new GM class '66s.' In this very early morning scene in May 1989 two of the class are seen at Goonbarrow Junction, No. 37675 *William Cookworthy* being the locomotive on the right.   *Author*

A photograph that shows the juxtaposition of Goonbarrow Junction signal box on the Newquay branch line to the sidings at ECC Rocks. Passing the site with a 'Pathfinder' railway enthusiasts tour from Manchester to Newquay on 23rd November, 1991 is NSE-liveried No. 50033 *Glorious*. Two other class '50s', Nos. 50015 *Valiant* and 50008 *Thunderer*, were at the other end of the train.
Author

Goonbarrow Junction is one of just seven locations in Cornwall where GWR/WR lower quadrant semaphore signals survive. The junction is also significant in that it is now the only passing place on the Newquay branch between St Blazey and Newquay. Leaving the loop in August 1992 an IC125 unit makes a change from the usual dmus and clay trains as it takes holidaymakers westward.
Author

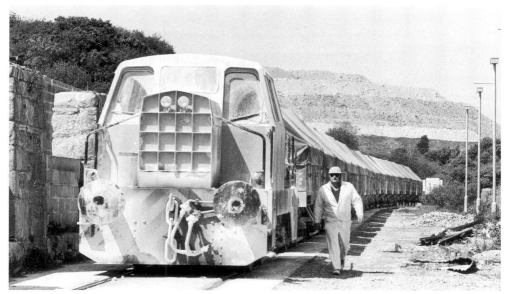

ECC Rocks (now owned by Imerys) is important enough for the clay company to employ its own motive power. Various shunters, including ex-BR class '08s', have been used at the site but in June 1986 it was a Rolls-Royce-engined Sentinel No. P403D *Denise* that was in daily use. The locomotive is seen beside the abandoned Wheal Henry at the start of the old Goonbarrow branch. *Author*

In days of old much of the china clay carried by rail for export was conveyed in casks, which each contained between 2 and 4 cwt of clay. Casks, or barrels, were delivered to the clay driers from the coopers by horse and cart. In this scene 78 casks are being delivered to a clay dry on the Goonbarrow branch. By the linhay are three privately owned wagons. *Author's Collection*

against possible invasion. A short siding was retained at the Luxulyan end of the tramway, complete with protective gate, but this was disconnected on 27th September, 1964.

From Ponts Mill ground frame the main Newquay branch climbs across the 52 yds-long Prideaux viaduct, the 92 yds-long Ponts Mill viaduct and the 52 yd Rock Mill viaduct before curving under Treffry viaduct. Still climbing, the single track enters a granite cutting and the 52 yds-long Luxulyan tunnel before curving into Luxulyan station, once known as Bridges. The 1890 guide book states that 'simple refreshments may be had at the Station Master's cottage'. The train ride up the Luxulyan Valley is one of the most spectacular on the UK rail network and a trip is recommended. In the old days, if there were more than 20 wagons on a descending train, the Luxulyan porter had to assist the guard with pinning down brakes.

When opened by the CMR on 20th June, 1876 there was an up and a down platform at Bridges (Luxulyan) station. A signal box controlled the passing loop and a siding. A simple station building was provided away from the platform and the GWR provided a pagoda hut shelter. In 1910 there were drastic changes to the station layout when a single island platform was provided. A new GWR signal box replaced the CMR example on 30th March, 1911. The goods yard was extended on the north side of the line in 1916 when Treskilling Clay Works was opened. The passing loop was extended in May 1936 and a holiday 'camping' coach appeared but, by and large, there was little change until 1964, when disaster struck.

On 27th September, 1964 the goods yard was taken out of use. The signal box closed, the station building was demolished and the passing loop was removed, as well as the Treffry refuge. Treskilling China Clay Works closed in 1975 and with it the narrow gauge feeder line, which at first used horses and later a capstan, to move small clay wagons onto the standard gauge loading wharf. At this time the last siding serving the works also closed, leaving just a single track through the entire area. All the trappings of the days of steam disappeared such as water tower and water columns. Early in the 1980s the GWR shelter was replaced by a tasteless hut and by the late 1980s the station became a request halt. It had been unmanned since 12th July, 1964.

West of Luxulyan the gradient eases slightly and relatively straight track takes the branch via Bowling Green and Goonbarrow Junction's fixed distant signal to Goonbarrow loop, adjacent to the vast Imerys Rock Works, on the fringe of Hensbarrow Down and clay country.

The Goonbarrow Branch

Although the GWR took over the operational side of the CMR in 1877, the CMR was still very much in existence. With the china clay business in the ascent following a slump in the mid-1870s, the CMR proposed a branch line which was to penetrate the heart of clay country to serve numerous clay works including Higher and Lower Ninestones, Carbean, Bluebarrow, Caudledown, Cleaves, Old Beam, Imperial Goonbarrow, Rock Hill and many others. With a capital of £24,000 work started in 1890. Construction was slow due to the difficult terrain,

The Goonbarrow branch was opened in 1893 and it served over 10 clay driers and an oil siding. This September 1965 view shows the Imperial/Carnsmerry complex that continued to be rail served until closure in the late 1970s, when most of the old coal-fired pan driers were being replaced. Note the massive clay tip in the background, a leftover from earlier excavations.

M. Dart Collection

Once closure of a branch line or clay works takes place in clay country it takes very little time for all trace of past installations to be lost, as a combination of earth moving, pit expansion and reclamation take place. This 1989 view is looking down the trackbed of the Goonbarrow branch towards Gunheath, where trains bound for Carbean would reverse. *Author*

which included embankments, bridges, a tunnel and severe gradients. An 1876-built Manning, Wardle tank locomotive called *Ringing Rock* was used on the construction of the line.

The 3 mile 39 chain branch line was duly completed and it opened on 2nd October, 1893 (*see map on page 194*). Leaving the Newquay branch at Goonbarrow Junction the line climbed at a steady 1 in 39 for nearly 2½ miles. At the start of the branch, and adjacent to the sidings of Rocks china clay works, which itself was built adjacent to the site of Hallivet, Wheal Anna and Rosevear driers, was Wheal Henry. This old pan dry was closed in the 1960s but the rails were set in concrete and in fact trains still use one of the sidings when shunting at Rocks. The stack survives, although reduced in height.

The line then curved towards the village of Bugle, climbing hard to cross the main street on a high stone arch which has been demolished since the line closed. The main road to Roche was also crossed on a high bridge which in 2008 was still *in situ*. The first crossing was at Old Beam which was immediately followed by Old Beam siding at the 288 mile 35 chain point. This was taken out of use on 20th May, 1969. After passing over Netley crossing a siding diverged on the up side at New Caudledown North and was crossed by a trailing connection from Imperial and Carnsmerry sidings. This 'loop' line then served New Caudledown before rejoining the branch at New Caudledown South. Beyond was Rock Hill siding, which closed back in July 1946. The ground frames at this point followed each other in quick succession, all on the up, or west, side; Imperial 288 miles 54 chains, New Caudledown North 288 miles 63 chains, Carnsmerry 288 miles 67 chains and New Caudledown South 288 miles 78 chains.

Some years after closure the preservationists arrived at Imperial Clay Driers and locomotives and stock belonging to the Cornish Steam Locomotive Preservation Society moved in. They accumulated a number of old goods wagons and other stock. Sadly, in 1987, the clay works environment was abandoned and the group moved their principal items to the Bodmin General preservation site. During their stay Open Days were held, where visitors could travel the short distance from Imperial to New Caudledown clay dry in brake vans.

The line continued to climb over the main St Austell to Bugle road and on the right was once located Caudledown (old) siding at 289 miles 18 chains. There was once a locomotive shed on the approach to Stenalees that housed the CMR locomotive *Goonbarrow* at the opening of the line. In later years the site of the long-demolished shed was located by a water tower. Next was the short Cleaves siding at milepost 289½, which closed in 1933. After passing under a minor road the line entered the 345 yds-long Stenalees tunnel and again crossed the St Austell to Bugle road, which marked the summit of the line. Immediately across the road on the down side was Oil Siding, 290 miles 9 chains, opened in 1926 and which was situated on an earlier alignment of the branch. The deviation took place early in the last century following the extension of Carbean Clay Pit. The line then descended at 1 in 39 past Gunheath New Siding to reach Gunheath, where there were sidings and loading wharfs, 290 miles and 48 chains from Paddington via Bristol!

To continue to Carbean trains had to reverse at Gunheath. A loop was provided and locomotives could run round their trains. The line dropped away at 1 in 40 and then at a staggering 1 in 35 towards Carbean and at 290 miles 51 chains Carthew Crossing was reached. After passing the crossing gates Carbean was reached a mere 24 chains further on. The track layout at Carbean was very cramped with a loading wharf, a short run-round loop and a head-hunt.

Restrictions have always been so severe that only short wheelbase tank locomotives have been passed to work the branch. Following the early workings by the converted CMR 0-6-0 saddle tanks, locomotives of the '2021' and '2181' classes worked the line. The latter were modified versions of the former, having increased brake power for heavy gradients, as found on the Goonbarrow branch. The final class of steam locomotive to work the line was the 41 ton '1600' class 0-6-0PTs. On rare occasions '4500' class Prairies worked over part of the branch, but special permission had to be given in such circumstances. In later years 350 hp diesel shunters and 'D63XX' diesel-hydraulics appeared on the branch, and once a class '25' diesel-electric appeared. However, in the case of the latter the train worked only to New Caudledown, the line beyond having been closed on 29th April, 1965.

Normally one train per day traversed the branch. In the late 1950s the branch freight left St Blazey at 8.10 am returning from Carbean at 1 pm. As sidings made both facing and trailing connections with the branch, a single locomotive would call at certain sidings on the way down and the remainder on the return journey. However, some days saw a locomotive at both ends of the branch freight, with each of the locomotives returning with its own train, normally one from the New Caudledown area and the other from Gunheath and Carbean.

Photographs of trains at Carbean are few and far between but this 1961 shot shows St Blazey allocated pannier No. 1626 with 20 ton brake van No. B954898 at the compact terminus. Note the old granite loading wharf on the left and the old clay tips along the background horizon. This section of the branch closed in 1965 but the last train ran some time earlier.
                                                                                    Terry Nicholls

After the Goonbarrow branch finally closed, the Cornish Steam Locomotive Preservation Society moved into the Imperial Clay driers area. The final train delivered stock to their leased site on 1st December, 1978. In this scene recorded on 17th May, 1984, 1923 Peckett 0-4-0ST No. 1611 and a fireless locomotive can be seen. After several open days the group moved to Bodmin General to join forces with the infant Bodmin & Wenford Railway.

Author

Traffic on the branch gradually declined due both to the closure of the old coal-fired pan driers and an improvement in pipeline technology. The last two miles of the branch closed in 1965, as mentioned above, and the section from New Caudledown to a point near Wheal Henry closed on 3rd December, 1978. The last train over part of the branch was on 1st December, 1978 when No. 25206 delivered stock to the Imperial Clay Driers preservation site. Today many remains of the Goonbarrow branch can be found, albeit with a bit of 'bramble bashing' at some locations. Much of the land remains in clay company hands. Only one of the four main road over bridges remains, although the sites of those demolished are readily identified with the aid of an Ordnance Survey map. The line was greatly under-photographed and illustrations of trains in action have been hard to locate.

The line never had a passenger service and there were no signals beyond Goonbarrow Junction. A couple of railway enthusiast special trains travelled over the line before closure, with the participants enjoying a journey in the much-lamented brake van. Now only a few hundred yards of the branch remains as testimony to one of the CMR's last significant developments.

The track between Goonbarrow Junction in the distant background and Bugle was originally single but was doubled in 1930. Following rationalisation in 1965 the tracks were operated as two single lines, one for Newquay branch trains and the other for Bugle and Carbis Wharf china clay traffic (but lifted in this view). Since 1987 locomotive workings west of Goonbarrow, such as this Sunday ballast train, have been exceptional. No. 37413 *Loch Eil Outward Bound* heads Dogfish wagons westward on 20th March, 1994. Bugle platform is at bottom left.   *Author*

The two-coach train reflects winter loadings at Bugle in the 1950s, when both faces of the island platform were still in use. Calling with a Newquay-bound train that seems to have an abundant steam heating supply, is 2-6-2T No. 4569.   *Maurice Dart*

Chapter Fourteen

Goonbarrow Jn-Bugle
and the Bugle Clay Branches

Goonbarrow Junction to Bugle

For a stretch of railway line with a length of only half a mile the Goonbarrow Junction to Bugle part of the branch has had a history of mixed fortunes. The alignment was part of the original Treffry Tramway, dating back to 1844 when horses hauled a wagon or two from the top of Carmears Incline near Luxulyan to Mollinis, near Bugle. With the coming of the CMR in 1874 the line was upgraded to take locomotives and heavier loads. At the site of Goonbarrow Junction signal box was once located Rosevear Siding signal box, which controlled a junction with the siding that served a clay loading point.

Rosevear signal box was closed in 1893 and Goonbarrow Junction box was opened. This was to coincide with the opening of the CMR Goonbarrow branch to Gunheath and Carbean. Also, Wheal Henry siding opened in the area adjacent to Rosevear siding. This was followed in later years by a series of sidings serving clay driers at Rocks, Wheal Anna and Hallivet. A new signal box replaced the 1893 product in 1909 which, at the time of writing, remains in use. The sidings on the south side of the signal box were added at the same time. An up siding was added in 1924. Not only does it survive but is still has some of the original chairs holding the track in place.

By 1930 seasonal passenger traffic was heavy and with more china clay trains operating than ever before pathing problems occurred in the area. To combat the increasing number of trains and the constant flow of holidaymakers to the resort of Newquay the GWR set about doubling the track between Goonbarrow Jn and Bugle. Work was completed on 20th July, 1930. The track between the two points was straight with a slight curve to the north approaching Bugle station. Just before Bugle at Mollinis level crossing a signal box was installed. Bugle was once another important railway centre, which was also subject to a number of changes over the years.

The original Treffry Tramway from Ponts Mill terminated at Mollinis, near Bugle station. The name Bugle is in fact derived from the bugle in the badge of the Cornish Regiment whose soldiers regularly frequented the Bugle Inn as they traversed the main Bodmin to St Austell road. At the site of the two down sidings at Bugle there was once a substantial clay loading wharf where horse-drawn wagons from nearby pits, such as Single Rose, would unload. Although long abandoned the wharf could still be seen a decade ago but new housing now covers the site. There was an up side goods yard that handled general produce, ranging from coal to cattle, and in 1874 and 1893 respectively the CMR opened branch lines to Carbis Wharf and Wheal Rose. In 1874 they also extended the railway to Roche and across Goss Moor to link up with the Hendra to Newquay tramway, at Bodmin Road Junction, later St Dennis Junction.

When the passenger service between Fowey and Newquay commenced in 1876 Bugle had a single platform with a CMR signal box at the east end. This was the last CMR box to survive - until 1916. The original wooden station buildings were allegedly once lived in by the navvies building the line. There were minor track

Another Plymouth Railway Circle railtour operated on 28th April, 1962 to commemorate the end of steam in the area. With the old loading wharf on the left and the island platform and up goods yard on the right, '4500' class tanks Nos. 5531 (1927 series) and 4564 (1906 series) pose on the Carbis and Wheal Rose line. The first of the two stacks belongs to the closed Wheal Hope kiln.   *Terry Nicholls*

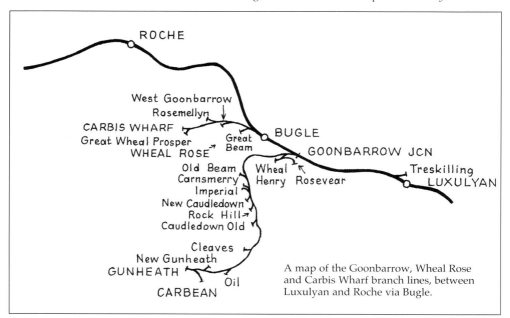

A map of the Goonbarrow, Wheal Rose and Carbis Wharf branch lines, between Luxulyan and Roche via Bugle.

It would be a strange thing indeed if a town called Bugle did not have a brass band! It is said that the town is named after the bugle incorporated in the badge of the Cornish Regiment whose soldiers frequented the establishment now known as the Bugle Inn. From 1876, when the CMR passenger service commenced, the band could have travelled by rail to attend special events.

Author's Collection

Photographing a train on the Carbis Wharf branch was very difficult because workings were very much 'as and when required'. To be in position on 5th May, 1989 it was necessary to be at Bugle station at 06.50. With no run-round facility at Carbis the single 80 tonne 'Tiger' wagon had to be propelled from Goonbarrow Junction, the out and back trip having to be achieved before the first Newquay branch train arrived. Just three months before closure No. 37669 has just reversed across Mollinis crossing on the down run.

Author

It looks as though there is a complicated shunt going on in this Edwardian view of Bugle station. There are wagons in the up goods yard, at the single branch platform road, on the Carbis freight line and at the china clay loading wharf but without any sign of an engine, although there appears to be some steam behind the original CMR signal box. The latter was replaced in 1916. Note the crane and the casks awaiting loading.   *Author's Collection*

Bugle station *circa* 1950. At this time both platform faces of the post-1930 island platform were in use, the GWR signal box at Mollinis (*top right*) has replaced the CMR example, the down wharf is just surviving and the up goods yard seems busy, with cattle wagons and box vans visible. Five passengers alight from an up train at lunchtime.   *Author's Collection*

Another 40 years or so has passed at Bugle in this fascinating quartet of views. In this depressing scene from August 1992 Regional Railways 'bubble' car No. 122100 runs through the station non-stop, there being nobody interested in alighting or boarding. The up goods yard has been reclaimed by nature, the main station building has gone, as has the signal box and the double track to Goonbarrow. The down branch line and both the Carbis Wharf and loading dock lines have also been lifted. *Author*

Completing a 100 years of 'development' at Bugle is this 8th September, 2007 view with modern housing having been built on the up goods yard site and, out of frame, on the down side as well. Trees have covered the old down branch trackbed and goods lines, a small bus shelter provides the total creature comforts and a single lamp provides illumination. Passing the station is a Midland Main Line HST set, which was on hire to Virgin Trains and working through from Manchester to Newquay. *Author*

Over the decades the author has spent very many hours at Bugle station and has observed that regular passengers are virtually non-existent. However, a most remarkable sight took place on Saturday 25th September, 1993 when a full IC125 set forming the 09.29 (Saturdays only) Plymouth to Newquay, which stopped at intermediate stations by request, was 'hailed' by this elderly lady, seen boarding the 125 mph unit! This could happen only on the Newquay branch. The unit would return as an up express later in the day.   *Author*

Over six months later, in March 1994, the author was again at Bugle simply to photograph the class '150/2' unit working the Newquay branch. Most unusually the late lunchtime ex-Newquay train stopped at Bugle and the only passenger to alight was the same elderly lady dressed in the same coat and shoes! This fact was only realised when compiling this book, some 15 years later. No. 150219 will shortly leave for Par and Plymouth.   *Author*

Towards the end of its days and with half a dozen photographers on hand to record the event, one of the surviving class '50s', No. 50008 *Thunderer*, is seen approaching a derelict looking Bugle station with an enthusiasts special from Manchester on 26th January, 1991. No. 50015 *Valiant* was on the rear of the crowded train. The large ECC Rocks works can be seen behind Mollinis crossing.   *Author*

Approaching Bugle from the Newquay direction in March 1991 is class '121' unit No. 55000. The train guard has joined the driver in the cab, which on its exterior has two exhaust pipes following the window frame line, taking spent gases to the roof line. On the left is the abandoned Carbis Wharf freight line that had closed some 18 months earlier and would soon be lifted. Note the fixed distant signal, by 1994 this had been replaced by a warning board, see page 192.

see page 192.

Author

This bizarre scene at the east end of Bugle station shows one of the most remarkable 'seminar' shots ever recorded on the Newquay branch. In the dying days of the class '52' 'Western' diesel hydraulics a large band of followers travelled behind these fine locomotives at every opportunity. The last chance to visit Newquay with a 'Western' was on 4th December, 1976 when the author organized the 'Western China Clay' railtour. The train had run from Paddington overnight, also visiting Falmouth and Carne Point, Fowey. The locomotive is the magnificent No. D1056 *Western Sultan*, which would be withdrawn just 11 days later. *Author's Collection*

changes in 1910 at the west end of the station and an additional siding was laid in the up goods yard. In preparation for the doubling of the track from Goonbarrow a single island platform was built, giving two platform faces. Access for passengers was by steps from the main road overbridge, which was modified to take the extra track. Bugle was at its peak in the late 1930s.

After World War II some of the clay dries never recovered, more buses and lorries came onto the roads, rail traffic dwindled and by 1964 rationalisation was in prospect. The Wheal Rose branch closed on 29th November, 1964, the same time as the up goods yard and effectively the line to Goonbarrow was singled for branch line working. The east end crossover was also removed. The other track (on the 1930 double track alignment) was used only for freight to Bugle down wharf or Carbis. The signal box located at Mollinis Crossing, at the up end of the station, was reduced to ground frame status and only a single platform face was used. In later years the down wharf sidings were removed and from 1973 Mollinis Crossing was 'open' as the gates were removed and the ground frame abolished.

After 1973 it was difficult to imagine that the scene could become much bleaker with just the two single lines from Goonbarrow taking trains to Newquay and very rarely to Carbis Wharf, without a siding or crossover in sight. However, from the end of August 1989 the Carbis Wharf line closed to traffic, leaving only a rotting hut on the single platform at Bugle station. In the 21st century the hut was replaced by a glass bus shelter, new lighting was installed and the platform resurfaced. Building developers moved in and having purchased old railway land on both sides of the line a housing estate appeared. The Bugle of 2008 is barely recognisable compared with days of old and the single line now runs between these houses but at least the frugal branch service still runs!

The Wheal Rose Branch

In common with the Goonbarrow branch the Wheal Rose branch was a late arrival. The name is capable of being confused with the East Wheal Rose line, the terminus of the original 1849 Newquay Tramway line from Tolcarn Junction, near Newquay. The branch was little more than a half-mile long siding which left the Newquay branch just beyond Bugle station. The branch opened in October 1893, although part of the line to the old Wheal Virgin Air Dry may have been opened some years before.

A single crossing gate protected the branch and this had to be opened by the train crew before proceeding. The main reason for the gate was a dirt road which crossed the line just beyond the St Austell to Bodmin road bridge. On the down side of the branch, just beyond the junction, was Wheal Hope Clay Driers (also known as Treleavens Kiln), followed by East Goonbarrow Kiln on the up side. Both had rail loading facilities facing the branch without individual sidings. There followed a shallow cutting and junction. The old line curving to the south served Wheal Virgin Air Dry and Boss Allen's Timber Wharf. The primary branch then looped, with the down track serving Martins Goonbarrow and Great Beam No. 1 and No. 2 kilns. All of these were of the old coal-fired pan dry type, most of which passed into oblivion during the 1960s. The Great Beam sidings were set in concrete and beyond the loop a single track continued to a stop block that was located but a few hundred yards from the Carbis Wharf branch.

The short Wheal Rose branch was little more than a ½ mile long siding. It was opened by the CMR in 1893 and it served several installations. Seen shortly after closure in 1964 this view down the branch finds Martin's Goonbarrow, Great Beam and Wheal Rose driers on the left, beside the loop and beyond.   *Maurice Dart*

This photograph taken at Carbis Bridge shows the appalling condition of the track, which was one of the reasons for the demise of the Carbis Wharf branch line. With just weeks left before the last train No. 37669 arrives to collect a single 'Tiger' wagon loaded with china clay for the Armitage Shanks company in Scotland. After closure in August 1989 Carbis Bridge, seen here, was demolished and the Roche to Bugle road alignment improved. The two stacks are located at the closed kilns of Rosemellyn (*left*) and West Goonbarrow (*right*), both once rail-served.

Author

One of the last wagons to leave Carbis Wharf was 80 tonne 'Tiger' No. TRL 11600, which was on hire to the Goonvean & Rostowrack China Clay Company by Tiger Rail Leasing. The wagon would be filled with china clay using a front-loading tractor. The track seems to disappear into the undergrowth down the short 1 in 44 gradient towards Carbis Bridge. *Author*

The line formally closed from 29th November, 1964. The track was left *in situ*, pending the outcome of evaluation of the transportation of acid by rail tanker to Wheal Rose but this came to nothing. The line gradually decayed and it became buried under a mixture of mica, stent and overgrowth. It is still possible to detect a little track just beyond the junction at Bugle and the track set in concrete at Old Beam (on private land). Curiously, despite years of research, no photograph of a locomotive on the line could be found. In 1988/89 the last two stacks at the junction were felled leaving only the Great Beam stacks as testimony to the once great industrial activity in the area. Wheal Rose china clay was, unusually, still laid out in blocks to dry in sheds at the turn of the 20th century but Wheal Rose and Great Beam both became part of the vast West of England and Great Beam China Clay & Stone Company who introduced more modern techniques. The company was later absorbed by English China Clays.

The Carbis Wharf Branch

The Bugle area was rich in china clay works and by the mid-1850s the transportation of an increasing yield was becoming a problem. As recorded elsewhere, the dependence upon horses drawing three ton wagons over very poor quality roads was slow and costly. A line of just over a mile from Bugle to Carbis was incorporated in the 1873 Cornwall Minerals Railway Act. Treffry had already reached Mollinis in 1844 and substantial amounts of clay were loaded from the wharf at the terminus. However, an extension of the railhead to the growing Rosemellyn clay dries and Great Wheal Prosper Clay Kiln was attractive for the clay producers, who in many cases were also the landowners of the envisaged trackbed.

By February 1874 work had still not been commenced on the line to Carbis (then Carbus) nevertheless it was ready for service, together with the rest of the CMR, on 1st June, 1874. William West's foundry at St Blazey produced the ironwork and a suitable inscription could be seen in the main iron support span beneath the weight-restricted Carbis Bridge, until it was demolished in the 1990s. Although towards the end of the short branch there was a 1 in 44 gradient the rest was near level and construction was relatively straightforward.

In the words of the original Act the line was to terminate at a point near Great St George Clay Works. At the end of the line accommodation was tight with the single-track line dividing into two for the last few yards to the end of a loading dock. One of the two lines served Great Wheal Prosper Clay Kiln, where the clay from the works of that name was dried, and the other was a general wharf where clay and other merchandise was loaded onto railway wagons. The two tracks at the terminus were so short that a run-round loop could not be provided, with the result that for the 115 years of the line's existence trains were always propelled on the outward (or down) run. In 1901 the length of the sidings was doubled and the agreement between the GWR and the Great Wheal Prosper China Stone and Clay Company shows the work cost precisely £331 16s. 7d.! The single point was moved nearer to Carbis Bridge but there was still no run-round provision. Originally a catch point was located on the west side

Just two years after closure the Carbis Wharf branch line started to become overwhelmed by foliage and gorse bushes. This is the point where the sidings to both West Goonbarrow (*left*) and Rosemellyn (*right*) china clay pan driers diverged from the main branch but it was no longer possible to 'walk the branch'. *Author*

By 1992 the Carbis branch track was being lifted by this digger/excavator, which is seen astride the old line at Rosemellyn crossing. The line had served its purpose for 115 years but gradually all of the works it served closed. The branch was only just over one mile in length but was a great favourite of the author. *Author*

This was the classic view of Carbis Wharf, as seen from Carbis road bridge with the aid of a medium telephoto lens. A Railfreight class '37' has just deposited a 32 tonne PGA wagon at Great Wheal Prosper Clay Kiln. This was the very last coal-fired pan dry/kiln in operation in Cornwall, with the coal visible on the left. The loading chute is for the Goonvean Company's lorries. In the background is the defunct Carbis Brickworks and its three foliage-covered bee hive kilns.

Author

of Carbis Bridge but in later years it was between the wharf and Rosemellyn Gates.

Shortly after opening, a siding at 288 miles 56 chains was provided to serve Rosemellyn Clay Works. The works produced fine quality clay, reputed to be the best available, which in 1877 commanded a price 50 per cent higher than its rivals. By the turn of the century the single track siding into the works had also been doubled. By 1912 a further substantial pan dry called West Goonbarrow had been opened, this time on the south side of the line. The junction for the West Goonbarrow siding was at 288 miles 54 chains; just 40 yards east of the Rosemellyn siding. ECLP acquired the Rosemellyn Works in 1936 and it was subsequently to be the first of the sidings to close, in 1948. West Goonbarrow closed in the early 1960s, although unlike Rosemellyn the track was still *in situ* in 1968. In the 1950s and 1960s it was observed that there were some vintage South Devon Railway chairs in the trackwork at Carbis Wharf - a leftover from the Victorian era!

The branch has always been worked as a siding; from Bugle between 1874 and 1973 and from Goonbarrow Junction from 1973 until the line closed in 1989. For many years the Carbis branch had a daily train which would propel empty clay wagons and loaded coal wagons to the various works and reverse the situation on the return journey. The line was worked by small 0-6-0 pannier tanks and on occasions two locomotives were used. The line had dedicated brake vans, which were stabled at Goonbarrow Junction. In recent years the token for the line had simply 'Carbis Siding' engraved in the alloy.

Once West Goonbarrow closed the only works served was the Great Wheal Prosper Clay Kiln, which was acquired by the Goonvean & Rostowrack China Clay Company in 1937. Gradually the output from this site was diverted from rail to road and a special loader for road transport was installed by the company, while retaining the rail option. This private company was one of the few not to have been subjected to the progressive ECC (now Imerys) takeovers and is the only company other than Imerys to have its own railhead. The principal shareholder and an extensive landowner in the area is Lord Falmouth. The service gradually dwindled from daily to weekly, as and when required. In the early 1980s there were reports that the line required renewal. In the early 1980s there were inaccurate reports that the line had closed and this seemed to coincide with the changeover on the long-distance trains from the wooden-bodied, short wheelbase, vacuum-braked PBA wagons to the new French-built, long wheelbase, 'Tiger' bogie wagons, in 1982.

It was decided that the track could support the weight of the new 80 tonne (gross) air braked wagons and the 107 ton class '37' locomotives. A Tiger wagon from the Tiger Railcar Leasing 'ECC International' fleet was used to convey clay to the Armitage Shanks Company in Glasgow. Between 1982 and June 1989 this dedicated Tiger wagon, No. TRL 11600, was used on the Goonvean circuit, which normally saw the wagon traversing the branch every three to four weeks. On rare occasions, and between June and August 1989, smaller 32 tonne PGA wagons were used. On occasions, the single wagon would be taken to Carbis where it would be loaded the same day, although sometimes it would be a next-day collection. While at Carbis wooden chocks were placed under the wheels of the wagon to prevent a runaway down the 1 in 44 gradient towards Rosemellyn

Crossing. The railway wagon was loaded by a front-loading tractor. For a very brief period during the 1988/89 winter, PGA wagons used the line on a weekly basis, no doubt reflecting customer demands.

Operationally the Carbis branch was a nuisance to BR. Especially after St Dennis Junction signal box closed it was difficult to find a suitable path for the branch freight. Due to the crossing mechanism at Mollinis, near Bugle, it was not possible for more than one train to be west of Goonbarrow Junction at the same time, even though the parallel Carbis line was all but separate from the 'main' Newquay branch (it was effectively the old down line of the former double-track section as far as Bugle). Accordingly, the Carbis service normally ran between 6.30 am and 7.15 am, before the first branch passenger train from Par reached Goonbarrow Jn. With slick working there was also a lunchtime path at 1.25 pm. With the slow speed restriction, gate opening, catch point changing and wagon coupling, a run to Carbis was time consuming, taking about half an hour for the two-mile out and back journey.

A number of circumstances contributed to closure. The condition of the track in places gave cause for concern and it was clear that substantial sums would need to be spent on renewal. For the volume of traffic the return on capital would have taken decades to recover. As already mentioned, the workings were operationally inconvenient and BR had deliberately not included the branch in the weed-killing itinerary for a couple of years. The Goonvean Company had installed a pipeline from Great Wheal Prosper to their other railhead at Trelavour, near Parkandillack, and the autumn of 1989 saw the interface equipment ready for service. There were also health and safety considerations because, latterly, train crews had to contend with a waterlogged track, clay slime and brambles. Although these problems could have all been remedied they would have exceeded the small fixed maintenance charge paid by Goonvean. Eventually even the 107 tonne class '37s' slipped badly on the grass over the track and it was clear the end was in sight. Closure was obviously on the cards because in the early months of 1989, following a gate-crushing contretemps, brand-new wooden crossing gates were fitted at Rosemellyn Crossing!

It is amusing to relate the story of the Carbis gateway. Effectively this gateway was an aperture in a hedgerow which was used by the Goonvean and Rostowrack China Clay Company for coal deliveries to the Great Wheal Prosper Clay Kiln. Lorries would use the unpaved track to provide coal for what was the last coal-fired pan clay dry in Cornwall. Under an old 1943 agreement the clay company paid the GWR and later BR an annual rent of 10s. 6d. for use of the road. No less than 45 years later BR woke up to the peppercorn rent and demanded £15 per annum from the clay company - a 28-fold increase!

The very last wagon arrived for loading at Carbis on the morning of Friday 25th August, 1989 and it was collected the same day at 5.25 pm. There followed a three month trial where, pending the completion of the aforementioned pipeline, Great Wheal Prosper's clay was delivered by road to Trelavour for loading into railway wagons. The trial was successful. Thus ended 115 years of railway history. The Carbis line was the last of its kind. It not only oozed with atmosphere and had eccentric workings but it served an old dry with a typical Cornish stack, which still carried its smoke and steam into the sky. The line

In the final years both road and rail were used to transport the china clay output from the Great Wheal Prosper Clay Kiln. Eventually the clay was conveyed by pipeline in slurry form to the Goonvean Company's Trelavour works near Parkandillack. In this view the kiln is becoming dilapidated and maintenance levels would appear to be low. In September 1988 we see a Goonvean lorry being loaded.   *Author*

never had a passenger service, although an enthusiasts special or two traversed the line. The little line will be held in the memory with considerable affection.

Since closure and removal of the track Carbis Bridge has been removed and Rosemellyn Crossing gates are no more. Vegetation has now consumed the old branch alignment in many places and nature has reclaimed much of the land. The old stacks at Carbis, Rosemellyn and West Goonbarrow are still standing but they are all silent. However after closure Colin and Anne Coad acquired the Grade II listed Great Wheal Prosper Clay Kiln and they have tastefully converted the old building into living and holiday accommodation, preserving many of the key features. They have also saved and converted the adjacent Carbis Brick Works, its beehive kilns and its unusual rectangular brick stack. Manicured gardens now occupy the space taken up by the clay trains! The site is well worth a visit.

In a truly remarkable 'before and after' comparison, this September 2006 photograph shows the complete restoration and conversion of the Great Wheal Prosper Clay Kiln into a family home and an overnight and holiday accommodation complex. The work was undertaken by Colin and Anne Coad and their family, in a style that was sympathetic and compatible with the building's Grade II listed status.   *Author*

One of the wilder areas in topographical terms between Bugle and St Dennis Junction is Goss Moor. Half way across the moor is Tregoss Moor crossing that once boasted a signal box and crossing gates. However, once a section of track beyond the crossing was singled and automatic barriers were installed the diminutive structure was demolished. Lewis Cross holds up the single line token in the 1950s. *Charlie Saundercock/Courtesy M. Dart*

This interesting view from the footplate was taken in the era when diesel was replacing steam. On 23rd September, 1960 'County' class 4-6-0 No. 1002 *County of Berks*, working the 12.40 pm Par to Newquay, is held at signals on the approach to St Dennis Junction while 'D63XX' class No. D6322 accelerates the 12.50 pm Newquay to Par away from the passing loop. *R.C. Riley/Courtesy Transport Treasury*

Chapter Fifteen

Roche-St Dennis Jn
and the Retew Branch

Roche to St Dennis Junction

The line from Bugle, once clear of the junction with the Carbis branch, heads in a north-westerly direction towards Roche. This section of track was always single as far as the loop at Roche station. The track is level for the first mile or so beyond Bugle but then it climbs steeply to the summit of the line just beyond Roche station. The line leaves china clay country and runs through pleasant rolling farmland. As mentioned earlier, this section of track was not opened by the CMR until 1874 and it was 1876 before passenger trains served the community.

Roche station was originally known as Holywell but the name was changed to Victoria in 1879, reflecting the name of the nearby hamlet. A third name was used from November 1904 when the station became Roche, the name of the village some three-quarters of a mile to the south. Roche is derived from the French name for rock and in fact it is Roche Rock which is the most famous of nearby landmarks. The 100 ft high rock has the ancient St Michael's Chapel built upon it and it contains a hermit's cell. The area is strewn with huge granite boulders (*see photograph page 107*).

The station was served by a single platform in CMR days but eventually a second platform was provided on the up side and a signal box controlled the passing loop and the sidings, which comprised the up side goods yard. Additional freight sidings were provided by 1920 and on 3rd July, 1936 the passing loop was extended to take full-length trains. On summer Saturdays, when some of the trains to Newquay had banking locomotives from Par, many engines were detached at Roche. Roche is one of the quieter stations on the branch; it never possessed any grandiose buildings and its decline occurred at the same time as other stations on the line. Goods facilities ceased at the end of 1964 and the passing loop was removed and the signal box taken out of use in 1965. From 3rd January, 1965 the down line was taken out of use, but in July 1965 BR decided it would be the down line which would be retained and the up line and sidings were removed in October that year.

The line continues through a cutting and under the old A30 road to reach Goss Moor. The railway crosses the old A30 on a narrow, low, girder bridge that has seen many high commercial vehicles 'reduced in height'. After crossing the old A30 the line descends from its 'skew' on an embankment which, during construction, required thousands of cubic yards of spoil from other excavation sites on the CMR. This gorse covered expanse is a wild and windswept area, steeped in history, at an elevation of over 400 ft above sea level. The line then runs across the moor for three miles to reach St Dennis Junction.

At the 292 mile 31 chain mark there is a level crossing called Tregoss Moor. The gates were controlled from a small cabin opened in 1914, which was replaced by a signal box on 10th September, 1921, when the two miles from Tregoss to St

Opened in 1876, the original CMR Roche station was called Holywell but was changed to Victoria from 1879. Finally, in November 1904, it became Roche after the major village located about one mile to the south of the station site. Under the auspices of the GWR a passing loop was later provided plus a small signal box and a goods yard. This 1950s view shows the up platform on the left with a couple of box wagons in the goods yard.   *Author's Collection*

Additional freight sidings were provided by 1920 and in July 1936 the passing loop was extended to accommodate full length passenger trains. However the decline started in 1964 when goods facilities were withdrawn and just one year later the passing loop was removed and the signal box closed. The down platform and the small wooden shelter (*left*) survive but there is now no trace of the old up platform or the buildings seen here.   *Lens of Sutton*

Passing a rather forlorn Roche station without attracting any revenue is single power car No. 55006 forming a Par to Newquay branch working in April 1991. Passengers must cross the line by a foot crossing to gain access to the platform, where two platform lamps and a small waiting shelter are provided. Note the 290½ mile post, the mileage from Paddington via Bristol. The goods yard was once located in the foliage behind the unit. *Author*

One of the most photographed locations on the Newquay branch is where the line crossed the old A30 road on a low 14 ft 3 in. headroom girder bridge. Over the years innumerable lorries have been part demolished as they ignored the low bridge warning signs. An interesting visitor on a dull day in April 1987 was a grubby No. 37207 *William Cookworthy* hauling the annual Chipman's weedkilling train from Newquay to Par.   *Author*

On 24th January, 1991 single power car No. 55026 climbs up from Goss Moor to the A30 road bridge with the 12.37 pm Newquay to Par. Since 2007 the A30 has now been diverted away from this alignment following the opening of a new dual carriageway to the north of the site.   *Author*

St Dennis Junction, originally Bodmin Road Junction, was once an important railway centre where lines from Par, Newquay, Drinnick Mill/Burngullow and the Retew branch all converged. The signal box was located immediately behind the leading coach of this Newquay-bound holiday train from Paddington. With the remains of the passing loop on the left a work-stained No. 50041 *Bulwark* negotiates the speed restricted curve on 3rd October, 1987. The sidings in the background were later removed leaving a rather desolate scene.   *Author*

The author was privileged to have a footplate ride on 'Western' class '52' diesel-hydraulic No. 1058 *Western Nobleman* from Newquay to Par on 6th August, 1976. This was the view from the cab as driver Prophet slowed his train to 15 mph at St Dennis Junction in order to collect the single line token from the signalman for the run to Goonbarrow Junction.   *Author*

The author's very first trip over the Newquay branch was not until June 1970, during an all line railrover. Here the driver of a three-car dmu successfully collects from the St Dennis Junction signalman the token that gives him authority to proceed along the single line to Newquay. In recent years trains passed here only on summer Saturdays and predictably the box was abolished in December 1986.   *Author*

Long after St Dennis Junction signal box was demolished and most of the once busy sidings were lifted, the site was used only as a ballast tip and, for a short period of time in 1991 to remove the inner lining of the CDA china clay wagons, which was breaking-up and contaminating the clay. Here the driver, second man and shunter pose for the camera in front of main line-liveried No. 37420 *The Scottish Hosteller* that had been re-allocated from Scotland to Plymouth, Laira.   *Author*

Dennis Junction were doubled. Trains passing this crossing once included not only the Par to Newquay branch trains but clay wagons to and from St Dennis Junction, from both the Retew branch and the Newquay & Cornwall Junction Railway (N&CJR) line to Drinnick Mill and Burngullow. The signal box was reduced to ground frame status on 3rd January, 1965 when the track was again singled and was closed altogether on 25th May, 1973, when the crossing became open with flashing-light warning signals and a railway speed restriction.

St Dennis Junction was once an important focal point for the Newquay branch and branches. Originally known as Bodmin Road Junction, because the Truro to Bodmin road passed nearby (the name had no connection with the distant main line Bodmin Road station), lines from Newquay, Par, Retew and Burngullow all met at St Dennis Junction. The village of St Dennis was nearly two miles away to the south-east. The site saw its first tramway in 1857 when Treffry opened his rail link between Hendra and Newquay as a means for shipping china clay from the pits he owned south and east of St Dennis. But it was the CMR which opened up the area with the completion of the line from Bugle, the N&CJR line to Drinnick Mill and the new Retew branch to Melangoose Mill.

The track layout on the south-west side of the junction was quite complex with not only the signal box but also five ground frames to control movements. However, St Dennis was not a marshalling yard as such and most of the track work comprised various loops for locomotives to run round their trains. All clay trains from St Blazey to Retew or Drinnick Mill had to reverse at St Dennis Junction and on the Retew branch, banking locomotives were removed there for up trains. A pair of sidings curving away to the east served as a tip for many years and spoil trains comprised of Grampus and Turbot wagons containing old ballast and waste discharged their loads at St Dennis.

The Retew branch was an 1874 CMR original, although the line down to Melangoose Mill was extended by 1½ miles to Meledor Mill by the GWR in 1912. There were 20 clay driers and other industrial installations served by the branch in just over four miles. In this exceptional view at Retew siding, looking north-east, a GWR wagon is being unloaded, with the spoil being taken by horse and cart to Wheal Remfry tip. The stack of Retew clay kiln can be seen, *top left*.

Cornish Studies Library/Courtesy M. Dart

Most of the clay works served were of the older type, producing small volumes that were dried in traditional coal-fired pan kilns. Half had already closed by 1950 and from that date it was a case of gradual decline. The last commercial traffic on the line was in September 1980 and the last movement by rail seems to have taken place in 1982. The weeds rapidly took over and by June 1989 this was the mica covered scene looking south at Melangoose Mill. The former branch is on the left and the loading area and linhay of Wheal Benallick on the right.   *Author*

From 1965 St Dennis was regularly used as a passing loop by up and down branch trains and the signalman was kept busy exchanging single-line tokens with train drivers. However, with the closure of the St Dennis Junction to Parkandillack section of the N&CJR line in 1966 and the gradual but relentless closure of the various clay works on the Retew branch from 1965 to the late 1970s, freight traffic all but disappeared. The Newquay branch lost its pick-up freight in 1964 and by the early 1980s St Dennis Junction was used as a passing place only on summer Saturdays. Predictably, the signal box closed in December 1986 leaving Goonbarrow Junction as the only passing place on the Newquay branch between St Blazey and Newquay. Newquay signal box also closed in October 1987 and, except for the St Dennis ground frame and a couple of rarely used sidings, rationalisation was virtually complete. However, it was only after the removal of all remaining track in the 1990s, except of course the single Newquay branch line, that the desecration of the once busy St Dennis Junction was complete.

The Retew Branch

The branch was a Cornwall Minerals Railway original. In the 1873 Act their railway No. 3 was shown as the Ratew [*sic*] branch and was described thus:

> A branch railway 2 miles and 1 furlong in length, commencing in the parish of Saint Columb Major by a junction with the existing New Quay Railway at a point about 260 yards (measured along the said railway) south eastward of the turnpike road from Truro to Bodmin, passing through the parish of St Denis [*sic*], and terminating in the parish of St Enoder at or near the Melangoose Clay works. The said railway is designated by the number 7 on the said plans.

The railway referred to was, of course, the Newquay Tramway line to Hendra and the road was the main A30 which still crosses the line at St Dennis Junction, then known as Bodmin Road Junction. Shortly after the start of the branch the line picked up the course if the infant River Fal and this facilitated the chosen alignment of the remainder of the branch, which opened on 1st June, 1874.

St Dennis Junction is on the edge of Goss Moor and after passing the sidings there the line descended to Gaverigan the first of the crossings, across the St Dennis to Indian Queens road (*see map page 224*). Continuing into the Fal Valley, at 1 mile and 55 chains the line fell at just over 1 in 200 to reach Trerice Crossing where, twice per day, gates were closed to the few vehicles using the Treviscoe to Indian Queens road. Immediately after the crossing the first siding was encountered on the up side. It was known as Trerice siding and an old brickworks on the site was an early casualty amongst the 20 or so sidings which once infested the next 2½ miles of 'main' branch line. The 'post-brickworks' Trerice siding closed in 1966.

A mere 16 chains further on, on the eastern (down) side of the line, was McLaren's siding, effectively a loop off McLaren's North at 1 mile 62 chains to McLaren's South at 1 mile 77 chains. The siding was opposite Wheal Remfry, McLaren's other name. It too succumbed in 1966. Falling still, at 1 in 149, Trerice New siding branched off at 2 miles and 4 chains on the down side, formed a loop and rejoined the branch at New Trerice South, 180 yards further on. It was taken out of use in 1966. At the same point, but on the up side, a siding (removed in 1972) served the Fal Valley or Retew Works. The branch and the siding crossed the third level crossing of Retew at 2 miles and 35 chains, with only the siding crossing the River Fal.

At this point it must be said that in addition to the Retew branch and the many sidings serving various works, several clay works had their own 'internal' tramway systems to move clay or waste products and their track layout was often changed from month to month. Most were narrow gauge but because many faded away years ago surprisingly little has been written on the subject. It is known that two tramways were active at Wheal Remfry. Just beyond Retew Crossing a siding (opened in 1939 and closed in 1973) serving South Fraddon (or Great Halwyn), branched away on the down side at 2 miles 25 chains, while at 2 miles 27 chains there were once loops on either side of the branch: Retew Loop on the down side and New Halwyn on the up. They rejoined the branch at 2 miles 34 chains and 2 miles 36 chains respectively.

Another fascinating aspect of the many works in this and other areas is the precise naming of the site. Often the railway had its name for the siding, the clay company another, while in some instances local names were used, sometimes reflecting mere nicknames. There was nothing ambiguous about the once busy Wheal Benallick siding or the Melangoose Clay Works at 2 miles 36 chains. This siding made facing and trailing connections on the up side of the branch, effectively forming a loop. After Melangoose Mill siding the line dropped away at a steep 1 in 40 for the short distance to Melangoose Mill Public sidings on the up (west) side. Adjacent to this site, at right angles on the south side, was the large Anchor Works and siding, which with Melangoose, closed in the 1972/1973 period. This location was significant in that it was the original terminus of the line. It is interesting to note that by railway milepost the distance to Melangoose is greater than that recorded in the Act. Early in the present century there was much development in this area and new clay works were opening and old ones were expanding rapidly. Accordingly, in 1912, the GWR extended the branch by just over 1½ miles to Meledor Mill.

After Melangoose the line turned quite sharply towards the south-east. One of the Melangoose Mill sidings dropped to connect into Grove sidings (closed 1963), and from there a trailing siding descended back into the rear of Melangoose Mill at 1 in 100. Apparently, a capstan was used to winch wagons back up to Grove siding. The clay driers here had deep wooden chutes which were angled down into the railway wagons for loading. At 2 miles 67 chains, and still falling at 1 in 40, the extensions of Grove siding trailed in, which was immediately followed by Virginia siding which also diverged on the up side. Here, the line ran through the delightful Treviscoe Wood with the massive Virginia China Clay Works to the south.

Virginia sidings were themselves something of a branch line extending over a quarter of a mile towards the clay loading point. The works also had its own tramway but there has been extensive expansion in recent years and since closure in 1965, all trace of the sidings has gone. The River Fal was again crossed at Virginia Bridge followed by the fourth crossing. Continuing at 1 in 40 West Treviscoe siding was reached at the 3 miles 3 chains mark on the down side. It was taken out of use on 5th March, 1965. The line continued to follow the river in pleasant wooded country with two crossings of the Fal before Tolbenny (sometimes known as Virginia) Crossing was reached. On the down side, until closed in 1972, was Tolbenny siding at the 3 miles 44 chains mark, and just beyond was the north end of Meledor Mill Loop North. Branching away from the 1 in 95 loop on the up side was Burgotha siding (which had been out of use for many years before the branch closed). The River Fal was again crossed to serve Melbur Driers and Mill on the up (west) side. Towards the end of the branch Meledor Mill was served on the up side and the main branch ended at Meledor Crossing, 4 miles and 2 chains from the junction.

However, that was not quite the end of the story for a siding continued across the road, which was gated, to New Meledor (opened 1929/closed 1965) and Collins Rotary Drier. At the very end the line was set in concrete, as it was in many of the driers. It should be added that at times there has been confusion over the opening and closing dates of the multitude of sidings. Some were closed so long ago that even railwaymen of the immediate post-war period do not remember them. Sometimes the closure date has no obvious link to the date that the last train worked the siding.

The gates at all the level crossings were worked by the train crews. Nearly all the sidings were controlled by single-lever ground frames and there were no signal boxes on the branch. In the absence of passenger trains there were no facing point locks with the sole exception of Tolbenny sidings. Tolbenny and Virginia sidings had multiple-lever ground frames. There were restrictions on motive power using the line, but St Blazey's small 0-6-0 pannier tanks and the

The Retew branch followed the course of the infant River Fal. The line never had a passenger service in its 108 year history. In the early days a little china clay traffic went to Newquay but the majority was shipped from the ports on the south coast. These 'platforms' are in fact loading wharves at Meledor Mill in July 1986, some six years after closure.   *Author*

small-wheeled Prairies presented no problems. The maximum permitted speed anywhere on the branch was 15 mph. On occasions two locomotives worked a single train onto the branch but in this event they had to be at either end of the train. Locomotives were not permitted at some sidings and so wagons could only be left or removed by means of a rake of wagons being between the engine and the relevant wagons. At some steeply graded sidings stop bars were bolted to the track to prevent runaways. With so many sidings to serve it was not surprising that only two trains a day were booked in the busiest years of the line.

With such activity it is not unreasonable to ponder over the reasons for the line's closure. In the first place most of the older driers were the classic coal-fired pan dries where a fire at one end of the long clay dry building was drawn by a tall stack at the other end, resulting in hot air passing beneath the clay which was spread over the floor (or pan) of the dry, after having surplus water removed in filter presses. Such driers were replaced by more modern methods such as rotary driers and buells, and so gradually the old inefficient, coal-consuming, low-output pan driers were all closed.

There had also been significant improvements in pipeline technology and clay in slurry form could be transported for a dozen or more miles to distant large driers, such as those at Par Harbour. Furthermore, the entire scale of the industry changed over the years and the small clay works were gradually phased out. Another important factor was the amalgamation and takeover of the various clay companies with, for example, English China Clays taking over control of more than 100 clay companies between 1919 and 1966. This naturally led to rationalisation in order to maximise the use of resources and eliminate duplication of effort and under-capacity.

Photographs from the 1950s show the line to be partly grass-covered and in a state of decline. One by one the works closed and consequently traffic dwindled. By the end of the 1950s only 10 intermediate sidings survived. By the end of the 1960s railwaymen observed that there was little traffic but, surprisingly, clay continued to be moved from the Retew branch until the late 1970s. The last recorded traffic from Collins Driers at the end of the branch was in September 1980. The line was traversed by the annual weedkilling train in the summer of 1981 and in mid-March 1982 a locomotive and a van worked to the end of the branch and back. This was the last movement before most of the track was lifted in 1983. A few weed-covered sidings remain to this day and, of course, the track set in concrete remains in places. However, nature and the clay companies have reclaimed much of the land and many areas are completely overgrown by foliage. The last recorded passenger train was an enthusiasts' special dmu in April 1977.

In addition to the china clay works, driers and sidings there were also brickworks on the line and many years before the railway, there were a number of iron mines in the area, including Kernick and Meledor. There were also many stone quarries but unlike the Luxulyan Valley area their history is essentially pre-railway. Many of the waste products from the china clay producing process lend themselves to manufacture into diverse by-products, such as bricks and blocks. In fact some companies mixed titles, such as the Wheal Remfry China

Clay Brick & Tile Company Limited, which was allied to H. D. Pochin & Company Limited, and which was absorbed into the ELCP and later English China Clays Group. Wheal Remfry Brick Works was at the end of Trerice sidings.

One of the operational problems concerning rail traffic on the Retew branch was the need for all trains to reverse at St Dennis Junction, and then to traverse the largely single-track line to St Blazey via Bugle. After the direct Fowey to St Blazey line closed, clay trains had to reverse again at Lostwithiel before reaching Fowey Docks. There had once been plans to extend the branch by several miles following the course of the River Fal all the way to St Just Pool in Carrick Roads, virtually across the river from Falmouth but, as with the majority of these somewhat grandiose schemes, nothing came of them.

The branch is now but a memory and despite the massive Wheal Remfry, Virginia and Melbur China Clay Works, each producing thousands of tons of clay every year, not one ton now moves by railway.

Unpublished photographs of trains on the Retew branch are hard to come by and even photographs with the track *in situ* are a rarity. This interesting view was taken near the end of the Retew branch where the line was extended across a local road to serve New Meledor Mill and Collins Rotary Driers. Note the 'Stop' board and the warning to open the gates before crossing the road! The gates look to be on their last legs in this June 1981 photograph. This land is now covered by a heavily wooded copse.   *Author*

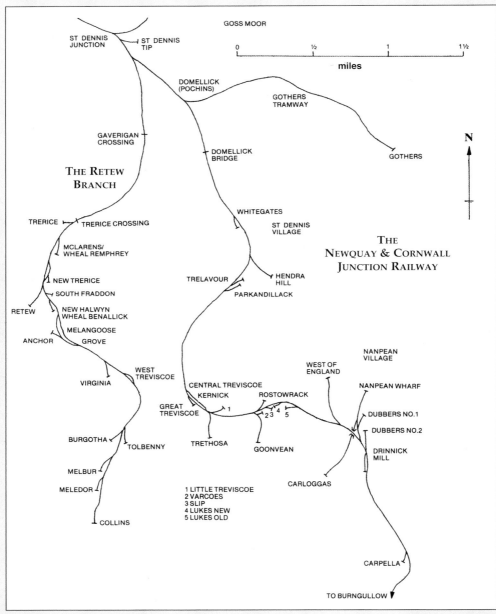

This map shows the various sidings on the Retew branch and the northern section of the Newquay & Cornwall Junction Railway

Chapter Sixteen

The Newquay & Cornwall Junction Railway

By the fourth decade of the 19th century the owners of the many clay pits which were expanding on the high ground north of St Austell, and across the greater Hensbarrow Downs area, had still not tackled their chronic transportation problems. Horses were still hauling three ton wagons over difficult terrain and appalling roads. The tramway from St Austell to Pentewan Harbour, with its primitive horse-drawn wagons, had opened in 1829 but with the terminus at St Austell being some distance from the clay driers, transhipment from road to rail at the railhead was still necessary.

There were a number of plans produced which included not only an extension of the Pentewan Railway but new ventures which would build a railway towards the St Stephens area and north-west towards the village of St Dennis. One of the most important proposals was publicised in November 1843 for a St Austell & St Stephens Railway. It would have been necessary to purchase 257 parcels of land and the railway would have linked Pentewan with Gover Mill and then run via Trewoon, north of Methroes, High Street, Carpella, Foxhole, Drinnick, Nanpean and ending at Little Treviscoe. The line would climb a total of 428 ft in 5¼ miles. The ruling gradient would have been about 1 in 60 but there would need to be one 1 in 12 incline. This and further schemes in 1858 and 1862 came to nothing. In the meantime, as detailed in Chapter Five, Treffry had opened his standard gauge tramway from Newquay to Hendra in 1857, although a short section up an incline to Hendra Downs, which included two inclines at 1 in 9 and 1 in 20, may have opened earlier.

In 1864 there was a proposal to build a 5 mile 13 chain single line from Burngullow, on the Cornwall Railway main line, through clay country (thereby serving several clay pits) to link up with the original Newquay Tramway near St Dennis. The line was to be known as the Newquay and Cornwall Junction Railway and it would, in common with the main line, be broad gauge throughout. The railway was authorized on 14th July, 1864 with capital of £27,000 in 1,350 shares of £20 each. Easy payments were advertised for those wanting to invest and deposits of £2 per share were invited. The Chairman of the N&CJR was to be Brydges Willyams of St Columb. The Prospectus made fascinating reading:

> The proposed line of railways is intended to be constructed from Burngullow station of the Cornwall Railway through the heart of the important china clay and china stone district of St Stephens and St Dennis to a junction with the St Dennis branch of the Par and Newquay Railway near the village of Hendra. [The announcement optimistically continued:] It is also intended to apply for powers to improve the Par and Newquay Railway so as to adapt it for locomotives as far as Ruthvoes within a little more than two miles of St Columb (to which it is intended to continue the railway if sufficient funds shall be prescribed for the purpose). The line to Hendra will be about five miles in length affording direct communication with Newquay, Par, Fowey and Falmouth.

When the first 2,700 hp class '50' appeared in large logo livery during 1980, with huge numbers, yellow cabs and silver roofs, there was much excitement, especially after so many years of the drab BR all blue colour scheme. Occasionally these thoroughbreds would find themselves diagrammed on china clay duties, such as on 4th October, 1985 when No. 50018 *Resolution* was photographed coming off the Drinnick Mill branch at Burngullow with air braked 'Tiger' wagons. The Plymouth to Penzance main line is in the foreground. *Author*

The old broad gauge Newquay & Cornwall Junction Railway opened from Burngullow to Drinnick Mill on 1st July, 1869. From 1874 it was theoretically joined to the CMR's standard gauge line that ran down to Drinnick Mill from St Dennis Junction. In this unusual picture from the 1950s, friends, railway employees and 2-6-2T No. 4552 have gathered at Drinnick Mill to celebrate the retirement of station master Bert Davy, notwithstanding the fact that there was never anything other than a goods station at Drinnick Mill. *Cornish Studies Library/Courtesy M. Dart*

There was also some quantitative information in the announcement:

The curves and gradients will be easy and there will be no tunnels, viaducts or other heavy works. It is estimated that 80,000 tons of merchandise would annually pass over the line besides passengers. Needless to say, this would afford a very handsome return of the limited capital required.

What was 'needless to say' was that the N&CJR were being economical with the truth!

The diaries of William Pease deposited in the County Records Office, Truro, make interesting reading. Pease had been the steward of Treffry but he was also a landowner in his own right. On 22nd February, 1865 Pease, by then the steward of the Fortescue family, walked the route of the proposed railway over his land and two weeks later one Mr Geech was valuing the land on behalf of the N&CJR. Finally, in May 1865, the railway purchased parcels of land from Pease at £100 per acre. There seems to have been something of a 'gentleman's club' with plenty of communication between the land and clay works owners. For example, William Pease makes note of a visit to Mr Lukes clay works (there were later sidings on the branch named after the owner). The N&CJR tried to tempt the important West of England China Clay Company to invest in the railway, but at the time of the approach they were carrying a £5,000 overdraft and the proposition was unsuccessful.

The first sod was cut in a field near Burngullow on 15th November, 1864 by the wife of the Chairman of the railway company and an inscribed wine cooler was presented to her by William West & Sons of St Blazey who had been nominated as contractors. The company was soon in difficulty with construction and financial problems. It was another well-known landowner of the period, George Fortescue, who although irritated by the N&CJR selecting broad gauge for the line, loaned the railway a further £1,000 in 1867 and allowed the monies from the sale of his lands to be appropriated to the construction of the line. In 1868 it appeared that a deviation line from the original 1864 plans would be necessary, and a further Act was secured to allow the 1 mile 2 chain deviation to be built, and for an extra £3,000 in funds to be raised. In 1869, after two further years of activity, the railway reached Drinnick Mill and the railway was opened on 1st July that year, but completely devoid of funds for the further work required to reach St Dennis.

William West & Son used two broad gauge steam locomotives in the construction of the line, although historians argue about the detail. One of the two engines was a Manning, Wardle 0-4-2T, No. 136 of 2/1866, purchased by the contractor from the South Wales Mineral Railway in 1869. The other was said to be built by (but more likely last overhauled by) the Brotherhood firm of Gloucester in 1863. It was a six-wheeled, four-coupled locomotive with 16 in. by 22 in. cylinders. They were named *Newquay* and *Pheonix* respectively. There are stories of a third locomotive called *Cornwall* working the line but there is no proof of this. The contractor's locomotives worked the line for some time, but when the GWR took over the running of the line in 1879, they refused to have them in their stock and both were sold to N.J. Barton, an iron dealer at Par, for scrapping.

The first two miles of the N&CJR to Higher Carpella had cost some £22,000 and the long cutting to Nanpean was through granite and very costly. Although the railway was operating it was not maximising its potential and it was not until the Cornwall Minerals Railway Act of 1873 that this situation was addressed. The 1873 Act recognised the N&CJR efforts but stated that,

> ... powers for the construction of the remainder of their railway ... have expired and they have not taken any land for the purpose of the said portions of their undertaking, but they have entered into contracts for the purchase of certain lands.

Details of the N&CJR's indebtedness were included in the Act, as was the CMR proposal to build a railway,

> 2 miles 4 furlongs and 5 chains in length wholly situate in the County of Cornwall and commencing by a junction with the N&CJR near the termination thereof at Drinnick Mill in the Parish of St Stephen in Brannell, and terminating by a junction with the New Quay Railway about 300 yards northward of a place called Hendra Crazey in the Parish of St Dennis.

Thus it was the CMR, headed by the entrepreneur Roebuck, that completed the link between the broad gauge N&CJR and the standard gauge CMR. The line opened throughout on 1st June, 1874, the date when the entire CMR network, as defined in the 1873 Act, also opened. The work was carried out with the full co-operation of the clay companies and many sidings serving various clay driers were paid for by the clay works owners. There was a break of gauge at Drinnick Mill, a situation which persisted until the abolition of the broad gauge in 1892. In fact the 1873 Act stipulated that a third rail should be provided from the end of the Newquay Railway to Burngullow to allow mixed gauge running, but the CMR did not comply. This was to lead to the Cornwall Railway insisting that the CMR provided a third rail to St Dennis and as a result of inactivity, the CR commenced legal proceedings against the CMR in 1875. The CMR consequently laid a third rail but in such a way that it was quite unusable and broad gauge wagons never worked beyond Drinnick Mill. The matter was never subsequently pursued by the CR.

Although provision in the original N&CJR Prospectus and the CMR Act was made for passengers in terms of publicity and rates per mile, the line from Burngullow to St Dennis Junction has never had a passenger service, and the only passenger trains to traverse the line have been occasional railway enthusiasts' specials. There was an unconfirmed report of a one-off diversion during World War II using the route. Curiously, there was at one time a sign at the entrance to Drinnick Mill Goods Yard which read 'To the Station'.

Just to the east of Burngullow station are the sidings of the massive Blackpool Driers loading point. In addition to powdered china clay the sidings are where English China Clay International (now Imerys) load china clay slurry into railway tank wagons for customers who prefer their white gold in liquid form. In the 1960s some huge concrete clay silos were constructed, which can be seen for miles around, but these turned out to be 'white elephants' and they are no longer used. In the past there were other clay driers in the immediate vicinity as well as Blackpool, including Wheal Louisa, Cornish Kaolin, Parkyn and Methrose.

Burngullow station was opened by the Cornwall Railway in 1863. The station was re-sited a little further to the west in 1901 but there was no significant centre of population and the GWR closed it as long ago as 14th September, 1931. Although the station was located at the junction with the N&CJR in the absence of a passenger service a branch platform was never built. There was a broad gauge engine shed located to the north of the station which once accommodated a broad gauge locomotive. The shed was demolished in the late 1920s. The signal box (former 'West') was closed in October 1986 but the 1901 structure was used by permanent way staff until it burnt down. Burngullow East signal box, opened in 1899, was closed from 24th March, 1935.

The N&CJR, also known as the St Dennis branch and sometimes the Drinnick Mill branch, curves sharply away from the main line at Burngullow at the 288 mile 50 chain mark. Within a few yards, the first of many clay company sidings was encountered; that to Burngullow West. Now an abandoned shell, the dry closed in 1974 after three-quarters of a century of clay production. The line curves to the north-west climbing at 1 in 38 and then 1 in 50. Although in days of old the direction from Burngullow to St Dennis was 'up', on the basis of the presently truncated branch, the 'up to London' approach has been adopted in describing the position of sidings. Only 200 yards beyond West Burngullow was Crugwallins siding where the adjacent driers had been producing china clay for loading onto railway wagons since 1907 but precisely 100 years later, in October 2007, the sidings were closed. Traffic was erratic and a photograph of a train calling at the driers was well worth having (*see photograph overleaf*).

The branch continues to climb at 1 in 50 to Lanjeth Crossing. Until the crossing gates were removed on 14th November 1966, trains stopped at the stop board and the train crew opened the gates. Except for a 'give way' road sign and a stop, and blast of the warning horn by the train driver, the crossing is now unprotected. At 289 miles 71 chains was Beacon siding, where in August 1928, the Beacon Clay Company brought the siding into use. The old wharf can still be seen but the siding closed in 1963. Immediately beyond Beacon and also on the up side was High Street siding. Here narrow gauge lines carried dried china clay from the linhay to the loading dock before closure in 1967.

In 1907 there was potential disruption for the branch line when the Carpella Clay Company gave notice of its right to extract china clay from ground beneath the railway line. The GWR took the matter to court on the grounds that the activities of the company were not tantamount to the extraction of minerals, which was permitted under their preserved mineral rights retained when the N&CJR first used the land. The House of Lords adjudicated that china clay was a mineral and the company had the right to require removal of the track while excavating. Accordingly, the line was severed between 290 miles 20 chains and 290 miles 40 chains as and from 16th December, 1909. From that date through running was not possible due to the 'Carpella Gap'.

On Tuesday 18th April, 1922 the GWR announced the opening of a deviation line to avoid the break and re-established through working between Burngullow and St Dennis Junction. South of the break, New Carpella siding had opened on 19th September, 1921 on the down side of the line and the truncated 'stubs' of the original route were retained as sidings for some years.

During June 1989 a new Railfreight-liveried class '37' eases out of Crugwallins dries with a rake of 50 tonne CDA china clay wagons, which will end their journey at Carne Point, Fowey. An English China Clays shunter shunted the wagons within the works. The main Drinnick Mill branch to Parkandillack is on the left. Crugwallins closed in October 2007.   *Author*

Operations on Cornwall's remote branches did not always have strict regard to the rule book but somehow the informality of times past was refreshing compared with today's obsession with 'Health & Safety'. On this day in 1985 class '45' 'Peak' No. 45072 had arrived at Drinnick Mill with an air braked freight from St Blazey. In the meantime and somewhat alarmingly, at least to the layman, 400 tons of china clay was coming down the bank behind Nos. 37181 and 37247, but the vacuum brakes were in order and no problems were experienced. Lunch was then taken in the goods office! *Author*

This unique and unrepeatable photograph of lines that have now been abandoned shows original Railfreight-liveried No. 37696 propelling a coal train from Nanpean Wharf (just behind the photographer) down to Drinnick Mill power station and Nos. 5 to 7 kilns, which were at a lower level than the main branch line. On 22nd July, 1986 the train had just descended from Drinnick Mill goods office via the steeply-graded line on the left and has reversed at Nanpean Wharf. Both lines were abandoned in May 1992. *Author*

The Drinnick Mill branch served over 25 individual clay works at its peak but with consolidation and centralisation within the industry only three modern plants are now active on the railway map; Kernick, Treviscoe and Parkandillack. Some of the old pan kilns closed over 60 years ago but in tonnage terms the three main sites now produce more china clay than all of the old works put together. On a very wet 20th April, 1983 No. 37181 climbs from Drinnick to Lukes Old siding with empty 'Tiger' wagons for Parkandillack. *Author*

Once a year the weedkilling train visits the clay lines and in April 1989 it was the turn of the Chipmans Company train to traverse the Drinnick Mill branch. Passing the junction at Drinnick Mill are Hunslet-Barclay class '20s', Nos. 20904 and 20901. The line to the right provided access to Nanpean Wharf and Drinnick Mill lower and the train is destined for Parkandillack. *Author*

The deviation was from the 290 mile mark to 290 miles and 62 chains. Old Carpella siding (which was part of the old pre-deviation line) closed in 1949 and at 290 miles 64 chains was Carpella siding on the down side, which lasted until 1968. The latter was served by the Mid Cornwall Tramway and its two distinct sections delivered the clay to the wharf at Carpella. Drinnick Mill's ringed fixed distant signal was located near to this point and 33 chains further on was Drinnick Mill South ground frame which, until May 1966, was the start of a 170 yard loop on the down side.

On the up side, at 291 miles 31 chains, was a very old clay dry dating back to the original line opening date. Known as Dubbers No. 2 siding the installation closed in 1973. Just beyond was the junction where a spur left the 'main' branch on the up side and ran down to Drinnick Mill Goods, known as Nanpean Wharf, 291 miles 60 chains. On the up side of the spur, at 291 miles 40 chains, was Dubbers No. 1 siding which opened and closed at about the same time as No. 2. At 291 miles 46 chains is a trailing connection which runs down under the 'main' branch to Drinnick Mill itself, where there were numerous clay dries, as well as coal staithes. It was here in 1936 that a power station was opened which, with the aid of 11 substations, provided the power for much of the surrounding area. Also served were Carloggas and Barne & Rottery sidings. In 1989 clay was again loaded at Drinnick Mill, although a brief resurgence of coal traffic, this time for local distribution, which had recommenced in 1985, ended in 1987. Cornwall's coal is now distributed by road from Exeter!

Nanpean Wharf dated back to the original days of the line. There was a head shunt with two tracks and one loading dock. Latterly only calcified seaweed was loaded at Nanpean, a long way from those far off days when teams of horses with their 3 ton wagons of china clay queued for unloading and transhipment. The reverse connection out of the wharf area dropped down to Drinnick and Carloggas, passing under the N&CJR via a limited clearance stone bridge. The last train worked over this section of line in 1992 and now substantial trees cover the spot.

At Drinnick Mill Junction there was once a signal box but this was closed in May 1966 and subsequently demolished, a fate shared by the Drinnick Goods Office located in the 'V' of the junction during October 1993. On leaving Drinnick Mill the West of England China Clay Company's siding branched off on the up side at 291 miles 47 chains. Snell's stone wharf was also served. This once important siding was served by the Hendra Tramway and china clay and stone from both the West of England China Stone Quarries and the Hendra China Clay Works was loaded there. After over a hundred years of service the siding was abandoned in 1973 and lifted in 1975. Climbing at 1 in 40 again, the branch curves around the clay tips. Luke's Old siding, which faced on the down side at 291 miles 63 chains, closed in 1960 and this was followed by Luke's New siding at 291 miles and 77 chains that closed in 1963. The next two short (and long removed) sidings, known as Slip sidings, belonged to the Goonvean & Rostowrack China Clay Company. Wagons were loaded with china stone until the early 1960s. Another Goonvean siding left the branch by a trailing connection on the up side just seven chains further on. Known as Rostowrack, china stone was loaded at infrequent intervals until 1984. The sidings now came thick and fast with Goonvean siding

In the heart of clay country at Drinnick Mill 0-6-0PT No. 9755 is taking water, while some enthusiasts obviously have permission to travel in the GWR 20 ton brake van. The line to the left leads down to Nanpean Wharf, while the main branch ahead meanders its way down to the main line at Burngullow. In this era the branch would normally be visited by at least two china clay and general goods workings per day. *Norman Simmons/Courtesy M. Dart*

The line from Burngullow to Parkandillack penetrates the very heart of china clay country and there is some wild and desolate scenery *en route*, with the remains of the activity of past industries everywhere to be seen. With a massive 1,000 tonnes in tow 1,750 hp class '37' No. 37673 was on full power as it passed Slip Bridge between Kernick and Drinnick Mill on its way to St Blazey in April 1993. *Author*

If any readers wondered what china stone looked like, well this is it! In this remarkable scene from the 1930s at the West of England Company's sidings, off the Drinnick Mill branch, an early 0-6-0 pannier tank gets to grips with 11 wooden-bodied wagons that had just been loaded manually. China clay and stone from Hendra China Clay Works was also loaded at this point. The siding was abandoned in 1973 and lifted two years later.   *English China Clays/Courtesy M. Dart*

In the right background is Slip Bridge, where there was once a siding and on the left is Rostowrack, where china stone was loaded until about 1983. The siding has now been lifted. The branch line normally sees at least two trains per day Monday to Friday, although the number of trains is determined by customer demand and traffic patterns can be erratic. *Author*

There was a period of only two to three years when English Welsh & Scottish Railways-liveried class '37s' worked china clay trains in the Royal Duchy. The first example to appear in Cornwall was during 1996 and by the end of 1999 North American-built class '66s' started to arrive in the south-west, eventually replacing the class '37s'. Negotiating the ferns and seen passing the abandoned Luke's clay works and approaching Slip Bridge in August 1997 with empty wagons is No. 37521, appropriately named *English China Clays*. *Author*

trailing on the down side at 292 miles and 21 chains. In 1895 this long siding, which once served the Goonvean Company's China Clay and Stone Works, was accessed by a single 13 ft turntable from a siding adjacent to the main line but in later years rakes of wagons would be propelled down the siding. The former siding had been provided for Robert and John Varcoe by the GWR in 1882. Now so many years after closure the remains of all these sidings can barely be detected in the ever changing topography.

Between 292 miles 30 chains and 292 miles 38 chains was the Little Treviscoe loop on the up side and off the loop was Little Treviscoe siding and, lost in the mist of time, Gears siding. This siding was served by a narrow gauge tramway and between 1907 and 1969 (when it was removed) it was extended on more that one occasion. An early closure in 1948 was Trethosa siding which trailed in on the down side at 292 miles 38 chains. Next on the up side is the still used Kernick sidings, followed by Central Treviscoe. These sidings still enjoy almost daily trains but the same cannot be said of Great Treviscoe siding on the down side at 292 miles 61 chains. Between the years of 1913 and 1950 there was a signal box at Kernick on the down side of the line. There were extensive track layout changes at Kernick and here, as with many clay driers, much of the track in the sidings is set in concrete. The line continues to descend, as it has from the summit of the branch at Slip siding, towards Parkandillack. The line is but half a mile from the Retew branch at this point.

The major clay works on the Drinnick Mill branch is Parkandillack. A signal box was in operation here between 1911 and 1922. This major works dispatches hundreds of tons of china clay by rail every day. Normally two trains per day serve the works, Monday to Friday. The leading point into the works on the up side is at 293 miles 34 chains. There are sidings serving a calciner and buell drying plant. At the back of Parkandillack is the Goonvean & Rostowrack China Clay Company's only railway siding, Trelavour, which is not used at the present time. The branch that once continued to St Dennis Junction closed beyond stop blocks at 293 miles and 60 chains on 6th February, 1966. The trackbed beyond can be traced and the old 1852 Hendra Incline to Hendra Downs, which was removed before the World War I, can be seen on the up side at the 294 mile mark. The works on the Downs are long abandoned with their spoil tips now covered in gorse.

Whitegate crossing was 1¾ miles to the south-east of St Dennis and there was once a siding there as well as a small wharf for local produce and inward coal deliveries. Passing the siding ground frame at 294 miles and 12 chains the line continued to Gothers or Pochins siding at Domellick where the 3 ft 1 in. gauge line from Gothers China Clay Works transhipped its loads. The substantial stone loading wharf is still much in evidence. A loop served the wharf at 295 miles and 5 chains. A final level stretch of line completed the route at St Dennis Junction (295 miles 61 chains).

There were once signal boxes at Burngullow, Drinnick Mill, Kernick, Parkandillack and St Dennis Junction. They closed in 1986, 1966, 1950, 1922 and 1986 respectively. Between 1950 and 1966 the branch was divided into two block sections; Burngullow to Drinnick Mill and Drinnick Mill to St Dennis Junction.

Probably taking the prize for the worst play on words of any railtour name was Hertfordshire Railtours 'Par Snip' tour in February 1993! Cornish class '37' No 37670 *St Blazey T&RS Depot* is seen approaching Slip Bridge on the Drinnick Mill branch while returning from Parkandillack with a rake of InterCity air conditioned coaches.   *Author*

A workaday scene in the heart of clay country on 2nd April, 1986 is this study of class '47' No. 47292 passing Rostowrack siding with 45 clay hoods loaded with powdered china clay. The disused siding can be seen to the right of the locomotive's cab and in the far distance is the vast Virginia Clay Works. The line here was broad gauge between 1869 and 1892.   *Author*

One of the best places along the branch to observe china clay trains is from the road bridge at Kernick driers, *provided* the observer knows there is a train in the area! Having worked up from Parkandillack along the old bullhead track on 5th May, 1989, new Railfreight-liveried No. 37673 has left its five 'Tiger' wagons on the main branch in order to propel a single VAB van into Kernick driers.   *Author*

Back in 1982 there were still wagons on the china clay circuit that were not clay hoods. The china clay in these wagons was protected from the elements by tarpaulins and they were used in the 'Clayliner' train to Stoke-on-Trent and also to Scotland. On 19th February, 1982 the shunter waits on the main branch while No. 37135 enters Treviscoe clay driers, along track set in concrete.   *Author*

Although there was some local concern when the French Imerys company acquired English China Clays International any fears were allayed when the company announced that although there would be some rationalisation there would also be some inward investment. China clay trains are now run by the English Welsh & Scottish company, recently taken over by Deutsche Bahn, such is the corporate world of high finance! On a delightful October evening in 2007 No. 66019 is seen shunting CDA wagons at Parkandillack, now the end of the line.   *Author*

An exceedingly rare movement at the time was when No. 50045 *Achilles* propelled a 'Tiger' wagon from Parkandillack into the Trelavour works of the Goonvean & Rostowrack China Clay Company. Photographed in February 1988 this was one of only two trains seen working at this location in dozens of visits over many years. Note the ancient granite building on the right.   *Author*

Originally the line was worked by the CMR under the train staff and ticket system but the GWR introduced the more sophisticated electric train staff. The branch tablet instruments at the St Dennis end of the line were located at St Dennis Junction ground frame. The ground frames controlling most of the sidings were locked by an Annett's key on the train staff. Some sidings had small cast nameplates attached to the levers, while some ground frames were located in small huts. Locking bars were used on some sidings. From 1966 Burngullow signal box controlled the branch, having telephone communications with Drinnick Mill. Now, the signals on the main line are under the control of Par.

In steam days there were always severe restrictions on motive power. With 18 chain radius curves, minor sidings and other restrictions the N&CJR was, in common with many other lines featured in this volume, restricted to small 0-6-0 pannier tanks and 2-6-2 Prairie tanks. Over the years some improvements have been made to the permanent way and most classes of diesel have worked the line. I must say the sight of a 136 ton 1 Co-Co 1 'Peak' class diesel at Nanpean Wharf was awe inspiring! In the days of non-vacuum-braked freight trains there were numerous places to pin down brakes, and double-heading of trains was not uncommon. From January 1991 class '47s' and '50s' were banned beyond Drinnick Mill but upon arrival of the GM class '66s' a weak bridge was strengthened.

Working such a multitude of sidings in the old days was a complex business, but with only two trains per day from Burngullow to Drinnick, and two from the St Dennis direction to Drinnick (one of which worked through to Burngullow), this was manageable. Towards the end of steam there was but one train per day from St Dennis towards Drinnick. By 1989 there was normally one morning and one afternoon train from Burngullow to Parkandillack calling as required at the remaining china clay driers. Traffic to Nanpean and Drinnick Mill, which has now ceased, was erratic but trains to Kernick, Treviscoe and Parkandillack are still regular. The N&CJR or Drinnick branch is a remarkable line. It traverses the bizarre, almost surreal, china clay country, passing old clay works and modern plant. There are mica dams, the old abutments of trolley ways, gorse-covered spoil tips and settling tanks. There are a few hamlets and villages.

Many years prior to the coming of the railway important clay works had been established on St Dennis Downs. These included Higher and Lower Gothers, and Wheal Frederick China Clay Works. The works were connected to the N&CJR by a two mile 3 ft 1 in. gauge railway, with a transfer loading wharf at Domellick, as mentioned above. Opened in 1884, the locomotive-worked tramway served a total of seven clay driers at Gothers and also Dick Runnal's and Stoneman's kilns. After several successful decades the tramway seems to have been in decline towards the end of the 1920s and various reports show the line as closing in the early 1930s. In 1932 the Pochin Company was absorbed by the ECLP (later ECC) and the site still enjoys industrial use under the guise of Gothers Concrete Works. Little remains of the tramway today. The locomotive shed walls survive in deep undergrowth and some of the old clay driers survive for storage purposes. The trackbed across Goss Moor is clearly visible beneath huge electricity pylons and the loading wharf at Domellick or Pochins siding remains. Although there were numerous tram and wagon-ways in a large number of clay works, the Gothers tramway was worthy of specific mention because of its length and because, although the line was narrow gauge, it was significantly larger than the more usual 2 ft gauge lines that were used within the various works.

Although the N&CJR line never had a passenger service during its long history, there were proposals in 1989/1990 for the line to be developed as the main route to Newquay and for the existing branch line between Goonbarrow Junction to St Dennis Junction to be closed so that the railway track alignment could be used for a new section of dual carriageway on the main A30 trunk road. Stations at Luxulyan, Bugle and Roche would have been closed but new stations on the old N&CJR at St Dennis, Treviscoe and either Nanpean or Foxhole would have been opened. The lifted section between Parkandillack and St Dennis Junction was to be re-instated. The new proposals would also serve another useful purpose: to take passengers to and from St Austell, the main local shopping centre and what would have been the new junction for Newquay. Few locals want to travel from Newquay to Par, unless continuing onward to Plymouth. However, the cost considerations were too high, land for the new road (which opened in 2007) was purchased to the north of the Newquay branch alignment across Goss Moor, and the whole idea was abandoned.

The line beyond Parkandillack once ran through to St Dennis Junction via Whitegate and Domellick but the link was closed on 6th February, 1966. The N&CJR never had much to do with Newquay as such, but partial closure over 40 years ago severed all links. With the village of St Dennis in the background Nos. 37222 and 37196, in all blue and original Railfreight livery, disturb the peace as they leave Parkandillack with clay hoods on 3rd October, 1985.   *Author*

Chapter Seventeen

St Dennis Junction to Tolcarn Junction

Beyond St Dennis Junction the line heads westward towards Ruthvoes. Although initially on the route of Treffry's old Newquay Tramway, at 294 miles and 55 chains there is a significant deviation from the original line. The original tramway incorporated the 530 yds-long Toldish tunnel which was not only damp but was a mere 8 to 9 ft high, sufficient for a horse and wagon but totally inadequate for the CMR's purposes. The old route is still shown on the current 1:50,000 Ordnance Survey map, even though abandoned on 1st June, 1874. The new line took a longer route to the north of Toldish tunnel and from 1904 there was a further minor deviation from 295 miles 39 chains to 295 miles 66 chains.

Just beyond is St Columb Road station which, for the first two years of its life was known as Halloon. The station is well over two miles from St Columb Major and in fact it is much nearer the curiously named Indian Queens. It opened in June 1876 and boasted two platforms, a passing loop and a goods yard. By 1910 the goods yard had been enlarged and a substantial loading dock was built. Between 1931 and 1933 two further extensions to the passing loop saw it lengthen by 60 yards to the west, and by 100 yards to the east. As with most other stations on the line the service varied from three trains each way in 1888, four or five in 1910, 11 or 12 in 1938 and 1958, six in 1989 and a rather miserable four in 2008, courtesy of the First Great Western Company. Over the years there were always more trains on summer Saturdays, albeit not all stopping at the minor stations such as St Columb Road.

The 3rd January, 1965 was rather a sad day when, in common with so many stations on the line, the passing loop, goods sidings and signal box were all axed. In the following years the station building became derelict and was finally demolished. Although a new 'bus shelter' and iron railings have recently been installed the scene is now quite desolate, although one should perhaps be grateful that trains still call! Beyond the station the line reaches Halloon Crossing, which even in the mid-1980s retained its crossing keeper's hut, cottage and gates across the A392 road. The line runs via White Cross over a level crossing at Coswarth before entering a deep cutting and the 33 yds-long Coswarth tunnel. After crossing under the A392 road and crossing it again on the level, Quintrel Downs is reached. This typical GWR wayside halt served a small community and was opened from 2nd October, 1911. It had a pagoda hut, oil lamps, sign and a signal cabin. It had been the site of a goods siding long before the halt was built.

At the site of the halt there was once a loop and a siding, but when the platform was built the layout changed to a single branch line and two sidings. The signal box at Quintrel was closed in 1911 in favour of a gatehouse containing signal levers. By the early 1920s the ground frame had been removed to the platform where it remained in use until 1981 when the gates were removed, the signals uprooted and the crossing keeper for 35 years, Gladys Sleeman, was retired. Years before one of the sidings was privately owned by Martyn & Lewarnes but in 1965 the sidings were closed and removed.

Charming crossings are located at Chapel and Trencreek, 300 miles 54 chains and 301 miles 35 chains respectively, as the line drops towards Newquay. Before conversion to open crossings the former crossing keepers operated not only the gates

It is sad to think that this busy scene at St Dennis Junction on 11th July, 1955 represents a way of life that has gone forever. Just a single track now runs past this area, without a siding of any kind. This load of china clay has just come off the Retew branch and it being transported to either Par or Fowey. Leading the formation is 0-6-0PT No. 3635 with 2-6-2T No. 4526 banking the train. The spoil tip sidings are visible just above the signal box.

R.C. Riley/Courtesy Transport Treasury

Heading towards Newquay the next station along the branch is St Columb Road, originally called Halloon. St Blazey's little pannier tank No. 3635 seems to have been a versatile machine because rather than working freight trains, as seen oppositee, in this view from 15th August, 1950, it is heading a four-coach local passenger train from Par to Newquay. Note the brick kiln on the right. *P. Ransome-Wallis*

In this June 1990 scene a thinly-populated single power car dmu, thought to be No. 55026, scuttles across Halloon crossing, just west of St Columb station, on its way from Newquay to Par. The building on the left of the crossing was the original crossing keeper's cottage, the crossing being gated until the beginning of the 1980s. *Author*

This interesting view from the 1950s shows all the major features at St Columb Road station, including the small signal box, the large running-in board, brick and wood station buildings, passing loop, down waiting shelter and goods yard (with wagon) on the right. The goods yard was enlarged in 1910 but closed in January 1965.   *Lens of Sutton*

The passing loop at St Columb Road was twice extended in the early 1930s but the branch reverted to single track at this point on 3rd January, 1965. On 5th April, 2007 track replacement was taking place on the Newquay branch and old track was dumped in the space previously occupied by the down passing loop over 40 years earlier. Approaching the refurbished station with new metal railings and bus shelter *in situ* is class '150/2' No. 150238. With no passengers to board or alight the train did not stop.   *Author*

but protective signals either side of the crossings. Just a few hundred yards beyond Trencreek was Tolcarn Junction, but over the years, the exact alignment of this large triangular junction changed and the history is best dealt with by describing each chord separately. The three chords ran east/west, south/east and south/west.

The junction of the east to west and south to west chords was originally known as Treloggan Junction. At the opening of the CMR it was renamed Newquay Junction. The south to east and south to west junction was known as Lane Junction but the signal box there was closed in 1888. The east to west and south to east junction was Tolcarn Junction but that box also closed in 1888 when the 1874-built south to east curve was closed completely. From 1888 the entire junction complex was controlled by a single signal box which was located on the inside of the 'triangle' between the 'V' of the east to west and south to west chords, with the entire complex collectively being called 'Tolcarn Junction'.

It made sense for the GWR to close the direct south to east line as all traffic was either to or from Newquay. The main branch into Newquay was realigned in 1904 just prior to the opening throughout of the Chacewater to Newquay branch. A north chord passing loop was provided and until 1910 there was a siding made out of the abandoned east to south chord. The single track south to west chord was doubled with the coming of the passenger trains from Chacewater. The abandoned chord was relaid east to south to single track in 1931 and a brand-new Tolcarn signal box was commissioned. The chord was provided to turn locomotives, especially tender locomotives arriving on main line trains on summer Saturdays, the Newquay turntable having been abolished at the same

It always seems a wonderful phenomenum when a sleepy rural station, completely devoid of special features or creature comforts, suddenly comes into focus for a few minutes. In March 1992 it was St Columb Road's turn as the Merlin Railtours 'Cornish Construction Crompton' tour featuring Southern Region motive power paused for a photographic stop on its way to Newquay. The locomotives are Nos. 33050 *Isle of Grain* and 33063, both allocated to Stewart's Lane in London.   *Author*

With forthcoming changes in Train Operating Company franchises the last weekend of the summer 2007 timetable was exciting in modern traction terms as GNER and Midland Main Line (MML) HST units and Virgin-liveried Voyagers made what was thought to be their last appearances on the Newquay branch. However in May 2008 an HST still in MML livery was hired by Cross Country to work the 09.40 to Newcastle! On 8th September, 2007 MML No. 43046, then on hire to Virgin Trains, passes St Columb Road station with the 15.22 Newquay to Manchester. *Author*

Through the decades long distance trains to and from Newquay in high summer have originated in an amazing variety of locations throughout the Midlands, the North of England and Scotland, not to mention the Capital. On 25th September, 1993 this IC125 unit with power car No. 43086 leading, is forming the 14.15 Newquay to Leeds, photographed east of Quintrel Downs. Notice the sea visible just above the distant buildings of Newquay. *Author*

The short 33 yds-long Coswarth tunnel in the background was on the alignment of the original horse-operated Newquay Tramway but it had to be enlarged in 1873/4 to accommodate CMR steam locomotives. In this incredibly rare picture No. 37413 is about to discharge track ballast from its hopper wagons during a Sunday engineers line occupation in March 1994. Locomotive workings west of Goonbarrow Junction have become scarce since track rationalisation in 1987.

Author

It would be difficult to find a better example of the branch line pick-up goods than this formation, seen rounding the curve at Tolcarn Junction on 20th July, 1954 behind 0-6-0PT No. 9655. The train had worked its way along the branch from Par, shunting wagons at most of the intermediate stations, and would soon be arriving at its Newquay destination. The only identifiable load is coal in the fourth of six wagons.

Les Elsey

Sporting an express passenger lamp headcode, this duo look powerful as they approach Tolcarn Junction with an up through train in the 1950s. 'Manor' class 4-6-0 No. 7816 *Frilsham Manor* and an unidentified 'Hall' are passing the Tolcarn Jn signal box up home signal with a lengthy holiday train. Arriving double-headed, locomotives were often turned on the triangle at Tolcarn, just outside of Newquay.
Author's Collection

The last station before Newquay is Quintrel Downs, which at times is also spelt Quintrell Downs (current First Great Western timetable and Quintrel Down (GWR cast-iron sign on the ground frame)). Opened by the GWR in October 1911, the single platform halt now serves a growing community. Departing for Newquay in the early 1950s is No. 4559. The siding on the right was once owned by Messrs Martyn & Lewarnes.
Donald Kelk

time, when the engine shed closed. It is said that when double-headed trains with up to 15 coaches arrived at Newquay they had to stop at the buffers, blocking the run-round loop points and accordingly it was sometimes the practice to reverse the entire formation to Tolcarn Junction for complete train turning on the triangle. Generally, however, the leading locomotive was detached outside of the terminus.

With growing holiday traffic and the limited capacity of the single-track former CMR viaduct across the Trenance Valley into Newquay, a new masonry viaduct was proposed in the late 1930s providing double-track access to the seaside terminus. The viaduct was all but ready before the start of the World War II and the double line from Tolcarn Junction was extended. Trains crossed the new viaduct from 27th March, 1939 but the second track was not brought into use until 20th March, 1946, after the end of hostilities. Additional sidings were installed on the west side of the Tolcarn triangle at the same time.

Although there was a brief period of respite in the early and mid-1950s, the 1960s brought nothing but decline. The closure of the Chacewater line in February 1963 and the withdrawal of freight facilities to Trevemper siding in October 1963 (*see next Chapter*) resulted in the closure of both south to west and south to east chords at Tolcarn. Furthermore, steam locomotives has disappeared from the main line scene and the diesel replacements had cabs at both ends and did not need turning. Train loads decreased and the diesels could use the run-round loops at Newquay without difficulty. On 23rd November, 1964 the signal box was closed and effectively Tolcarn Junction disappeared from the railway map. Worse was to come as developers moved in and by the early 1980s an industrial and housing estate covered the entire site, with no trace whatsoever that a railway ever passed the place except, of course, for the single line of the surviving Par to Newquay branch.

Another remarkable anachronism that occurs on the Newquay branch on summer weekends is a streamlined Voyager unit, working through to Glasgow Central, stopping for the road crossing on the single track at Quintrel Downs, just five minutes into its 9½ hour journey to Scotland! Here on 9th September, 2007 the very last Virgin-badged Voyager to traverse the branch forms the 11.33 Newquay to Glasgow, with only the author present to witness the event.   *Author*

The origins of a GWR branch line linking Truro with Newquay date back to Victorian times when the GWR wanted to head-off any likelihood of the London & South Western Railway invading southern Cornwall. However by the time the circuitous Chacewater to Newquay branch was planned in its final form old rivalries had subsided. In this historic picture a horse has just delivered in-fill for an embankment at Perranporth during the 1902/3 construction period.   *Cornish Studies Library*

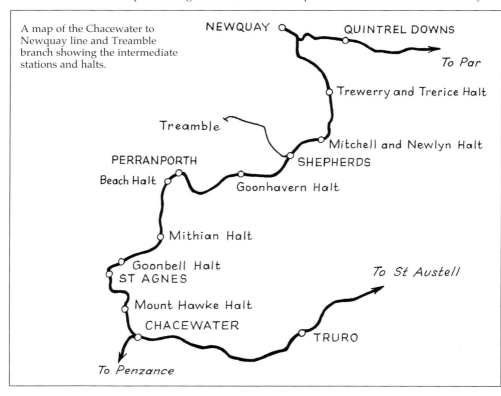

A map of the Chacewater to Newquay line and Treamble branch showing the intermediate stations and halts.

NEWQUAY

QUINTREL DOWNS

To Par

Trewerry and Trerice Halt

Treamble

Mitchell and Newlyn Halt

PERRANPORTH

SHEPHERDS

Beach Halt

Goonhavern Halt

Mithian Halt

Goonbell Halt
ST AGNES

To St Austell

Mount Hawke Halt

CHACEWATER

TRURO

To Penzance

Chapter Eighteen

Chacewater to Tolcarn Junction and the Treamble Branch

In February 1849 the first load of lead ore had been transported by rail from East Wheal Rose Mine to Newquay Harbour over the original Newquay Tramway. Subsequent developments included not only the arrival and takeover of the Treffry lines by the CMR, the extension of the East Wheal Rose line to Treamble and Gravel Hill in 1874, the opening of the line through from Fowey to Newquay, but also in 1896, the final takeover by the GWR of all the CMR lines.

The LSWR had taken over responsibility for the Bodmin & Wadebridge Railway (B&WR) in 1846, although it did not address the Parliamentary formalities until 1883. However, despite rivalries between the railway companies there had been agreement in 1888 to allow trains on the extended GWR standard gauge branch from Bodmin Road and Bodmin General, to work through to Wadebridge; the first time the isolated B&WR lines had been connected to the main railway network. The two lines joined at Boscarne Junction. However, the GWR still regarded the LSWR as a threat and in 1894 it proposed a direct line from Truro to Newquay to effectively 'cut off' a LSWR proposal to open a line from Wadebridge to Truro, possibly via Newquay. This proposal was rejected by Parliament but, in 1895, the LSWR did arrive at Wadebridge via its North Cornwall line and so the threat was real.

There had been many previous schemes to link the LSWR via the Bodmin and Wadebridge lines to the CMR and as already mentioned, in 1873 there had been a proposal to link Ruthern Bridge with the CMR at a point near Roche, a distance of only four to five miles. The reason for the proposed link was a more direct access to a port with better facilities than the restricted Wadebridge. There were other schemes outside the scope of this book but development by the LSWR continued when its 1895 North Cornwall line was extended to Padstow in 1899.

Although there remained a competitive spirit between the GWR and the LSWR, typified by the boat train 'races' from Plymouth to London on their respective routes, by the end of the 1890s the two giants had agreed to stop the fruitless competition in the County of Cornwall, even though the LSWR did run bus connections from Wadebridge to Newquay! At the end of the decade the GWR lodged its Truro and Newquay Railway Act which included a proposed route greatly different from its earlier initiatives.

The railway was to leave the GWR main line at Chacewater, where a station had been opened as part of the West Cornwall Railway route from Truro to Penzance in August 1852. The station was about a mile north of the village it purported to serve and from 1903/1905 its importance as a junction increased with the opening of the line to Perranporth and then Newquay. Its operational inconvenience was recognised when, in 1912, extensive modifications including the provision of an island platform were made. The station approach and the main buildings were on the down side, as was the signal box. A pair of sidings were provided at the down end of the down side forming a small goods yard.

This photograph shows the construction of an overbridge on the Chacewater to Perranporth section at the 0 mile 44 chain point, just north of Blackwater Junction on 5th June, 1902. Note the wooden forms on the left, used to support the brick arch above the trackbed.

Author's Collection

Another early shot from 1902 shows that concrete was used in the construction of overbridges on the line. Note the contractor's line veering to the right beyond the overbridge, no doubt used to supply spoil for the infill of the gradient each side of the road bridge. What is curious is the soot on the metal girder section, which suggests heavy use of a contractor's locomotive. *Author's Collection*

In fact these sidings were the last vestige of commercial activity at Chacewater, which continued to be used for cement deliveries long after the branch and the complete station were closed.

However, the GWR did not do things by halves and in addition to the Newquay branch alignment from Chacewater, there was also a direct link to the branch from the Redruth direction, which formed a triangular junction at Blackwater. In fact the north to west spur was very much a secondary link being used by infrequent passenger trains only between the years 1903 and 1916. It continued to be used by the occasional freight train until 1919 and was closed shortly afterwards. It was not until 1924 when an independent line was provided from Blackwater Junction to Chacewater (which ran parallel with the main line) that three signal boxes - Blackwater West, North and East were finally closed. To provide the half-mile independent line the north side of the cutting to the west of Chacewater had to be widened. The evidence can still be seen as can the remains of part of the embankments forming the triangular junction at Blackwater, now severed by the A30 highway.

Although it could never be said that the Chacewater to Newquay line had conveniently located stations for all the villages and hamlets it served, the meandering alignment clearly attempted to have regard to the local community. The only villages with a population worth mentioning were St Agnes, which had been a focal point for mining in days before the coming of the railway, and Perranporth, which subsequently owed much of its development to the railway. The latter village was the initial target of the railway builders and after inspection by Colonel Yorke of the Railway Inspectorate the Chacewater to Perranporth section opened on 6th July, 1903, a distance of just over eight miles.

The railway building continued towards Shepherds, where it would form a junction with the former CMR line to Treamble. Although upgrading was necessary, the alignment from East Wheal Rose, near St Newlyn East, followed the early 1849 Newquay Tramway alignment. Even then it was 18 months later, on 2nd January, 1905, before the 18 mile 49 chain branch was opened throughout. On the opening day 300 Newquay schoolchildren and eight teachers were treated to a free round trip to Perranporth. At the time of opening the only intermediate station between Perranporth and Newquay was Shepherds. Extensive modifications to track, signalling and platforms took place at Newquay during 1904/1905 in anticipation of the new route to the town.

In the best of GWR traditions half a dozen halts were opened from 14th August, 1905. These modest single-platform halts with a couple of lamps, a sign and a basic pagoda hut for passenger accommodation, completed the plan to provide a service for minor communities along the route. A small concrete halt at Perranporth Beach was opened in 1931 to cater for increasing holiday traffic and trips to the seaside. St Agnes station was greatly altered in 1937 when an island platform was built and the track re-aligned. The branch had an overall speed limit of 40 mph.

The line was essentially rural in character and after leaving the embankment at Blackwater Junction it climbed for just over 1½ miles to Mount Hawke Halt. The hamlet the halt served was over a mile away and as in the case of the other halts there were no sidings. The brick-faced platform was situated in a now

The branch line from Chacewater to Perranporth opened on 6th July, 1903. However by 1912 it was recognised that changes needed to be made at Chacewater to accommodate branch and main line traffic. Accordingly Chacewater was rebuilt with an island platform, the outer face of which would be used by Newquay trains. Looking towards Plymouth, this 1912 postcard shows the new layout to advantage. *Cornish Studies Library*

The first station on the branch was Mount Hawke Halt, 1½ miles from the junction. In this August 1955 photograph the Perranporth portion of a down Paddington to Penzance express is seen passing behind 2-6-2T No. 5500. This halt was not opened until 1905 and it comprised a single platform and a GWR pagoda hut waiting shelter. *G. Clarke*

infilled cutting. To this day the embankment between Mount Hawke and St Agnes is visible from the B3277 road.

It must have been disappointing for the inhabitants of St Agnes when they realised that the much heralded new railway was to locate its station some three-quarters of a mile from the village centre. It could be argued that in 1903, as the village was the most important on the line, more money should have been spent on a more convenient alignment, but a glimpse at an Ordnance Survey map reveals that insurmountable topographical problems would have been encountered in crossing Trevellas Coombe. The red brick station initially had a single platform and boasted a station master. Some 34 years after opening, in 1937, a long 300 ft island platform, with passing facilities, was built and connected to the original station area by an overbridge. A 30-lever signal box was opened at the same time replacing the existing ground frame. Unlike the halts, the station had goods facilities with a goods shed, cattle pens and the usual paraphernalia.

Leaving St Agnes, 3 miles 26 chains from Chacewater, the line veered sharply eastward and a mere 45 chains from St Agnes the halt of Goonbell appeared, which like Mount Hawke, was situated in a cutting. Goonbell could perhaps have been called 'south-east St Agnes', although the halt was located immediately adjacent to the few buildings that comprise the hamlet of Goonbell. The line continued across a five-arch masonry viaduct which shares the name of the previously mentioned Goonbell hamlet. At the 5 mile 46 chain mark was yet another halt called Mithian. Again, the halt was conveniently located to to serve the small community.

The line then descended the Perrancombe Valley at gradients of up to 1 in 45 to within a short distance of Cornwall's north coast at Perranporth. However, from 1931 Perranporth Beach Halt was used by the bucket and spade brigade, thus saving them a quarter of a mile walk from the main Perranporth station. At Perranporth the direction of the line changed abruptly from north-north-east to south-south-east. From the date of opening Perranporth had a substantial island platform, goods shed, cattle dock, signal box and other associated railway buildings. The station was notable for its deep awnings. The resort so increased in popularity that in the 1950s there was, almost unbelievably, a through train to and from Paddington on summer Saturdays. For example, in 1958, a first and second-class, restaurant car express left Perranporth at 8.15 am, arriving in the capital 7 hours and 40 minutes later at 3.55 pm. The down train ran to Perranporth and Penzance, with the former portion arriving at its destination at 4.20 pm after a 7 hour 55 minute marathon.

After leaving Perranporth the railway builders again respected the terrain by running the branch line along the Bolingey Valley in a generally easterly direction, across a further viaduct to reach Goonhavern Halt at 10 miles 38 chains. Here the line crossed the main Newquay to Redruth road. The halt was easily accessible by the local inhabitants. The line curved to the north-east and through a cutting before descending to Shepherds, the junction for the freight-only line to Treamble. As distinct from Perranporth and the rebuilt St Agnes, Shepherds was built on more traditional lines with separate up and down platforms. It, too, had a goods depot, a passing loop controlled by a signal box on the up platform and was 12 miles and 38 chains from Chacewater.

As illustrated in Chapter Seven, the track layout at St Agnes station was radically changed in 1937 when the platform in front of the main brick station building was demolished and an island platform was constructed. A 30-lever signal box was also opened as seen in this view. In front of the large goods shed are two camping coaches, which proved popular in the summer months.
Author's Collection

Just under four miles from the junction was Goonbell Halt, which in common with most other halts on the line was opened in August 1905. The halt was a short distance from St Agnes, indeed a name of 'south-east St Agnes' would not have been out of place, even though there was a tiny hamlet called Goonbell nearby.
Author's Collection

At the 5 mile 46 chain point there was another of the diminutive halts, called Mithian Halt, which was conveniently located to serve a small local community. By the late 1950s there were between 10 and 12 trains per summer weekday serving Mithian Halt and half a dozen trains each way on summer Sundays. *Author's Collection*

Perranporth Beach Halt was the last station on the line to be opened, in 1931. The concrete halt was built to serve the tourist trade and the platform was located within a ¼ mile of the beach. The line closed in 1963 and seven years later part of the Perranporth Beach Halt platform was removed and used in the construction of The Dell station (later Falmouth Town) on the Falmouth branch. *M. Dart Collection*

Perranporth was the major intermediate station on the Chacewater to Newquay branch. The station comprised a large island platform with a subway entrance/exit, a signal box, goods shed, many sidings and it was an important passing place. Direct trains to and from Paddington worked into the station during the height of summer, taking under eight hours for the journey. The GWR introduced steam railmotors in 1905, the same year as the whole line opened, and a pair of these machines are seen passing at Perranporth in Edwardian times. *Author's Collection*

In an era when few enthusiasts pointed their cameras in the direction of the new diesels, North British type '2' No. D6316, arrives at Goonhavern Halt on 29th September, 1961 in pouring rain with the two-coach 4.40 pm Newquay to Chacewater. The halt was 10 miles and 38 chains from Blackwater Junction. *K.D. Jubb*

Little has been written about the Treamble branch. There had been evidence of mining to the north and west of Penhale Sands for centuries, but of primary interest was the Perran Iron Lode which ran from Holywell to the downs around Newlyn East. In the 18th and 19th centuries iron ore had been raised in the area, but due to the heavy costs incurred by the method of working, and the ore having to be carted some nine miles for shipment, few profits were made – until the railway arrived. Although there had been an application to Parliament in 1865 to construct a railway from the iron lode to Newquay it was the CMR which, by virtue of its July 1873 Act, continued the old Newquay Tramway line from East Wheal Rose to Treamble, as described in Chapter Five.

It had been said in support of the application that there were millions of tons of ore in the lode, that it was specially adapted for making Bessemer steel and that it needed only railway communication to develop it. The ore was near the surface but at certain points the lode was only a foot or two wide. The main mines in the area were at Gravel Hill, Duchy Peru and Deer Park. This potential was recognised by the CMR entrepreneur W. Roebuck who included in his application to Parliament 'Railway No. 4'. It was described thus:

> A railway four miles seven furlongs in length, commencing in the Parish of Newlyn by a junction with the existing tramway from New Quay [sic] to East Wheal Rose Mine about eight hundred yards or thereabouts from the termination thereof, and terminating in a field in the Parish of Perranzabuloe at a point one hundred and sixty yards or thereabouts to the southward of a mill known as Treamble Mill.

It was also stated, somewhat prophetically, that the success of the working would depend on the output, which would require opening up of the deposits at many more points than was done at present. In addition to the Treamble line, a 1 mile 4 chain extension from a trailing point near the terminus to Gravel Hill, at the easterly end of Perran Beach (*see map page 46*), was built in a period of only 10 days with landowners', but not Parliamentary, authority. The line to Treamble and Gravel Hill was opened on 1st June, 1874, in common with the rest of the CMR network. Despite early optimism the mines were not efficiently worked, production slowed and following a downturn in the industry and a slump in world commodity prices, the Cornish Consolidated Iron Mines Corporation was dissolved in 1884. The Gravel Hill extension was finally closed in 1888 and the track lifted.

Traffic was not particularly lucrative at Treamble and, despite the presence of a goods agent, the line from Shepherds closed in 1917. In common with so many other minor lines and light railways the track was lifted and the metal used in World War I munitions' manufacture. By this time Deer Park, followed by Duchy Peru and Treamble, had seen the last iron ore mined. Deer Park had its own trailing siding on the up side of the line, but this was closed by the time the April 1897 GWR Service Book was issued. It seemed that after a life of 43 years a small piece of the CMR had been lost for ever.

It was therefore with some surprise that following the necessary reinstatement works, the GWR proudly announced in Notice No. 2131 that, 'The Treamble Branch which forms a junction with the Perranporth Branch at Shepherds, has now been reinstated and would be opened for Goods Train traffic on Tuesday February 16th 1926.' The 3¾ mile branch would provide

Photographs of green-liveried dmus without yellow warning panels on the Chacewater to Newquay line are uncommon. However, during the last summer of operation in 1962 this Chacewater-bound branch working was recorded at Shepherds, former junction for the Treamble branch. Brick-built station buildings and small awnings are available for passengers travelling in both directions.   *R.K. Blencowe Collection*

This fine view shows Shepherds signal box that controlled the station passing loop and, while open, the Treamble branch, just visible on the extreme left. The sidings contain a handful of goods wagons and a clerestory-roofed camping coach.   *Lens of Sutton*

accommodation for 14 trucks at the Private Siding terminus. The line was controlled by Shepherds signal box on the one engine in steam or 'two coupled' principle using a train staff. The wonderfully precise timings showed trains running on Tuesdays, Thursdays and Saturdays.

For the first mile the line descended at 1 in 60/88/41, followed in the second mile by the line falling at 1 in 40/100/60. At the two mile mark the falling gradient was even more pronounced at 1 in 50/40 for over half a mile. There were similar 'ups and downs' before and after the three mile marker. The 1926 trackwork was single from Shepherds to the loop just outside Treamble. The loop was 276 ft long commencing at the 3 mile 1¼ chain point. The locomotive would always run round in the loop and propel wagons into the main private siding. There was a short, second siding on the on the down side but 'not to be used by engines'. Both sidings were beyond the 'end of GWR maintenance' point at 3 miles 12 chains. There was a gate across the track just beyond the GWR boundary.

Beside the loading wharf at Treamble there was a 2 ft gauge tramway worked by a pair of diminutive 0-4-2T steam locomotives (Kerr, Stuarts No. 812 of 1903 and No. 1169 of 1911, both from Dalcoath Mine, near Camborne). They served a quarry where gunpowder was manufactured by the C.M. Powder Co. Ltd works. The tramway was closed and lifted by 1942. Although other produce was loaded at Treamble the volume was very small and the capacity provided by the 13-wagon loop was never required.

Notwithstanding the steep gradients the permanent way was such that the speed limit over the entire line was a miserly 10 mph. Stop boards were fixed at 0 miles 47 chains and 2 miles 59 chains and, in accordance with incline instructions, brakes had to be picked up at 2 miles 41 chains and at Treamble Loop. Whistle boards were situated either side of the crossing near Rejarrah. Propelling along the line in either direction was not permitted.

After a handful of wartime troop trains (that may have served Penhale Camp) and a few 'as and when required' runs, traffic finally petered out in the summer of 1949 with closure formally posted in January 1952, followed by track lifting in 1956. The line can still be traced in a couple of locations but most of it is heavily overgrown, especially in the Treamble area. Curiously, Network Rail still have maintenance obligations on the line; a bridge and bridge abutments at Rejarrah, 1 mile 44½ chains, and Treworthen, 2 miles 72¾ chains!

From Shepherds station, where in times gone by a holiday camping coach with a clerestory roof was located, the Newquay line passed Fiddlers Green before crossing Penhallow Moor. There was some difficulty in laying the original track at this point. The next halt was Mitchell and Newlyn, at 13 miles 60 chains. In common with all GWR stations and halts with the words 'and' or 'road' in the name, it was convenient for neither Newlyn East nor Mitchell! There were no houses nearby, just the waste from the East Wheal Rose Mine which, during the 19th century, had become a legend in its time. After the CMR extension from East Wheal Rose to Treamble the mine had its own siding at a point 1 mile 57 chains from Shepherds and 4 miles 53 chains from Newquay.

Old Wheal Rose mine opened in 1814 and by 1818 it had become a major producer of lead. The price slumped in the late 1820s and it ceased production

Right: The 1874-built 5 mile Treamble branch and the 1 mile 4 chain Gravel Hill extension were originally built to serve the iron mines of the Perran lode. The line was an extension of Treffry's old Newquay Tramway that ran from Newquay to East Wheal Rose lead mine. Once the Chacewater to Newquay line opened the junction for Treamble was at Shepherds and the dedicated line was then only 3¼ line miles long. In later years the line served a gunpowder works at Treamble where this picture was taken in the 1930s, looking towards Shepherds.

Clinker Collection/Courtesy Brunel University

Below: The iron ore traffic failed to materialise and the branch was closed and lifted in 1917. It was surprisingly re-opened by the GWR 'for goods traffic' on 16th February, 1926. Traffic was thin and after World War II the line effectively closed, formal closure notices being posted in 1952. Action photographs on the line are scarce but here we see a '4500' class 2-6-2T trundling down the 10 mph restricted branch during December 1935.

H.G. Ordish

in 1831. However, in 1834 a new mining venture started at East Wheal Rose and, as stated in Chapter Five, by 1846 no fewer that 1,200 men, women and children were employed in the mine. Unfortunately the lode was very soft, resulting in many rock falls and the use of enormous amounts of timber. Also at the lower levels, water infiltration was a major problem and by 1842 pumping engines were removing no less that 734 gallons per minute! In 1846 there was a terrible disaster at the mine when flash floods resulted in the loss of 39 miners who were drowned as the pumping engines failed to cope. By the time Treffry had put down his tramway to the mine in 1849 it was already in decline, 1845 having been the peak year. The mine finally closed in August 1885.

The final halt on the line was at Trewerry and Trerice, 16 miles and 76 chains from Chacewater. This halt, in common with Mitchell and Newlyn, originally had a wooden platform but in later years they were rebuilt, looking more like a Southern Railway halt with an entirely concrete structure and small basic waiting shelter. In the *Country Homes of Cornwall* publication the fine nearby Elizabethan mansion of Trerice is featured, and in the tourist season it is open to the public. A coal siding at Trewerry was closed in 1948. Early maps showed the siding just north of the level crossing as Trewerry siding or Trewerry Mill. The building by the level crossing was once a CMR crossing keeper's house. Between here and Trevemper siding the CMR line deviated slightly from the old Newquay Tramway.

Trevemper siding was less than half a mile south of Tolcarn Junction. After the branch closed to passengers and freight in February 1963, just the short section from Tolcarn to Trevemper siding remained open. However, it too succumbed on 29th October, 1963 and the line was lifted by January 1964. The triangular junction at Tolcarn was the point where the line joined the Par to Newquay branch, which was described in the last chapter.

When services ended in 1963 there were 24 working levers in St Agnes signal box including seven for signals, six for discs, five for points and six for facing point locks. Perranporth had 20 working levers including 10 for signals, three for discs, four for points and three for facing point locks. Shepherds had just 14 working levers including eight for signals, two for discs and four for points.

When the closure notices appeared there were rallies and protest groups fighting the decision. The typical Dr Beeching era procedures took their course with the Western National Omnibus Company Limited providing the alternative service. Except for Trevemper siding, both passenger and freight services ceased on and from Monday 4th February, 1963. One curiosity on the formal closure notice read:

As an experiment a parcel depot will be maintained at Perranporth Beach Halt until the end of the 1963 Summer Season. The retention of the facility after this period will depend on the use made of it.

Readers were invited to ring the station master, Perranporth, telephone 3211 for further information. Years later, part of the Perranporth Beach concrete platform was used in the construction of The Dell station, later Falmouth Town.

From six trains in each direction Mondays to Fridays in April 1910, timetabled services increased on the same basis to eight in January 1927, 12 in July 1938 falling to 11 in 1958. In later years there was also a Sunday service plus

From Shepherds station the next halt along the Chacewater to Newquay branch was Mitchell & Newlyn Halt. Photographed in September 2003, exactly 40 years after closure, the corrugated iron hut and concrete platform were revealed after some 'bramble bashing' and seemed remarkably intact, despite nature having almost reclaimed its land. The brief visit was utterly fascinating.   *Author*

The final halt on the line was Trewerry & Trerice. In common with other halts it originally had a wooden platform but was later rebuilt with an all concrete structure and small waiting hut that was much less stylish than the GWR pagoda. There was a nearby siding that served Trewerry Mill, later used for coal and finally closed in 1948.   *R.K. Blencowe Collection*

This view shows the Tolcarn Junction complex from the south. In the foreground is Lane Junction with the line to left changing from single to double as it heads off in the Newquay direction, with the right-hand chord forming a triangle with the Par to Newquay branch. The latter was rarely used, except for turning locomotives and occasionally complete trains.   *Author's Collection*

seasonal adjustments. The trains varied from single-car railmotors in the early days to typical two- to four-coach branch trains in the days of steam. During the last decades of steam the normal branch tank locomotives were based on Truro shed. From mid-1962 diesels locomotives and units took over all services and the last train on the branch was a four-car diesel multiple unit. As a means of getting to Newquay from Plymouth and London the branch was a duplication of the line from Par. But the Chacewater line always had a better service than the Par line and it was reckoned that some 600 passengers used the line daily for return journeys. However, on the basis of the accounting principles then used the line lost money and against those criteria, closure was inevitable. The loss-making Par line received a subsidy in later years, a situation which prevails to this date.

The Lappa Valley Railway

After closure of the Chacewater to Newquay branch line in 1963 there was a plan to reopen part of it. But, like most similar projects, such plans seemed to be more romantic notions rather that practical possibilities. In 1968 Eric Booth saw the potential for a narrow gauge steam railway running along the Lappa Valley and he commenced negotiations with British Rail. After six years of work a 15 inch gauge line was laid from Benny Halt to the East Wheal Rose Mine, where there are many attractions for the traveller and holidaymaker. The line to this leisure area in just over a mile in length. The Lappa Valley Railway now has a small fleet of steam and diesel locomotives. This length of track is all that remains of the railway that once ran between Tolcarn Junction and Blackwater Junction.

After closure of the Chacewater to Newquay line in February 1963 it was rather harrowing to observe all of the railway infrastructure that had been so carefully and skilfully created just 59 years earlier being demolished. In this scene at Perranporth a crane in the background is lifting the track, the water column filler has gone, some of the windows in the signal box are broken and soon there would be no trace of the branch railway that once promised so much. *Royal Institution of Cornwall*

With the town of Newquay in the background this record of Tolcarn Junction dates back to 28th April, 1962 and the end of the steam era. This pair of prairie tanks, Nos. 4564 and 5531, are seen taking water before continuing with their railtour duties. The locomotives are on the Chacewater line, while to the right are the lines to Par. Main line corridor stock is berthed on the far left. *Terry Nicholls*

Chapter Nineteen

Tolcarn Junction to Newquay

The origins of this section of line are detailed in Chapter Five. However, just to recap, although Joseph Austen Treffry had given notice in 1835 that it was his intention to link Par and Newquay by a tramway, it was not until he had acquired Newquay Harbour in 1838 that the prospect became a reality. Following the purchase of land and the agreements from other landowners that the tramway could run across their land, work commenced on tramways from Newquay Harbour to St Dennis and Hendra in clay country and to East Wheal Rose in mining country. By 1849 the East Wheal Rose line was ready and, following the opening of the most important structure on the line, Trenance viaduct, on the 29th January, 1849, loaded wagons found their way to Newquay Harbour for the first time. The wooden structure on part-granite piers was chosen because the building time of one year was only a third of that required for an all-masonry example.

The tramway, having crossed the Trenance Valley, curved towards the infant town and harbour. When the Cornwall Minerals Railway was surveying the area for its proposed Fowey to Newquay route the ideal station site was found just across the Trenance Valley, only ¾ mile from Tolcarn Junction, and just a few hundred yards from the cliffs above the shore of Newquay Bay. Although the new station area was open for goods traffic from June 1874, it was 20th June, 1876 when the first passenger train drew into Newquay station, having crossed the Trenance Valley on the rebuilt 1874 viaduct with stone piers, and iron girders forged by William West & Sons of St Blazey.

The station, built by John Ennor, had a single platform with unpretentious but permanent stone buildings on the north side of the site. A few yards outside the station was a CMR signal box and a stone-built locomotive shed. At a much later date a goods shed was provided. At the western, buffer stop, end of the station there was a small turntable which the CMR tank engines used either to run-round their train or visit the engine shed. Beyond a couple of goods sidings a single line (effectively the old tramway) crossed the main road to the harbour. With a service of only three or four trains per day plus a modicum of goods traffic this arrangement was to be adequate for a number of years, but with the coming of the Chacewater to Newquay branch trains and the start of through working potential following the GWR's abandonment of the broad gauge main line in 1892, consideration was given to likely growth.

Accordingly, during the 1904/1905 period, substantial changes were made. The CMR platform was extended considerably and a further island platform was built, giving three platform faces. The old CMR signal box was taken out of use and replaced by a GWR box on the opposite side of the line and to the east. The end of platform turntable was abolished and the old engine shed was demolished. The goods yard was enlarged and a new locomotive shed was built, served by a new and larger turntable.

Although the old harbour branch closed in 1926, the heyday of the seaside tripper and holidaymaker was about to occur. The original platform was

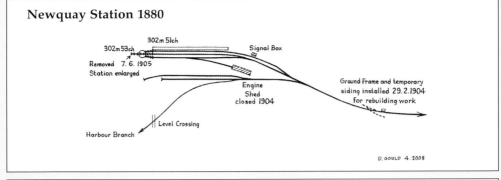

Newquay Station 1880

302m 51ch
302m 53ch

Removed 7.6.1905
Station enlarged

Signal Box

Engine
Shed
closed 1904

Ground Frame and temporary
siding installed 29.2.1904
for rebuilding work

Level Crossing

Harbour Branch

D. GOULD 4.2008

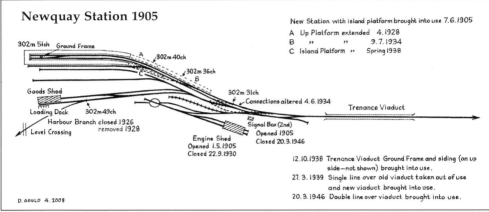

Newquay Station 1905

New Station with island platform brought into use 7.6.1905

A Up Platform extended 4.1928
B   ,,   ,,   9.7.1934
C Island Platform ,,   Spring 1938

302m 51ch Ground Frame

A 302m 40ch
C
302m 36ch
B

Goods Shed

Loading Dock 302m 49ch
Harbour Branch closed 1926
Level Crossing   removed 1928

302m 31ch
Connections altered 4.6.1934

Trenance Viaduct

Engine Shed
Opened 1.5.1905
Closed 22.9.1930

Signal Box (2nd)
Opened 1905
Closed 20.3.1946

12.10.1938 Trenance Viaduct Ground Frame and siding (on up
           side—not shown) brought into use.
27.3.1939 Single line over old viaduct taken out of use
           and new viaduct brought into use.
20.3.1946 Double line over viaduct brought into use.

D. GOULD 4.2008

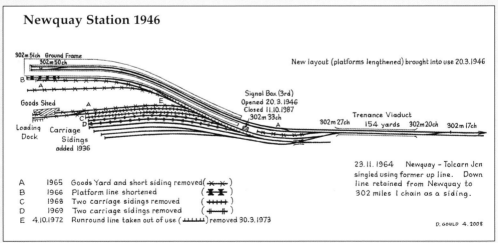

Newquay Station 1946

302m 51ch Ground Frame
302m 50ch

B
A

New layout (platforms lengthened) brought into use 20.3.1946

Goods Shed

E

C
D

Loading
Dock Carriage
      Sidings
      added 1936

Signal Box (3rd)
Opened 20.3.1946
Closed 11.10.1987
302m 33ch

Trenance Viaduct
302m 27ch   154 yards   302m 20ch 302m 17ch

23.11.1964 Newquay – Tolcarn Jcn
            singled using former up line. Down
            line retained from Newquay to
            302 miles 1 chain as a siding.

A	1965	Goods Yard and short siding removed (✕—✕)
B	1966	Platform line shortened (✕—✕)
C	1968	Two carriage sidings removed (++++)
D	1969	Two carriage sidings removed (+—+)
E	4.10.1972	Runround line taken out of use (⊥⊥⊥⊥⊥) removed 30.3.1973

D. GOULD 4.2008

Track plans showing the Newquay station area between 1880 and 1946 adapted from plans by R.A.
Cooke. On 11th October, 1987 all remaining permanent way was taken out of use except for a single line
into platform 3. On 18th January, 1988 the single line was diverted to run into platform 2 and shortened
by 2 chains.

This building was the second and last engine shed at Newquay, which opened in 1905 and closed about 1930. Beside the two-road shed is the second signal box that also opened in 1905 but which closed in 1946. The buildings were photographed in April 1936.   *SLS/W.A. Camwell*

The one major feature between Tolcarn Junction and Newquay is Trenance viaduct. Crossing the third version of the viaduct on 17th July, 1954 is a 12 bogie Paddington to Newquay working double headed by 'Hall' class 4-6-0 No. 6911 *Holker Hall* and 'Grange' class No. 6808 *Beenham Grange*. The double-track viaduct was not fully operational until 20th March, 1946.   *Les Elsey*

Perhaps the finest steam locomotives to work on the Newquay branch were the 'Castle' class 4-6-0s. These graceful engines could be seen hauling crack express trains all over the GWR and the Western Region. Arriving at platform 1 with an excursion from Exeter is No. 5021 *Whittington Castle* on 20th July, 1954. The gasometer is now merely a memory.   *Les Elsey*

On occasions the local branch service was worked by a tender locomotive, including this 'Modified Hall' class 4-6-0 with 6 ft diameter driving wheels. No. 7909 *Heveningham Hall* has a strengthened six-coach load of suburban style non-corridor compartment coaches as it prepares to leave for Par on 26th July, 1958.   *Terry Nicholls*

extended with wooden platforms in April 1928 and lengthened again in July 1934. At the same time the crossover connections were replaced to reflect the new length of platform. The engine shed closed in September 1930 as there was no need to berth locomotives at Newquay overnight. There were water cranes at the platform ends for any necessary locomotive replenishment. In expectation of additional traffic and the replacement of the CMR Trenance viaduct by a new double-track masonry viaduct, the island platform was extended in the spring of 1938 and a significant number of carriage, as distinct from freight, sidings were added in 1936.

The double-track viaduct was not fully operational until 20th March, 1946 when the 1905 signal box was replaced by a later GWR model. This was to be the last of the long series of developments. After the mid-1950s peak, when 20,000 passengers would arrive at Newquay by rail on Summer Saturdays, the picture was one of decline and rationalisation. Again, it was the closure of the Chacewater to Newquay line in 1963 and the general Beeching era climate which started the rot. The double-track section from Trenance viaduct east to Tolcarn Junction was singled on 23rd November, 1964 and Newquay goods yard was lifted shortly afterwards. One of the platform lines was shortened in 1966 and in 1968 two of the carriage sidings were removed. Two further carriage sidings were removed in 1969, severely limiting the number of trains that could be berthed at Newquay. The old up platform, which was supported on concrete stilts on the extended portion, became unsafe. The long platform awnings were severely pruned in 1964 and all the trappings of the days of steam were removed. Notes from the demolition contractor's notebook show the scale of rationalisation:

On 10th June, 1964 seats were removed from platforms, the day after the roofs of platforms 2 and 3 were demolished, and the day after that, glass, wood and lead were removed from the platforms. By the 25th June, 1964 lamp standards had been cut down and the wrought iron removed. On 29th June it was reported that the water column on platform 1 had been very hard to break up, will try and finish it tomorrow. Platform 2's water column was broken up on 2nd July, 1964 and that from platform 3 the day after. Two further water columns were broken up on following days.

The three demolition men arrived by train at 10.15 am and departed at 5.30 pm. An amusing note on 20th June 1964 recorded that, 'three men commenced to cut off purlins on platforms 2 and 3 but had to stop as passengers wanted to board their train at 11.00 am. Started to work again at 12.30 pm'!

Further sidings were closed in the mid-1980s and platform 1 was regarded as dangerous and was no longer used beyond the station buildings. As a result only three trains and a dmu could be accommodated at Newquay. It seemed that the final act of official vandalism took place in 1987 when, at the end of the summer timetable, the last scheduled locomotive-hauled train called at Newquay, the run-round crossover was abandoned and all signals were removed, the signal box closed and only a single platform was in use from Monday 5th October. The only bright spot was the retention of through IC125 trains from distant destinations on summer Saturdays, including, through trains to Glasgow Central and the 'Atlantic Coast Express' to London Paddington.

With the gasworks dominating the background another grubby St Blazey prairie tank, No. 5562, arrives at the Newquay terminus with a train from Par on 23rd April, 1960. Notice the GWR station seats on the left and the old-fashioned confectionery machine on the right. Two Tannoy speakers are ready to blast any message for passengers down the lengthy platforms!   *Author's Collection*

Four-wheeled diesel railbuses never regularly worked Par to Newquay branch services. However, after arrival at St Blazey in 1962, primarily for use between Boscarne Junction and Bodmin North, a test run was made to Newquay and back. The train crew and inspector pose in the sun on platform 1 beside AC Cars Ltd 150 hp railbus No. 79977.   *Carey Bachelor*

Towards the end of the age of steam it was depressing to see such fine engines as the '4500' class prairie tanks in such grimy condition but then there was little incentive for depot staff to keep locomotives clean when they were about to be withdrawn. A typical branch train headed by No. 4570 waits to leave platform 2 at Newquay with a train for Par. *M. Dart Collection*

One of the classic train movements at branch line termini was the locomotive 'run round' and here we see the crossover being used at Newquay on 6th August, 1976. One of the glorious sounding twin V12 engined 'Westerns' with driver Prophet at the helm runs round its stock. No. D1058 *Western Nobleman* has its number shown in the train indicator blind because in January of that year displayed train headcodes were abolished throughout BR. *Author*

Between 1970 and 1985 the class '45' 'Peaks' were regular performers on the Newquay branch at weekends during the summer months, especially at the head of inter-Regional trains to the north-east of England. In this sparkling summer scene from 1980 a class '45/0' leaves platform 1, while the local dmu is at platform 2. By this time drastic rationalisation was in the planning stage. *Author*

In 1986 platform 1 became unsafe and was used only by short local trains comprised of 2-car dmus. Passengers were warned of the potential danger. On 30th August, 1986 large logo class '50' No. 50008 *Thunderer* was at the head of 11.35 Newquay to Paddington, while on the left the 09.18 Newquay to Newcastle was in the hands of sister locomotive No. 50039 *Implacable*.

Author

The first through carriages from Paddington to Newquay were introduced from May 1906 when the journey took 7 hours 55 minutes, compared with the best 'ACE' 1989 timing of 4 hours 43 minutes and in 2007 five hours. Ironically, the best trains in terms of speed and comfort to visit Newquay have been the original pre-refurbishment InterCity 125s. Over the years overall journey times have barely changed, with in 2007 a non-stop High Speed Train taking 45 to 50 minutes for the 20¾ miles from Par to Newquay, compared with 55 minutes for a stopping local steam train in 1910!

Over the years Newquay has played host to an amazing variety of trains, ranging from the 4- and 6-wheelers of the early days, with their small tank locomotives of first the CMR, and later the GWR, through the Edwardian era of bogie coaches and clerestory roof lines to the non-corridor compartment coaches of the latter days of steam. Unusual workings were many and varied, ranging from Royal Trains throughout the 1874 to 2008 period, the steam railmotors of the Edwardian era, streamlined GWR railcars in 1932, through to a 4-wheeled railbus in the early 1960s. Then there were the full-length holiday trains, sometimes weighing over 500 tons and hauled by two locomotives with a banker for part of the journey to and from Par, bringing a wide range of GWR and BR (WR) main line steam engines to the seaside. Diesel locomotives and diesel-mechanical multiple units took over branch workings in the early 1960s and lasted until the 1990s. Most classes of main line diesels working on the Western Region have found their way to Newquay, including the memorable 'Western' and 'Warship' diesel-hydraulics. There was still room for novelty in 1989 when the annual weedkilling train brought Hunslet-Barclay class '20/9s' to Newquay. Enthusiast specials have produced everything from Southern Region class '33s' to EWS GM class '66s'. Normal weekday branch trains are now usually worked by class '150/2s' or single car class '153s'.

This photograph was taken on the last weekend when the WR lower quadrant signals would remain *in situ* at Newquay and the final weekend that the 1946 signal box would remain open. Within 36 hours the signals would be felled and the box decommissioned. Large logo-liveried No. 47459 waits in the soon to be removed sidings with stock for an inter-Regional train, on 3rd October, 1987.   *Author*

During 1986/7 an allocation of 2-car four-wheeled class '142' diesel units were dispatched to the west country, where they were known as 'Skippers'. Unfortunately they were destined to be a failure on Cornish branch lines, with excessive flange wear due to the long wheelbase, flange noise - particularly 'squealing' on bends, a complete lack of sanding gear - sometimes required on steep gradients in inclement weather, and power doors that were unreliable. Their stay was short-lived! Here No. 142025 stands at Newquay in October 1987.   *Author*

From 1987 it was downhill all the way at Newquay as various forms of rationalisation seemed perpetual. In this October 1988 view not only have the signals been removed, resulting in only a single platform being available, but much track lifting has taken place. The planning of the madhouse has placed buffer stops beyond the protective station awnings, no doubt to afford passengers additional compulsory exercise and a soaking if the weather turned inclement. No. 55006 takes a break between runs.   *Author*

The 3rd/4th October, 1987 and the 8th/9th September 2007 were two really significant weekends at Newquay, albeit some 20 years apart. In October 1987 there was a grand gathering of enthusiasts to celebrate the last weekend of locomotive-hauled passengers trains. No doubt discussing the various travel/bashing options this group have two class '50s' and a class '47' to choose from in terms of morning departures from Newquay. *Author*

On the following Sunday, 4th October, 1987, BR showed great enterprise in running a special 11-coach train all the way from Paddington to Newquay. Furthermore it was double-headed by a gleaming pair of Network SouthEast class '50s', Nos. 50034 *Furious* and 50035 *Ark Royal*. This general scene of the gathered masses would soon change as the five lines and sidings seen here would be reduced to a single line, allowing only multiple unit operation. *Author*

This great rarity was photographed in March 1991. Early in the morning the Royal Train conveying HRH The Prince of Wales had arrived in Newquay for the Prince to visit his Duchy of Cornwall estates. With but a single usable platform the first local dmu of the day from Par was stopped at the far end of the platform, beyond the Royal Train. Passengers had to walk past security guards and the Royal Train to reach the town. The 'bubble' was No. 55000 and the Royal engines were class '47s' Nos. 47835 *Windsor Castle* and 47834 *Fire Fly*.   *Author*

The abandoned Newquay signal box was used by permanent way workers after closure in 1987. Passing the structure on 8th March, 1997 with the 11.40 Newquay to Par is single car No. 153380. Just three months later the box burnt to the ground, apparently little being sacred in this day and age. By this time the terminus was of course a single line stub.   *Author*

Until March 2005 a member of the class '52' 'Western' class had not reached Newquay since December 1976. However the Diesel Traction Group, in conjunction with Pathfinder Railtours, rectified that situation by bringing their beautifully restored 'Western' No. D1015 *Western Champion* to Newquay with the 'Western China Clay' special. The original 'RPPR' tour, which carried the same headboard and used the same class of motive power in the shape of No. D1056 *Western Sultan*, was organized by the author over 28 years earlier (*see page 200*). *Author*

At the other end of the 'Western China Clay' special was a very rare sight for the seaside terminus, GM class '66' No. 66248, which would haul the chartex back to Plymouth where the 'Western' would take over for the return journey to the London area. In the 2008 timetable there was no branch train departure from Newquay between 3 pm and 8 pm, a long 'window' for such a special train to be accommodated! *Author*

On Sunday 9th September, 2007, the very last Virgin-liveried Voyager worked out of Newquay with the 11.33 departure for Glasgow Central. Virgin Trains were about to lose the Cross Country franchise to the Arriva Company. The train can be seen at the only operational platform. The only public seats are on in-filled ground between the old platforms 1 and 2 and they are not sheltered by the surviving station awnings! The First Great Western timetable shows Newquay as unstaffed, although TOC staff are present on summer weekends.

Author

This view shows the current Newquay station concourse and the only seating placed on ground in-filled between platforms 1 and 2. Trains now stop well short of the shortened awnings.
Author

There is no doubt that even the most cheerful and optimistic amongst us could not argue that the railway companies, including good old British Rail, and the local authorities have done anything other than destroy the wonderful CMR/GWR terminus of Newquay. This is the utterly depressing 2007 entrance to the station with graffiti on the left, peeling paint on the roof and patchy tarmac on the floor of this shoddy 1960s structure. There can be few sights less welcoming but at least after 132 years there is still an infrequent train service in operation - for now.
Author

With the sun breaking through the early morning fog, a GNER set on hire to Virgin leaves Newquay with the 09.40 to Newcastle on 8th September, 2007. GNER, Midland Main Line, Virgin Trains (Cross Country) and Valenta-engined HST power cars were all doomed and yet all appeared at Newquay for the last time. *Author*

On a delightful 25th February, 2008 a typical Newquay branch train poses at the terminus during its very brief stopover before returning as the 12.42 to Par, one of only four departures Monday to Saturday (there is no winter Sunday service). The unit is a refurbished First Great Western class '150/2', No. 150247. The palm trees add a tropical touch to the otherwise austere scene. *Author*

Having agreed to the demolition of the lovely old granite Newquay station building and having deprived passengers of any form of weather protection while standing on the platform, the local town council erected this 'Welcome to Newquay' sign over the filled-in trackbed during 1992. The station building was once located to the right of this view, while on the left is the end of the rationalised single line stub and the local Burger King!

Author

By 1990 it seemed that no more official damage could be done to the bleak and unwelcoming Newquay station but that turned out to be a misguided view. In 1992 the original granite station building was demolished to make way for car parking and a taxi rank. With so much utterly bland architecture in the town of Newquay it is hard to believe that local Councillors and developers did not recognise that they were destroying a part of Newquay's local history and heritage. It is inconceivable that an innovative use could not have been made of such a fine building. Sir John Betjeman, the late Poet Laureate and public transport fan, would have been appalled at such moronic actions.

In 2007 a small ticket office was open on summer weekends and a tiny shelter was provided for the handful of passengers on the few branch trains that run. A general concourse area was retained but with seating provided only in the unprotected and roofless central area. The seats are mainly used by passengers boarding the through holiday trains on summer weekends. At other times main line connections continue to be nonsensical and it is clear that the compilers of timetables have no practical experience of travelling by rail in this part of the world. The Newquay branch survives, indeed many miles of track were upgraded in the 2006/2007 period. But with so few passengers and such a meagre branch service it will take decades for the cost of permanent way renewals to be recovered. One can only hope that subsidies continue to be paid but with the train operating company running both the trains and the buses it is hard to envisage vigorous competition or an elaborate and expensive advertising campaign promoting rail travel!

Acknowledgements

The information and illustrations contained in this book have been amassed over several decades. A detailed list of the hundreds of data sources would fill several valuable pages of this book but it would be inappropriate not to record my thanks and gratitude to a number of organizations and individuals who have directly and indirectly helped with this particular project. The cheerful co-operation and natural enthusiasm shown by all contributors was greatly appreciated.

In no particular order I would like to thank Maurice Dart, Joyce Greenham of the Newquay Old Cornwall Society, Newquay Library, Kim Cooper and her willing staff at the Cornish Studies Library at Redruth, the County Records Office at Truro, Robert Cook of the Royal Institution of Cornwall at Truro, John Aanonson of Brunel University at Runnymede, Terry Nicholls, Peter Treloar, John Hicks, Bill Walker, R.A. Cooke, Roger Lacy, Steve Davies, Steve Chandler, Stan May, David Gould, British Rail and EWS staff at St Blazey, the staff of the old English China Clays Company, Courtenay Smale of the Goonvean & Rostowrack China Clay Company, the late Charles Clinker, the late John Penderill-Church, the late Les Elsey, the late Dick (R.C.) Riley, the late John Frith, the late Charlie Saundercock and all of the photographers credited in the captions to their photographs. I would also like to thank my publishers and in particular Ian Kennedy, for the freedom afforded in terms of specification, content and layout. Finally I would like to pay special tribute to my wife Maureen and to dedicate this book to her. During a period of convalescence following an accident she was an immense help with word processing and showed endless patience in understanding why her husband was incarcerated in his office for many, many months!

Bibliography

Anderson R.C., Frankis G.G.A., *A History of Western National*, David & Charles, 1979
Bartlett, John, *Ships of North Cornwall*, Tabb House, 1996
Barton R.M., *A History of the Cornish China Clay Industry*, Bradford Barton, 1966
Bennett, Alan, *The GWR in Mid-Cornwall*, Kingfisher, 1988
Clinker, C.R., *The Railways of Cornwall 1809-1963*, David & Charles, 1963
Cooke, R.A., *Track Layout Diagrams East Cornwall*, Author
Cornwall Archaeological Unit, *The Luxulyan Valley*, Cornwall County Council, 1988
Dart, Maurice, *East Cornwall Minerals Railways*, Middleton Press, 2004
Dart, Maurice, *West Cornwall Minerals Railways*, Middleton Press, 2005
Dunning, Martin, *Francis Frith's, Around Newquay*, Frith Book Company, 2000
Goddard, Fanny, *Newquay*, Homeland Handbooks, 1922
London, Peter, *Aviation in Cornwall*, Air Britain, 1997
May S.C., *A History of the Railway - Newquay to Fowey*, Author, 1982
Mitchell, David, *British Railways Past and Present East Cornwall*, Past and Present, 2006
Noall, Cyril, *A History of Cornish Mail and Stage Coaches*, Bradford Barton, 1963
Pearse, Richard, *The Ports and Harbours of Cornwall*, H.E. Warne, 1964
Penderill-Church, John, *Treffry's Tramways*, English China Clays, 1979
Riley, R.C., 'The Cornish China Clay Traffic', *Trains Illustrated Summer Annual*, Ian Allan, 1957
Vaughan, J.A.M., *Diesels in the Duchy*, Ian Allan, 1983
Vaughan, J.A.M., *An Illustrated History of West Country China Clay Trains*, Oxford Publishing Co., 1987, 2nd Edition, 1999
Vaughan, J.A.M., *Diesel Days Devon and Cornwall*, Ian Allan, 2005
Vaughan, J.A.M., *Branches & Byways: Cornwall*, Oxford Publishing Company, 2002
Vaughan, J.A.M., *The Newquay Branch and its Branches*, OPC/Haynes, 1991
Vaughan, J.A.M., 'Bugle's Railways Remembered', *Steam Days* magazine, 1997
Vaughan, J.A.M., 'The Newquay Harbour Branch', *Steam Days* magazine, 2005

Copies of *Bradshaws* and British Railways timetables, the *West Briton* newspaper, Acts of Parliament, *Royal Cornwall Gazette*, papers lodged with the County Records Office at Truro, Royal Institution of Cornwall, Truro, County Records Office at Truro, Brunel University at Runnymede and the Newquay Old Cornwall Society and the local library at Newquay.

Index

287